MUSINGS ON MONSTERS

OBSERVATIONS ON THE WORLD OF CLASSIC HORROR

MUSINGS ON MONSTERS

OBSERVATIONS ON THE WORLD OF CLASSIC HORROR

EDITED BY

RICH HANDLEY

LOU TAMBONE

SEQUART ORGANIZATION   EDWARDSVILLE, ILLINOIS

Musings on Monsters: Observations on the World of Classic Horror
edited by Rich Handley and Lou Tambone

First edition, October 2020, ISBN 978-1-9405-8923-7.

Cover art by Leah Battle. Book design by Julian Darius. Interior art is © by various respective rights holders.

Published by Sequart Organization. Edited by Rich Handley and Lou Tambone.

For more information about other titles in this series, visit Sequart.org/books.

Contents

I Was a Grade-School Monster Kid – Growing Up Ghoulish with Classic Creeps: A Foreword

by Jim Beard

It seems as though I've always been musing on monsters.

As a kid, I absorbed things like monster movies through my pores, via osmosis, or by some other strange and arcane means. A horror host out of Detroit with the to-me-clever moniker of Sir Graves Ghastly fed my appetite for black-and-white blood early Saturday afternoons, and my dad – a big movie buff – would always keep an eye out for spooky viewing in primetime for me. It pays to have fellow horror hounds in the family, I guess.

Toys supplied the scary stuff, too – everything from the Herman Munster Talking Puppet I inherited from my older sibs to the Mego Mad Monsters action figures later on. I came in at the tail end of the glory days of *Famous Monsters of Filmland* but still enjoyed seeking out new issues at the pharmacy right next to the grocery store my mom frequented. Heck, I even enjoyed the *Star Wars*-heavy issues in the late 1970s that real *FM* aficionados seemed to loathe.

As an adult (I hang that term loosely around my neck), I was blessed to share the beasts with a girl of my own heart and mind, and even marry her.

Becky loved *Dark Shadows* (yes, she was a run-home-after-school-to-watch-*DS* kid), Hammer films, and Bela Lugosi. Together, we cemented our adoration of Universal Monsters and tended to focus on the films that others tended to dismiss, such as *Dracula's Daughter*. For those of you who know that feeling of being an outcast for devotion to the nerdly things in life, I hope you know what it's also like to find and be able to cherish a kindred soul who never, ever questions your firm belief that Hjalmar Poelzig is as much a monster as Frankenstein's tatterdemalion man or poor, doomed Larry Talbot's hirsute alter-ego.

This book began as a dream of mine to create a forum for musings on the monsteriffic mayhem so many of us grew up with, but alas, Becky's untimely death took me out of the picture. Fortunately, two dear friends, Rich and Lou, picked up the reins of the Borgo Pass carriage and got it to the castle on time. I'm eternally grateful to them. Such fiends are hard to find in this strange, waking world.

Somewhere out there, I'd like to think Becky's sidling up to Bela, Boris, Christopher, Lon, and his pop to ask them all the questions we mere mortals would love to ask ourselves... and that she's getting some answers, too. Until such a time when we pass into that twilight dimension, it will have to simply suffice to muse on monsters through tomes like the one in your hot little claws.

Happy Hauntings!
Jim Beard
July 2019

 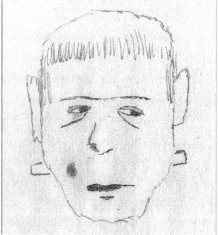

Left: future monster kid Jim Beard, circa 1966; right: Becky Beard's interpretation of Boris Karloff's classic Frankenstein's monster, including the cheek hollow made possible by the actor removing his dental appliance.

It Was a Graveyard Smash: An Introduction

by Rich Handley

> And though you fight to stay alive, your body starts to shiver.
> For no mere mortal can resist the *evil* of... the thriller!
> — Vincent Price, Michael Jackson's *Thriller* (1982)

Monsters are real. They ooze, creep, slither, and shamble. They terrify, horrify, devour, and destroy. They live, die, and live again. They hunger. They *crave*.

You'd thought the monsters weren't *really* hiding in your closet, waiting under your bed, and haunting your dreams. You'd thought you were safe and it was all in your imagination, because everyone knows monsters don't exist and can't hurt you. But you were wrong... oh, so horribly, dreadfully, heart-stoppingly wrong. They're real. It's midnight and the moon is full and the forest has gone silent, and the monsters are real. The fog is descending across the moor and your car is out of gas right next to a graveyard, and they're real. Your date is suddenly sprouting body hair and enlarged incisors and, oh dear lord, *they're real!*

Remember when you were young enough to believe in the kinds of monsters who bloodied the silver screen and went bump in the night? The kind who graced the covers of old comic books and magazines, their faces as ugly and distorted as their demented minds, who wanted nothing more than to hurt, kill, possess, or consume you, not necessarily in that order? That was before you became an adult and realized that while monsters *do* exist, they're of the plain ol' human variety and look like you and me. They don't have fangs, flippers, protoplasm, neck bolts, insect wings, antennas, or vapor trails; they don't levitate, mutate, or reanimate; and they can't transform into animals or transfix their prey through supernatural means or breathe atomic fire. They're flesh and blood, bone and muscle and soft tissue, and the horrors they visit upon this world are far more damaging.

But that's the real world. Who wants to live *there*? Certainly not me.

I was born in 1968, so my childhood spanned the early to mid-1970s, during the age of bell-bottoms, flared collars, unkempt hair, lava lamps, paneled station wagons, and far too much second-hand smoke. I was too young to benefit from one particularly popular aspect of that era – free love – but I found other ways to enjoy myself. I remember watching programs on the small, static-obscured, 13-channel black-and-white box that was my family's only television. Anything with a science fiction, horror, or mystery slant drew my attention. My cousins and I would go see monster movie matinees for only a dollar or two, and we'd be mesmerized despite the herky-jerky stop-motion animation, the papier-mâché buildings that crumbled just a little too easily, the visible prop strings on anything that was meant to look like it could fly, and the outdated acting styles that had become a bit humorous with the passage of time. It was monstrous and it was wonderful.

My personal favorites were the classic Godzilla films, which aired every Thanksgiving and periodically during local TV station film festivals. The cheesiness of Japan's *kaiju* films never bothered me – it just made me love them more.[1] I also enjoyed repeat showings of the Universal Monsters movies on late-night television,[2] particularly any featuring the Wolf Man[3] or the Mummy[4] (not so much the Gill-man[5]), and I made a point of reading Bram

---

[1] See my essay "Godzilla vs. Continuity: Toho's Shōwa-Era Shared Film Universe."
[2] See Joseph Berenato's essay "A New World of Gods and Monsters: Universal Studios and the First Shared Cinematic Universe."
[3] See Robert B. Nejman's essay "The Tragic Heroism of Larry Talbot, the Wolf Man." Rob is a close friend of mine going all the way back to high school, when he and I quickly bonded over our shared love for horror. When Jim Beard had to step down, Rob graciously filled in by writing Jim's intended essay about the wolfish Talbot.
[4] See Frank Schildiner's essay "Kharis: The Unsung Legend of Mummy Fiction."

Stoker's *Dracula*[6] and Mary Shelley's *Frankenstein*[7] after a friend told me how different the movies were from the source novels. The main protagonist of *Dracula* was the handsome Jonathan Harker and it was *he* who got to slay the Count, but I was more fascinated by Abraham Van Helsing because the old man possessed an impressive knowledge of a great many arcane subjects... and I've always been more Van Helsing than Harker anyway.

This explains why, while marathoning the monster-themed 1960s soap opera *Dark Shadows* a few years back, I quickly deemed Professor Timothy Eliot Stokes – brilliantly portrayed by Thayer David, one of the show's greatest assets – to be among the most intriguing characters. I also adored Jonathan Frid's reluctant vampire Barnabas Collins, Lara Parker's breathtakingly bewitching Angélique Bouchard, David Selby's immortal werewolf-ghost Quentin Collins, and practically every character played by Jerry Lacy, Grayson Hall, John Karlen, Nancy Barrett, Humbert Allen Astredo, and Christopher Pennock.

Dark Shadows was a daily monster-fest once the show moved past Victoria Winters' search for her parentage, Roger Collins' frequent outbursts, and Burke Devlin's cannery connivery, and I loved every minute of it... even the minutes I didn't love quite so much (yeah, I'm looking at *you*, Leviathans, Dream Curse, 1841 Parallel Time, and *Night of Dark Shadows*). For horror fans, the series' 1795 flashback storyline, revealing at last the tragic tale of Barnabas's vampiric origins, was a master stroke of gothic storytelling that stands up remarkably well on repeated viewings, even now.[8]

One effective cheat I've discovered when searching for items on eBay is to figure out the most likely misspellings ("Star Wras" for *Star Wars*, "Star Terk" for *Star Trek*, that sort of thing), as it's a good bet no one else will bid on those items since they won't come up in auction searches when the names are spelled correctly. I'd decided to buy *Dark Shadows: The Complete Original Series*, beautifully packaged in a coffin design, but everywhere I looked, the box set was priced from $400 to $900, which was far more than I was willing to spend on a TV show – and a soap opera, at that. So I searched for "Drak

---

[5] See Lou Tambone's essay "What's So Special About the Creature from the Black Lagoon?."

[6] See Charles R. Rutledge's essay "A Monstrous Regiment of Draculas."

[7] See Kelli Fitzpatrick's essay "*Frankenstein*: Defining Monstrosity."

[8] See Ross Johnson's essay "Modern Mythology on a Micro-Budget: Reinventing Classic Monsters on *Dark Shadows*."

Shadows." To my surprise, I found one listed with an opening bid of only $60 – and I had a $50 eBay gift card I hadn't redeemed.

I bid the minimum, crossed my fingers, and waited for the auction to end, hoping no one else would find it – and that the exasperated seller wouldn't refuse to let it go for such a low price. I won the auction without fanfare, then redeemed my $50 card and wound up with the casket set containing all 1,225 episodes, worth hundreds of dollars, for a mere ten bucks out of pocket. It was money well spent. I'm currently re-watching the show in its entirety – this time with the spinoff novels, comics, and audios added into the mix – and I'm enjoying it even more... though if I were playing a *Dark Shadows* drinking game and had to take a shot every time someone said "Vicki Winters," "Maggie Evans," "Roger Collins," or especially "Burke Devlin" instead of just using first names, I'd be drunk after only one episode.

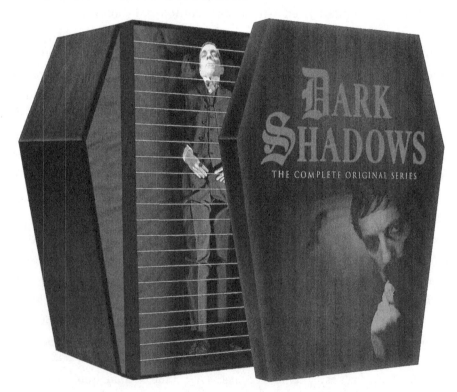

Dark Shadows: The Complete Original Series rests in its DVD coffin case, along with Barnabas Collins.

I'd missed out on *Dark Shadows* until adulthood, but I know I would have loved it as a kid. Monsters offered a refuge for the short, awkward, bullied bookworm I was in those days (as opposed to the tall, awkward, non-bullied bookworm I am now). If there were creatures in a story, I'd watch it, no matter how fake-looking they might be. I delighted at catching episodes of *The Twilight Zone*,[9] *The Outer Limits*, *One Step Beyond*, *Chiller Theatre*, *The Munsters*, *The Addams Family*,[10] *Star Trek*, *Lost in Space*, black-and-white *Doctor Who*, you name it. It was a treat to find these on TV, and I would wrest control of the channel from my sister Jody, who preferred *Good Times* or *Little House on the Prairie*, and later my other sister Susan as she watched *Gone With the Wind* for the hundredth time. This was before the ubiquity of modern home-viewing options, so if I didn't happen to be there when it aired, I was out of luck and would miss it – and that would never do.

I often pored through tattered copies of *Famous Monsters of Filmland*, *Monsters of the Movies*, and other magazines[11], awed and repulsed by the gruesome images staring up at me from the pages – and if there were vampires involved, all the better. I had a thing for vampires as a kid (did I mention I was bullied?), and if any blood-sucking movies starring Bela Lugosi (Universal's *Dracula*[12]), William Marshall (*Blacula*), or Christopher Lee (Hammer's *Dracula*[13]) were on TV, I was glued to our couch. I listened to LPs of Bobby Pickett's "Monster Mash," Sheb Wooley's "The Purple People Eater," Billy DeMarco's "Drac's Back," John Zacherley's "Coolest Little Monster,"[14] the Addams' and Munsters' theme songs, and other groovy-ghoulie tunes, memorizing the lyrics and singing along in what I thought must surely be an authentic Transylvanian accent. And I gazed wistfully at Aurora's *Monster Scenes* model kits that taunted me from their perch in a local toy store's front window.

---

[9] See Joe Bongiorno's essay "The Devil Has All the Best Films: Silver-Screen Satans and Boob-Tube Beelzebubs."

[10] See Robert Jeschonek's essay "Hippie Freaks in Monstrous Clothing: *The Addams Family* vs. *The Munsters*."

[11] See Samuel Agro's essay "Continuity of Terror: The Horror Comics of Warren Publishing."

[12] See Greg Cox's essay "Boris and Bela: The Best of Fiends."

[13] See Glenn Greenberg's essay "Dracula Gets Hammered."

[14] See Matthew Sunrich's essay "Hosts with the Ghosts: Horror Hosts in Comics and Television, 1940–1969."

Top: (left) Bobby Pickett's "Monster Mash," a graveyard smash since 1962, and (right) "Stanley and His Monster," which thrilled young monster kids in DC Comics' *The Fox and the Crow*, Bottom: (left) a vintage Universal's Movie Monsters lunch box, and (right) a Japanese LP recorded by Masato Shimon to promote *Ebirah, Horror of the Deep* at the 1972 Toho Champion Festival, featuring the songs "Bride of Godzilla" and "Rock Rock Godzilla."

I read the exploits of "Stanley and His Monster" in Frank Tashlin's 1960s comic *The Fox and the Crow*, any horror-themed anthologies my teachers had in their classrooms,[15] and all the delightful Crestwood House Monster books available in our school library.[16] When I was perhaps too young to appreciate it, I tried to read *Varney the Vampire*,[17] a Victorian-era novel by James Malcolm

---

[15] See Joe Bongiorno's essay "The Search for Monsters." Joe's vast vocabulary can best be summed up by the word "dictionary." Every time I work with him, I learn new words I'd previously not known. With this essay, I picked up "abstruse" and "ensorcelled," which I shall begin using in daily conversation, no doubt to my family's dismay.

[16] The Crestwood House books, aimed at young readers and recognizable for their orange or purple covers, featured such creatures as Dracula, Frankenstein's monster, King Kong, Godzilla, the Gill-man, the Blob, the Mummy, and more.

[17] Which I can no longer say without immediately thinking of Barney the Dinosaur.

Rymer and Thomas Peckett, first published in the mid-1850s as a series of penny dreadfuls. To my disappointment, I found the book tedious and never finished it. *Varney* is important to horror fans, though, not only because it predated *Dracula*, but because it introduced many now-common vampire tropes, such as neck-biting fangs, supernatural strength, and hypnotic powers – not to mention sympathetic self-loathing, an archetype exemplified by many subsequent creatures of the night, notably *Buffy the Vampire Slayer*'s Angel, *Forever Knight*'s Nick Knight, Anne Rice's sensuous vampires, and of course *Dark Shadows*' Barnabas Collins.

Six of the Crestwood House Monster books.

My parents brought me to wax museums, haunted house attractions, and theme restaurants with a monster motif. I marveled at a friend's monster-themed trading cards (*You'll Die Laughing*, *Mars Attacks*, *Monster Laffs*, *Creature Feature*... I'm sure I'm forgetting a few), then bought packs of my own with whatever was left of my 1970s allowance after I finished buying Topps baseball cards and *Planet of the Apes* trading cards.[18] And I reveled in the rare opportunity to enjoy General Mills' so-called "monster cereals" (Count Chocula,

---

[18] I eventually sold all of the cards to buy an Atari 2600 game system sometime around 1981, when I was thirteen years old – and I was majorly ripped off by the dealer who bought them, as I recall.

Franken Berry, Boo Berry, and Fruit Brute[19]) – at other people's houses, that is, since my folks never bought such products. I even went to school proudly carrying my "Universal's Movie Monsters" lunch box and thermos (again... bullied).

In the afternoons, I would hang out with two boys who lived across the street, and we'd stop playing and pay attention whenever a station aired the original *King Kong*, Vincent Price's *The Fly*, RKO's *The Thing from Another World*, the Steve McQueen B-movie *The Blob*, George Romero's *Night of the Living Dead*,[20] Val Lewton's *Cat People*,[21] or pretty much any movie featuring Ray Harryhausen's dazzling visual effects work.[22] We'd get particularly excited when *The 7th Voyage of Sinbad*, *The Golden Voyage of Sinbad*, *Jason and the Argonauts*, *Mighty Joe Young*, or *One Million Years B.C.* came on. I seem to recall that my friends' dad, who rarely said much to us otherwise, pointedly stuck around in the living room whenever *One Million Years B.C.* was playing; I'm sure it had nothing at all to do with the outfit that Raquel Welch was almost wearing in that film. We were there for the cavemen and dinosaurs.

There's something that touches a nerve deep inside us whenever we're scared or creeped out. It's why we watch TV late at night with the lights off. It's why we ride rollercoasters even though they sometimes make us vomit. It's why we go trick-or-treating after dark and force ourselves to walk past tombstones even when there are alternate routes we could choose instead. It's why we laugh after our friends jump out from behind a doorway and yell "Boo!" at us, causing us to shriek and drop whatever we're holding. It's why those of us

---

[19] There was a fifth monster cereal, Fruity Yummy Mummy, but that didn't debut until my college years and was discontinued a mere five years later; I never even knew it had existed until well into my forties.

[20] See Robert Smith?'s essay "The Plague of the Plague of the Zombies" – and yes, the question mark really is part of his name.

[21] See Corinna Bechko's essay "I Like the Dark: An Exploration of the Monstrous Feminine in Val Lewton's *Cat People* Duology."

[22] I still laugh at the memory of one of the boys across the street adamantly insisting, after we'd watched the 1977 horror film *The Car*, that the demon-possessed vehicle couldn't drive over "hollowed ground." I pointed out that the character who'd said this had stated "*hallowed* ground," referring to holy land (a cemetery) consecrated by the Catholic Church. My stubborn friend stone-facedly replied, "Well... it was hollowed, too. There were a lot of holes in it." And he was serious.

born before the 1980s told ghost stories around campfires – and why the legacy of classic monsters continued on into the modern age, not only with the Vincent Price lyric quoted at the start of this essay, but also in movies like *The Monster Squad*.[23]

It's also why we watch movies and TV shows about monsters, ghouls, freaks, and phantoms. Beautiful people on celluloid are a dime a dozen, and in the early days of Hollywood, they tended to get by on their chiseled jawlines, their perfectly coiffed and sprayed hair, and their heavily mascaraed eyes. But the beasts and brutes, the spectres and fiends – ah, now *they* were far more interesting to behold than the breathless beauties and the heartthrob heroes.

This, no doubt, explains my love for DC Comics' *Swamp Thing* mythology.[24] Characters like Alec Holland (a well-meaning scientist turned shambling bog-creature), Anton Arcane (an evil sorcerer), the Patchwork Man (a Frankenstein's monster analogue), Cranius and his fellow Un-Men (reanimated zombies), Ian MacCobb (a werewolf), Rebecca and Timothy Ravenwind (witches), M'Nagalah (a Lovecraftian entity), Auntie De Luvian and Black Jubal (ghosts), and other creations from the minds of Len Wein, Bernie Wrightson, and their successors provided wonderfully creepy takes on classic monster archetypes. They strongly resonated with the horror fan inside me, inspiring a decades-long obsession with the muck-encrusted mockery of a man and his macabre mythos.

That love of *Swamp Thing* led me even deeper into the bayou. When the series debuted in 1971, Wein and Wrightson were following in the footsteps of giants. The 1940s had seen the publication of Theodore Sturgeon's short story "It!" in pulp-fantasy magazine *Unknown*, about a plant monster with a human skeleton; Harry Stein's and Mort Leav's "SkyWolf," in Hillman Periodicals' *Air Fighters Comics* (later renamed *Airboy*) #3, which featured a bog beast called Heap; and Alfred Bester's "Fighters Never Quit," in *All-American Comics* #61, which presented the first appearance of DC's undead swamp-spawned super-villain monster, Solomon Grundy. So when Swamp Thing entered the bayou, it

---

[23] See Greg Mitchell's essay "Rock Until You Drop: The Enduring Legacy of Classic Monsters in *The Monster Squad*."

[24] Introduced in DC's *The House of Secrets* #92 by legendary writer-artist team Len Wein and Bernie Wrightson, then expanded upon the following year as a monthly *Swamp Thing* comic book.

was already bogged down with muck-men. Naturally, after reading *Swamp Thing*, I began checking out those other titles as well.

Marvel Comics, meanwhile, had unveiled its own swamp-beast – the giant-sized Man-Thing, from Roy Thomas and Gerry Conway (then Wein's roommate) – in *Savage Tales* #1, a month before Swamp Thing's debut. That series I admittedly never got into, but the late 1960s and early '70s saw the release of other stories featuring swamp beings, and I found many of them quite fascinating as well. DC tales published around that time which featured plant monsters included *The House of Mystery* #195 and #217, *The Phantom Stranger* #14, *World's Finest* #219–220, *Forbidden Tales of Dark Mansion* #10, and *The Unexpected* #152, among others. They're all on my shelves, and they're all worth a read if you can find them. But it was Swamp Thing that emerged as the most enduring of all bog-monsters, and I remain a major fan to this day.

Jim Beard shared my love of monsters when he invited me to pitch and helm this anthology with him in 2018, then under the title *I Was a Grade-School Monster Kid*. A lifelong fan of movies, television shows, comics, and pulp literature from before the 1970s, Jim has impressively made a career out of his nostalgic passion for that era, and Sequart was glad to publish a collection of essays on that subject coedited by the two of us. We invited contributors to join us in our quest, most of whom we'd worked with before, as we set out to define what it is about classic monsters from the 19th century to the early 1970s that had so enthralled us when we were young – what it is that made us "monster kids." I staked my claim on the Godzilla films of the Shōwa era, while Jim knew what he'd write about: Universal's Wolf Man character, Larry Talbot. We'd each snagged our favorite niche in the world of monster mayhem from the outset because, hey, rank hath its privileges.

After the contributors had signed aboard and were busily writing their articles, a schedule conflict forced me to step down temporarily as coeditor. It wasn't an easy decision, believe me. Jim and I had previously coedited a Titan Books fiction anthology, *Planet of the Apes: Tales from the Forbidden Zone*, and it had been a greatly rewarding collaboration, so I was thrilled to join him again. Sometimes, though, life throws you a curve ball and you have no choice but to adapt. For me, that meant moving on – though I did remain aboard as a contributor. After all, I wasn't going to hand custody of my favorite atomic-powered dinosaur over to just *anybody*.

Tragically, Jim received a thrown curve ball of his own a month or two later, and it was a devastating blow. Hollywood has perpetuated the myth of soul mates and fairy-tale romances, leading many to become depressed due to their inability to find a perfect match like those depicted onscreen. Well, Jim had actually found his soulmate, his fairy-tale love, his perfect match, in the form of his wife Becky, and the two had enjoyed a wonderful marriage, friendship, and creative partnership of equals that had lasted for decades until 2019, when Becky was unexpectedly stricken with a fatal illness.

Sadly, cancer is one insidious monster. There's no Abraham Van Helsing to outthink it and no Jonathan Harker to slay it. Torch-bearing villagers with pitchforks have no effect on tumors, nor do garlic, sunlight, wolfsbane, wooden stakes, silver bullets, salt, holy water, running water, freezing, fire, magic, electrocution, prayers, incantations, or any other popular methods of defeating movie monsters. Cancer often wins in the end... and in this case, it did. It was heartbreaking to hear that Becky had passed away, and Jim found he could no longer edit the book, as he quite understandably needed time to focus on grieving the loss of his wife and best friend. Therefore, I immediately came back to finish what Jim and I had started. How could I not? I'm no monster.

Then history repeated itself. Joe Bongiorno had briefly been slated to coedit this anthology with me, but he soon faced the same problem I'd run into: schedule overload. As it happened, Joe and Jim hadn't yet begun working on the book, so our buddy Lou Tambone, with whom I'd produced two other essay anthologies for Sequart,[25] took Joe's place. Together, Lou and I closed the revolving editorial door and, from false starts to satisfying finish, put together the book now staring you in the face with its beady monster eyes. Lou and I are proud of how *Musings on Monsters: Observations on the World of Classic Horror* turned out, and that the book's Halloween 2020 release synchronizes nicely with the upcoming 90th anniversary of Universal's *Dracula* – the first Universal Monsters movie[26] and thus the reason this book exists – not to mention Godzilla's 67th birthday.

---

[25] *Somewhere Beyond the Heavens: Exploring Battlestar Galactica* and *From Bayou to Abyss: Examining John Constantine, Hellblazer.*

[26] Although Universal's *The Phantom of the Opera* had reached the silver screen in 1925, it's not really part of the Universal Monsters series. *Dracula* (1931) is the film that truly launched the franchise.

Thanks to the immensely skilled essayists, as well as cover artist Leah Battle and the folks at Sequart, Lou and I, acting as a surrogate Victor Frankenstein and Ygor, gave life to mad scientist Jim's creation. I also need to thank my family — Jill (my beautiful Bride of Frankenstein), Emily (my Daughter of Dracula), and Josh (my Son of Godzilla), along with my parents Vinnie, Joni, and Carol (a monster triple-feature) — for their endless support and encouragement.

The lightning has struck, the electrodes are aglow, and our monster from his slab has begun to arise. As we triumphantly yell "It's alive!", I can only hope that when Jim reads the final product, he'll deem it worthy of his vision — that he'll consider this little monster mash a graveyard smash. For you, the living, this book was meant, too; when you get to our door, tell them Boris sent you.

The Frank 'n Stein roadside restaurant in Indiana, circa 1973. Sadly, this establishment and statue, once located on U.S. Route 20, are long gone.

The editors wish to dedicate this anthology to monster kid-at-heart Becky Beard, who was taken from this world far too soon and would surely have had a monstrously good time reading it.

The Search for Monsters

by Joe Bongiorno

For every monster, there's a hero. This essay is dedicated to my former teacher, the late Joseph C. Ingulli (1931–2004), to my high-school librarian, Harvey Brody, and to all the positive influencers of children who often pass unremarked, but are not forgotten...

There are none who truly know why we love monsters.

Oh, there are plenty of pop-psychology theories that were bandied about in the mid-20th century, and while there may be validity to some of them, mainly they allowed doctors and scientists to smugly assure parents that they didn't have to worry about their child's obsession with such strange fare. After all, polite society didn't talk or think about such things.

But for those of us who *do*, who suspect the conventional world hides a different sort of monster, all the rationalizations put forth to explain away monsters and the wondrous dread they evoke ultimately feel hollow... false... a form of whistling past the graveyard, empty authoritarian word salad made up of pat explanations, abstruse concepts, and highbrow language intended to cow the poor, irrational plebeian. Now, when the subject comes up, polite society can claim to understand – and laugh – at such things.

And yet, relegated as they are to modern myths, monsters refuse to go away. Maybe it's because there's something truer about them than there is about our conventional society and its pernicious obsession with superficiality and material acquisition, all of which is so easily stripped away. It doesn't take much, after all – a disaster, war, or pandemic – for the façade to come crumbling down, for the rotting accoutrements of civilization to be exposed for its hypocrisy, greed, apathy, and weakness, for the human monster and its ugly, grasping heart to be stripped bare.

The monsters we love – the ones that come from the pages of old books and stories and movies – have a kind of purity in their chilling commitment to our destruction or seduction. All monsters hide from the light, even the hideous human kind, but our monsters are so beloved precisely because they're *not* human. They possess a mythic power, deriving as they do from an ancient and alien *otherworld*, a hidden, supernatural *shadow world*. Even those impoverished "naturalistic" monsters – birthed in 1950s sci-fi books and Hollywood films – forged by human endeavors, mad science, or environmental degradation, hearken to the underlying feeling that we are being offered a glimpse into hidden realms. Behind the curtain is no mere man pulling the levers – as we've come to expect, thanks to *The Wizard of Oz* – but something truly terrifying, unnatural, and inexplicable that cannot so easily be dismissed or defined.

My fascination with monsters was born in the 1970s from reruns of *Lost in Space,* countless monster movies, *Star Wars*, and the book of Revelation (with its hybrid beasts and dragons), but it wouldn't be until 1978, at the ripe old age of eight, that my ardent passion for the macabre would creep into being. That was the year I discovered *Monster Tales: Vampires, Werewolves, & Things* sitting on the shelf of my elementary school library.

I still remember the first time I found it. It was a purple hardcover, upon which were painted strange red monsters floating on what looked like yellow smoke (later, when I saw the color, non-library edition, I realized it was the psychedelic head and mouth of another creature). The anthology was published by Rand McNally and edited by Roger Elwood, with black-and-white interior illustrations by Franz Altschuler of that particularly haunting variety that tends to stay with you in the deepest parts of the night.

The book immediately called to me. It was like finding something lost that I didn't realize was missing, a hidden treasure to which I knew I somehow belonged.[1] But what was such a wondrous thing doing *here*, in an elementary school library of all places? Did the librarian *know* this book was on the shelf? Or had it been smuggled in by someone who decried the poor state of children's literature and wanted to offer those who could appreciate it something greater than *Tales of a Fourth-Grade Nothing*? Would I even be allowed to check it out? I noted that three people had taken it out before me, but maybe they were older students or staff.

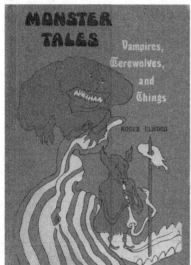

Monster Tales: Vampires, Werewolves, & Things (1973, library and standard editions), edited by Roger Elwood.

When I made up my mind about something, there was little anyone could do that could dissuade me. *I would have this precious relic.* Making myself look as tall and mature as possible, I walked to the checkout counter, wrote the date (April 25) on the card, and concealed my satisfaction as the librarian stamped it.

The entire rest of the day was spent in anticipation of going home. I was tempted to begin reading it in my more boring classes (which amounted to all but English), but I wouldn't do the book that injustice. Something of this magnitude required proper time and space.

My fellow students – obstreperous, mewling, obnoxious dullards – held little interest for me at the time. I ignored them and promptly rushed home, ate

---

[1] I would feel this way again a year later when I came upon *Dungeons & Dragons* for the first time on the shelf of a local Woolworth store.

the obligatory snack, and withdrew into the solemn privacy of my bedroom, where the outside world promptly vanished away, leaving only the view of the sun and the giant oak tree in the backyard, its large boughs swaying in the breeze, to penetrate my inner sanctum.

Robert Bloch's introduction was of the condescending type (and a long way down from his days of "Notebook Found in a Deserted House,"[2] which I read a few years later), and it spoke of monsters being the product of caveman superstition and the modern child's ability to scare them off by turning on the light. As if.

I didn't let it dampen my enthusiasm for what was to come.

"Wendigo's Child," by Thomas F. Monteleone, was the first. A deeply haunting tale, it's the one readers tend to remember the most – possibly because they were too scared to read beyond it. Near his Arizona home, young Marty Alvarez uncovers a small mummy in a recently excavated dig...

> His stomach churned as he uncovered the thing, and he pulled his trembling hands away – he had almost touched it. It looked vaguely like a little baby, with its curled-up legs and thin, sticklike arms. It was about two feet long and covered with dark brown skin that looked like cracked, cry leather. The head was like a human skull, but instead of teeth, it bore a sharp, curved beak like a big bird. Marty couldn't really see the thing's bones, but they were almost visible under the skin, which was stretched tightly over them. The eye sockets were empty – big and dark and round, but the face seemed to be almost grinning.

Thinking he'll make good money selling it to the researchers arriving the next day, Marty smuggles it out. From local Native American storyteller Charlie Longhand, he learns of the *weonee*, the offspring of the Wendigo, an evil god, who places them as guardians at the burial sites of the Indians who worship him. Undaunted, Marty sneaks it into his cellar. Later that night, awakened by his dog's howls, Marty is led into the dark cellar, where his flashlight reveals the *weonee* is not where he'd left it!

As with most of the tales in this anthology, "Wendigo's Child" is a masterwork of short prose that builds an atmosphere of ever-mounting unease. The protagonist feels wholly authentic, without any of the "funny," self-aware quips that have come to mar modern stories for younger readers. In fact, the anthology's greatest strength is that it doesn't seem to know it's geared toward

---

[2] A Cthulhu Mythos short story that debuted in a 1951 issue of *Weird Tales*.

a young demographic, giving it an off-kilter, subversive quality, as if somehow Elwood had ensorcelled the librarians of America to let this book slide into their schools. No more is this evident than in the next story, which centers on human sacrifice and devil worship.

"Torchbearer," by Arthur Tofte, is the collection's longest tale, and another treasure. Sold by his father to pay off his debts, young Rolf comes to live at the dark and haunted castle of his new master, Count Monterrant. An odd witch, Old Berthe, informs him of the evening's infernal proceedings. By torchlight, Rolf leads his master to the courtyard, where an assortment of freaks has gathered to witness the Count condemn a local magistrate, tied to a stake, who had put to death hundreds of innocents on the charge of witchcraft. Moved by the man's proclamations of innocence, Rolf sneaks out of his room later that night to free him, but when the judge threatens to kill him, he runs off! The next day, the Count informs the boy that he's glad he gave the judge false hope, for he was soon caught again, and will burn that very night...

> Rolf tried to look away, to close his mind to the sight. Everything about it was unreal, unclean, unholy. The utter blackness of the sky overhead. The stillness of the night air. The steady keening of the watchers. The hideous, foul movements of Count Monterrant as he proceeded with the blasphemous ritual. It was a ghastly thing that was happening. And yet he could not take his gaze from the scene. It was as though some force, greater than he, was holding him in a tight grip and was making him look.

An evocative examination of how the actions of evil people can drive others to become monsters, "The Torchbearer" is a layered story with interspersed supernatural and psychological aspects. Because the narrative is so steeped in dread and is driven by a protagonist who feels like a real person, the doom-laden events have the phantasmal quality of a living nightmare.

Dread haunts Brian Ball's "The Call of the Grave," a Welsh ghost story of a young girl whose father and brothers had died in a mining accident that had killed many of the men in town. The women of the village go out to "call on the dead." Although the girl's mother prohibits her from following the old legends, she is captivated by the idea. She finds an out-of-the-way ventilation shaft, where she can commune with her dead father and brothers in secret. Three weeks into her daily pilgrimage, she finds a local English businessman named Mr. Jackson at her spot, calling upon the deceased Morgan Lewis. Then, on the third day, she sees something that no one believes...

> Mr. Jackson had just finished his conversation when it happened. He turned and I hid. He was grinning. I am sure that he did not see the long,

thin arms that rested on the brickwork behind him, nor the long, emaciated, and blackened fingers. I saw them. To this day I swear that I saw them.

With a palpably moody setting, and the way the tension mounts towards its uncanny ending worthy of M.R. James, "The Call of the Grave" proved so effectively unsettling, it kick-started my love for ghost stories.

Left to right: Franz Altschuler's artwork from "Wendigo's Child," by Thomas F. Monteleone; Nic Andersson's "Werewolf Boy"; and "Precious Bodily Fluids," by Mario Martin Jr.

Nic Andersson's "Werewolf Boy" is the second longest entry in the book, and another standout that builds on the theme presented in "Torchbearer," with a unique take on werewolf lore...

> To pass through the black forest alone at night was a fearsome thing. Stefan knew that unless he hurried, he would not be through before dark. He held the brown-and-white puppy close in his arms. He had stayed too long, selecting from among the lively young dogs in the litter... Now it was getting late. Nightfall was only about two-and-a-half hours away. It would take him a good three hours to pass through the dense woods.

Unfortunately, the cruel baron and his deadly hounds arrive, and Stefan's puppy does not survive the encounter. The baron whips the grief-stricken boy across the face and departs. Helga, a witness to these events, brings him to her hut, where she reveals that she is, indeed, a witch. Stefan asks her for a way to avenge his lost puppy, vowing to do whatever it takes to kill the hounds, including becoming a werewolf. She agrees, though once he has committed this deed, he must return to her to pay whatever price she demands. The boy accepts these terms.

Discovering that magic is the only viable option for turning him into a werewolf, Helga gathers the ingredients and begins the enchantment. Once this is complete, she tells him that he will become a wolf from midnight to dawn. The following midnight comes with agonizing pain as Stefan transforms into a lycanthrope. Overcome with bloodlust, he uses his intelligence and animal instinct to defeat and kill the hounds — but upon returning home, he forgets to wash the blood off, and the baron's men trace it to his family home. Stefan then runs to the witch's hut to learn the terrible price he must pay.

Although I'd seen Universal's *The Wolf Man*, this was the first of the subgenre that I'd ever read, and it made me a lifelong devotee, paving the way for my love of *An American Werewolf in London* and *The Howling*, as well as my utter disdain for the gelded pop-werewolves of the *Twilight* series.

"Precious Bodily Fluids," by Mario Martin Jr. (a pseudonym for Thomas F. Monteleone), is arguably the creepiest tale in the anthology, which is saying quite a bit! Inheriting his late uncle's mansion on the moors of Midwich, England, 12-year-old Michael moves with his father into the large estate, inhabited only by the caretaker, Mr. Gaskell. While his father is at work, Michael explores and uncovers several mysteries. There are no animals, save for what appear to be buried in graves and a box of dried-up rats. Far worse, his father begins to inexplicably become gaunt and frail...

> Gaskell was as kindly attentive to Michael's father as he was mockingly hostile to Michael... Michael noticed that the old man's walk had acquired a spring, his sallow face was looking better, and he seemed to be young. Gaskell knew that Michael was aware of the changes in both men. Every time Michael would look at Gaskell, he would feel the tiny birdlike eyes burrowing into his soul, seeing his inner thoughts. Then old Gaskell would give a slight hint of a smile and wink at him, frightening him even more than before.

One day, while examining his uncle's papers, Michael finds old notes written about vampires and lamias. Then one night, Michael catches Gaskell sneaking into his father's bedroom. In the dark, he hears horrid sounds and runs off to hide in the large cellar. It's not long before the sounds of footsteps are heard descending behind him.

One thing that Roger Elwood did so brilliantly when choosing these tales was to find protagonists who were relatable, and often isolated. As each one stumbles upon the fantastical, there is a sense of wonder that accompanies it, not unlike the classic fantasy stories, but darker, as these doors do not open to magical worlds, but to the shadow realm.

"The Vrkolak," by Brian T. LoMedico (another pseudonym for Thomas F. Monteleone), sees young Billy as a victim of bullying at his upstate New York summer camp. One day, while scouting alone in the woods, sent ahead by his tormentor to locate the group's campsite for the night, Billy finds himself lost...

> He passed the hours by thinking about the woods he walked through. Sometimes his mind would wander, and he wouldn't even remember where he had been for several minutes, so intense were his fantasies about the forest. He recalled reading stories and seeing movies about strange creatures and monsters that lived in the woods, far away from men. These monsters took on many shapes, and they hid in the thick forest waiting to catch unwary visitors. Sometimes he would hear a rustling in the branches or bushes as he walked, and the hair on the back of his neck would grow stiff, like bristles on a brush.

After realizing that it's not a trick being played on him, Billy is forced to press on in the cold and dark woods for hours until, in terror at a noise, he runs headlong into a candlelit shack. There, a nose-less, toothless old woman invites him in. Her son had died recently, and she gifts him with herbs that she calls the charm of the Vrkolak, the spirit and ancient protector of the bogs, which will give him strength and cunning, ensuring that no harm can come to him. Billy eats the herbs and quickly departs to the nearby road she directs him to, where he's picked up by the police. After the next few days, Billy is shocked to discover that the nighttime brings about his transformation into a giant toad – but that maybe it's not so bad.

Echoing Franz Kafka's "The Metamorphosis," the final story in the anthology ends on more of a fantasy note than a horror one (arguably, the book has earned its semi-happy ending), though the description of being lost in the woods has rarely been conveyed with such genuine terror.

There's a lot to be said for reading well-told stories when you're young and your imagination more readily and intensely supplies the sights, sounds, and feelings beyond what's been sketched on the page. As an only child with few friends and a strong imagination, I was fortunate to have had parents who left me alone to enjoy my hobbies, as well as that rare sympathetic, intuitive teacher in Mr. Ingulli, who encouraged my reading and writing – no matter how bizarre it was.

I continued to take the book out subsequent times in the years that followed, along with other gems I found at the Scholastic Book Fair (which, thankfully, had no short supply of horror and fantasy) until I graduated and moved on to junior high school. By then, I had begun to fantasize about a future telling such tales, impractical as that seemed.

High school had a larger library, and though *Monster Tales* was not in it, I was blessed with a wonderfully astute librarian in Mr. Harvey Brody, who had been crafty enough to sneak in the works of H.P. Lovecraft, Clark Ashton Smith, Robert E. Howard, and others who specialized in weird fantasy and horror, solidifying a love of the genre that would keep me occupied for a lifetime.

Many years would pass before I would think upon *Monster Tales* again. Then, around 13 years later, I ran into Mr. Ingulli at the shopping mall (he'd become a deacon by that time), and nostalgia began to kick in for that old book. This was in the days before eBay and Amazon, so tracking down old books posed more of a challenge – particularly if you'd forgotten the book's title!

My elementary school was only down the road. Would the book still be there? Would they allow a grown man to even look for it? It all seemed a bit far-fetched, but it was worth the effort to at least discover the title.

The school's interior was far smaller then I'd remembered, and I felt a bit like Lemuel Gulliver amongst the Lilliputians. I waited until the final classes were out before approaching the principle, who proved nice enough. Before I knew it, I was scouring the library shelves, admittedly feeling a bit out of place. All I recalled was that the book was purple and had "monster" in the title. I searched every shelf in every aisle. Nothing.

But then, in the very last aisle, I saw a purple spine, and the words "Monster Tales" on it!

It felt oddly talismanic, as if greeting a long-lost friend. Checking the card on the back, I could see my handwriting all over it on various dates. Returning triumphant to the principal's office, I was greeted with a surprise: "Keep it," he said, "as a reminder, and in case it helps you become a writer."

My reread of it was met with trepidation. What if it wasn't as good as I'd remembered? Would I be ruining that special place it held in my memory?

Thankfully, that fear proved groundless. The stories stood the test of time, and now I noticed other things, such as how well-crafted they were, and the nuanced way in which they treated their monsters. For example, each of the book's three witches has a kind of nobility. In their own way, they help the protagonists seek the justice of which they'd been robbed in times past.

The fact that so few readers knew about this book gave it a kind of mythical quality, which made it all the more fascinating to discover online that several others had a very similar experience upon reading it in their elementary school libraries.[3] It's also been good to discover that Rand McNally had published it as part of a series, alongside *Horror Tales: Spirits, Spells & the Unknown, Baleful Beasts and Eerie Creatures, Tales of Terror*, and two science-fiction anthologies.

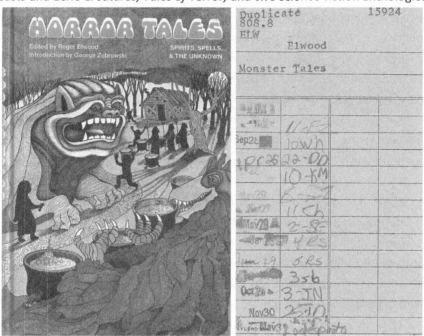

Horror Tales: Spirits, Spells, & The Unknown (1974, a related volume also edited by Roger Elwood), plus the library card from the actual copy of *Monster Tales* I read as a child and now proudly own.

The search for monsters continues, but now, at least, I understand them a bit better. They don't mind if you see them solely as metaphors. They don't care if you buy into the psycho-science claptrap about them. The living embodiments of nightmare remain hidden, yet accessible, for they fill a need in those of us willing to spend time with them. For some, they're just a pleasing diversion. But for others, they're a portal to the world as it really is. Beyond the façade of conventional wisdom, beyond the fabric of lies, villainy, and stupidity, they offer a glimpse at the shadow-realm beneath, shrouding our world in a deeper, darker cast – and yet, ironically, making it a brighter place for it.

For those who are brave, cautious, and wise, monsters open the door to a greater reality.

---

[3] See http://the-haunted-closet.blogspot.com/2008/10/monster-tales-vampires-werewolves.html. Also, see the reviews on the book's Amazon page.

A New World of Gods and Monsters: Universal Studios and the First Shared Cinematic Universe

by Joseph F. Berenato

In 1943, with the uttering of a single word by an old Gypsy woman, the shared cinematic universe was created.[1]

That was the year that saw the release of *Frankenstein Meets the Wolf Man*, the first crossover film featuring two movie monsters – and, no doubt, saw tens of thousands of monster lovers scream with delight. Though Universal Studios had been making horror pictures for some time – arguably starting in 1923 with *The Hunchback of Notre Dame*[2] – this was the first time that two of its marquee monsters had been featured in the same film. Sequels were, of course, nothing new for Universal creature features – *Frankenstein Meets the*

---

[1] Okay. Perhaps it wasn't that simple, and perhaps it wasn't that mystical. It was, however, no less magical.

[2] "Arguably" because, while that film's main character, Quasimodo, has been branded an official Universal Monster for years, the case could be made that there are no horror elements to the film, except for Quasimodo's appearance.

Wolf Man was, in itself, simultaneously a direct sequel to 1941's *The Wolf Man* and the fifth installation in the *Frankenstein* series that began in 1931, but nothing like this had been attempted before.

The Universal Monsters cinematic universe was wholly unique for its day, incorporating elements from, ultimately, four of its character series. Some monsters, for various reasons, never saw incorporation into the grander universe, either because their characters had long since shuffled off their mortal coil, or there was no practical way to incorporate them no matter how much the writers tried. Those who did come together, however, remain among the most legendary film monsters of all time – and it all really started with the first talking horror movie.

Dracula (1931)

Originally approved as a vehicle with silent film legend Lon Chaney[3] in mind, *Dracula*'s production received its first setback in August of 1930 when Chaney died of lung cancer. A treatment and a partial script had been completed, but these were later completely retooled in order to more closely follow John L. Balderston's 1927 play rather than Bram Stoker's original 1897 novel.[4]

The role of Dracula was masterfully played by Bela Lugosi, but he wasn't the studio's first choice after Chaney – nor the second, nor even the third. Producer Carl Laemmle Jr. auditioned several actors for the role, including Conrad Veidt, Paul Muni, and Ian Keith – with trade publications even reporting that Keith had been given the part – because they felt that Lugosi, who had performed the role on Broadway for a year and on a national tour for two, had no name recognition. However, by 20 September 1930, Lugosi was signed for the role.[5]

---

[3] Star of, among other things, *The Hunchback of Notre Dame* and *The Phantom of the Opera*, both of which, it could be argued, inhabit the same universe as they both take place in Paris, though almost 500 years apart, as the façade built for Notre Dame Cathedral in 1922 can be clearly seen during the climax of the later film. It's a tangential connection, at best.

[4] Riley, Philip J. *Dracula Starring Lon Chaney – An Alternative History for Classic Film Monsters*. BearManor Media, 2010.

[5] Rhodes, Gary Don. *Lugosi: His Life in Films, on Stage, and in the Hearts of Horror Lovers*. McFarland, 2015.

Another transplant from the stage production was Edward Van Sloan,[6] who was cast as Professor Van Helsing. Van Sloan's pitch-perfect performance led to his becoming Universal's go-to actor when they needed a character who knew enough about science and modern medicine to get by, but also knew that there are such things as vampires and curses and forbidden knowledge, as he would portray almost identical roles in *Frankenstein* and 1932's *The Mummy*.

Professor Van Helsing (Edward Van Sloan) and Count Dracula (Bela Lugosi) square off in *Dracula*, the first-ever talking horror movie, which spawned an incredible monster franchise.

---

[6] Ibid.

Because the script closely followed the stage production instead of the novel, a number of characters were excised or combined with others. Gone, for example, were both Arthur Holmwood (later Lord Godalming) and Texan Quincey P. Morris, two suitors of Lucy Weston (Frances Dade).[7] Her third suitor, Jack Seward, was transformed into Dr. John Seward (Herbert Bunston), the father of Mina Seward (Helen Chandler), formerly Mina Murray in the novel. John Harker (David Manners) still survives, though he exists simply to serve as Mina's love interest, as opposed to the real estate man who facilitated Dracula's move to London. That role is supplanted by Renfield (Dwight Frye) in the film.

The end of the movie is also quite different than that of the novel, in which Van Helsing, Harker, and the three suitors pursue Dracula back to his castle in Transylvania and destroy him. Here, Dracula flees to Carfax Abbey with Mina and is pursued by Harker and Van Helsing. The rising sun forces Dracula, after strangling Renfield, to retreat to his box of earth, wherein Van Helsing drives a stake through his heart.

Critical and popular reception for *Dracula* ensured that the world's first horror film with sound certainly wouldn't be its last – nor, as time would tell, would this be the last time the world saw Count Dracula, though it would be another 17 years before Lugosi once again played the role for which he is still remembered.

Frankenstein (1931)

Hot off the heels of *Dracula* – and the money that it helped put in Universal's coffers – Robert Florey was hired, in March of 1931, to write a script adapting Mary Shelley's classic novel, *Frankenstein; or, the Modern Prometheus*, from 1818, and to direct the film. His original script contained elements that made it into the final version of the film, including the climax and fire at the windmill and the use of a criminal brain in the creation of the Monster. Lugosi's success in *Dracula* made him Florey's choice for Frankenstein – the scientist, not the creation.[8]

However, Laemmle Jr. had other things in mind.

---

[7] Lucy Westenra in the novel.
[8] Riley, Philip J. *Frankenstein (Universal Filmscripts Series: Classic Horror Films)*. MagicImage Filmbooks, 1989.

In April of 1931, Universal secured the rights to a play adaptation of *Frankenstein* by Peggy Webbling and paid Balderston to adapt it into a screenplay. Laemmle Jr. also wanted Lugosi to test not for the scientist role, but for the Monster.[9] Scenes were shot, but Lugosi was not pleased with the character, which had been reduced from an intelligent, erudite being in Shelley's novel to a grunting brute in Florey's script.[10]

Soon Florey and Lugosi were out, and veteran director James Whale was in. Not long after his hiring, Whale spotted an individual eating lunch in the Universal commissary and knew he would be perfect for the role. Whale slipped him a note, and soon thereafter, William Henry Pratt – now known to the world as Boris Karloff – signed on as the Monster.[11]

Even with Balderston's and Whale's changes to the script, the film – like *Dracula* – represents a significant departure from the source material. The Monster cannot speak, though Whale did reinsert much of the pathos and sympathy of the novel. Victor Frankenstein is now Henry (Colin Clive), the name presumably coming from Victor's friend in the novel, Henry Clerval. Henry the friend, however, is now named Victor Moritz (John Boles[12]), whose last name is derived from Justine Moritz, a character killed by the Monster in the novel and axed from the movie script altogether. The movie has no wedding night murders, nor does it feature the creation of a mate for the Monster,[13] nor a chase through the arctic. Frankenstein's mentor, Dr. Waldman (Van Sloan), is present, though his role has been altered to be more of a cautionary Van Helsing – fitting for Van Sloan. Henry's bride-to-be, Elizabeth (Mae Clark[14]), is presented as a much more headstrong and modern woman than her novel counterpart. Added to the film is Fritz (Frye again, just as memorably as his performance in *Dracula*), Frankenstein's hunchbacked dwarf lab assistant.

---

[9] Ibid.

[10] Vieira, Mark A. *Hollywood Horror: From Gothic to Cosmic.* Harry N. Abrams, Inc., 2003.

[11] Riley, *Frankenstein*.

[12] Whose suspension-of-disbelief-destroying Texan accent is incredibly distracting, and one wonders if Balderston, when adapting *Frankenstein*, remembered something about a Texan from *Dracula* and simply got confused.

[13] The monster *will* demand a mate; just not for another four years.

[14] Perhaps best known to modern audiences for having been on the receiving end of a grapefruit to the kisser from James Cagney in *Public Enemy*.

Boris Karloff's portrayal of the Monster in *Frankenstein* captured some of the sympathy of Mary Shelley's character.

When the film was released, audiences were shocked, horrified, and enthralled. The picture was an instant success, with Karloff being hailed as the next Chaney,[15] causing his star to begin to burn very brightly at Universal.

---

[15] Ibid.

Interlude I

The success of both *Dracula* and *Frankenstein* caused Universal to focus rather heavily on horror pictures, with Lugosi and Karloff starring together in *The Black Cat* (1934) and *The Raven* (1935), both of which derive their titles from the works of Edgar Allan Poe, and neither of which bears any resemblance to the works of those names.

Karloff enjoyed success following *Frankenstein* as the title character in *The Mummy*, starring as the disgraced ancient Egyptian priest Imhotep. The script was written by Balderston, who covered the opening of King Tutankhamun's tomb in 1922.[16] Thematically, *The Mummy* bears a striking resemblance to *Dracula*: an ancient evil is in search of a bride, and when science fails, it's up to the mystic (played in both by Edward Van Sloan) to help put the evil down forever.

James Whale revisited the horror genre in 1933 with *The Invisible Man*, based on the 1897 novel of the same name by H.G. Wells. Karloff was attached to star as Dr. Jack Griffith (the eponymous invisible man), but, after a salary dispute with Laemmle Jr., Whale decided to go with Claude Rains.[17] The film follows the overall storyline of the novel rather closely: a scientist creates a formula that renders him completely invisible. A major difference between the two is that in the movie, the potion drives Griffith insane, whereas in the novel he is insane to begin with.

In 1935, Universal tried its hand at the werewolf genre for the first time with *Werewolf of London*, directed by Stuart Walker with a story by Robert Harris and a screenplay by John Colton. Henry Hull was brought on board to play Dr. Wilfred Glendon, a botanist who is bitten by a werewolf in Tibet while searching for the Mariphasa plant, which only blooms by the light of the silvery moon. The makeup for Glendon's transformation was done by Jack Pierce, who had so masterfully created the look for both Frankenstein's monster and Imhotep, and early tests show that it bore a remarkable resemblance to Pierce's later work in the genre. However, Hull suggested that the makeup be toned down, as the script required the other characters to recognize the werewolf as Glendon. Hull took the issue to Laemmle Jr., who handed down word to Pierce

---

[16] Vieira.

[17] Tom Weaver, Michael Brunas, John Brunas. *Universal Horrors: The Studio's Classic Films, 1931-1946.* McFarland, 2007.

to scale it back a bit.[18] The result is a werewolf who looks like he needs a good shave and who takes the time to put on his hat and cloak before roaming the streets.

While *Werewolf of London* was being filmed, Universal was hard at work on another horror film – the first of many sequels which would lead to the eventual creation of the shared universe.

The Bride of Frankenstein (1935)

After spending a few years in developmental hell – including a treatment by Florey titled *The New Adventures of Frankenstein – The Monster Lives!*[19] that Universal returned to him – and with Whale claiming that he had milked all he could from the tale of Frankenstein, the studio slowly started to move forward on *The Return of Frankenstein* in 1933. Whale eventually came on board with a concept fleshed out by Balterston and William Hurlbut and, by January of 1935, filming had begun on *The Bride of Frankenstein*.[20]

Karloff and Clive returned in their roles, though Clive now found himself with second billing. Clark was out, having been replaced by Valerie Hobson (who also starred as Lisa Glendon in *Werewolf of London*, shot at the same time). New to the story was Dr. Septimus Pretorius (Ernest Thesiger), one of Frankenstein's old mentors who had been asked to leave the university because of the nature of his experiments, and who coerces Henry into stepping back into the laboratory once more. Also new was, of course, the Bride herself (Elsa Lanchester), who doubled as Mary Shelley in the film's opening and was onscreen for fewer than five minutes in total.

The main narrative of *Bride* picks up immediately after the end of its predecessor, where we learn that the Monster did not perish in a burning windmill but did, in fact, survive by falling into the stream that ran underneath the structure. After a murder or two he flees into the forest, but not before

---

[18] Hull, Cortlandt. "Henry Hull & Josephine Hull: It's in the Blood!" PreserveHollywood.org, 2014.
https://www.preservehollywood.org/DungeonWebNew/In_The_Blood.html
[19] Yes, really.
[20] Riley, Philip J. *The Bride of Frankenstein (Universal Filmscripts Series: Classic Horror Films Volume 2)*. MagicImage Filmbooks, 1989.

scaring the bejesus out of Minnie (Una O'Connor),[21] the housemaid at Castle Frankenstein. There, in a touching reversal from the previous film (in which he inadvertently drowns Maria, a little village girl), the Monster this time *saves* a village girl from drowning, and his kindness is repaid with shrieks of terror and a bullet wound. The other villagers hear the screams and descend upon him, then overpower him and haul him off to the town dungeon, from which he summarily escapes.

The Monster finds his way into the hut of a blind monk, who showers him with friendship and kindness, teaching him how to speak in the process... before villagers show up, the hut burns down, and he runs away, eventually stumbling into the very cemetery from the beginning of *Frankenstein*. It is there, in one of the crypts, where the Monster meets Pretorius, and the plan to make the Monster a mate is hatched.

Reception for the picture was overwhelmingly positive. Reviews for *The Bride of Frankenstein* praised the cast and the story, but also made mention of the directing, the sets, and the scoring.[22] One reviewer even went so far as to state, "The picture again ends with the apparent demise of the Monster – and his mate – but Mr. Karloff's best make-up should not be permitted to pass from the screen. The Monster should become an institution, like Charlie Chan."[23]

Clearly, Universal agreed, but it would be four more years until the Monster would rise again.

Dracula's Daughter (1936)

In the meantime, Universal revisited the world of its first horror talkie, and ultimately had rival film company Metro-Goldwyn-Mayer to thank for it.

In 1933, MGM's executive, the legendary David O. Selznick, bought the rights for Stoker's short story, "Dracula's Guest," from his widow. Selznick

---

[21] According to Riley's book in the previous citation, O'Connor was a favorite of Whale's. They had worked together previously on *The Invisible Man*, in which her portrayal of Mrs. Hall was lauded by none other than H.G. Wells himself. For *this* author's money, however, every film in which she stars that is sold on physical media should come with complimentary ibuprofen.

[22] Variety staff. "Bride of Frankenstein." *Variety*, 15 May 1935.

[23] F.S.N. "Bride of Frankenstein At the Roxy". *The New York Times,* 11 May 1935. It's worth noting that Frankenstein's Monster remains universally (ahem) known, whereas Charlie Chan has faded into cinematic obscurity.

commissioned Balderston to write a script based on the story; instead, Balderston took the opportunity to pick up immediately following the events of the 1931 film, with – among other things – Dracula's daughter, Countess Szekelsky, travelling to London. The problem was that Selznick's contract with Stoker's widow forbade the use of any characters who did not expressly appear in "Dracula's Guest," so MGM could not use Balderston's screenplay. Selznick then sold the rights to both the original story and the screenplay to Universal, who would not be bound by such a stricture.[24]

Whale was initially attached to direct, at Laemmle Jr.'s insistence, even though back-to-back horror flicks left Whale itching for something else, which came in the form of *Show Boat*, so he was off the project – and done with horror. Laemmle Jr. finally settled on Lambert Hillyer, who had previously delved into the world of horror directing Lugosi and Karloff in *The Invisible Ray*.[25]

Lugosi was originally slated to return for the sequel, and Universal also announced that he would be joined by Karloff, Clive, Jane Wyatt (more popularly known for her role on *Father Knows Best* and as Spock's mother, Amanda Grayson, on *Star Trek*),[26] and Cesar Romero (perhaps best remembered by modern audiences for his role as the Joker on the 1960s *Batman*[27] television series).[28] None of them ended up being in the picture.

The actual film, with a script by Garrett Ford based around Balderston's story, also begins right after the end of *Dracula*, in the bowels of Carfax Abbey. The police arrive, finding two corpses – Renfield and Dracula – and Von Helsing (Sloan; the character's name has, inexplicably, changed its spelling), whom they arrest for murder. Von Helsing is told he has two choices: the gallows or the asylum (presumably that of Dr. Seward) and is advised to retain counsel, and he calls upon an old student of his, psychiatrist Jeffrey Garth (Otto Kruger).

---

[24] Skal, David J. *The Monster Show: A Cultural History of Horror*. Penguin Books, 1993.

[25] Curtis, James. *James Whale: A New World of Gods and Monsters*. Faber and Faber, 1998.

[26] Rhodes.

[27] Explored in great detail in *Gotham City 14 Miles: Fourteen Essays on Why the 1960s Batman TV Series Matters*, edited by Jim Beard.

[28] Mank, Gregory W. *Women in Horror Films, 1930s*. McFarland, 1999.

A problem with the case quickly pops up, however, as one of the bodies goes missing – that of Count Dracula, stolen by the mysterious Countess Marya Zaleska (Gloria Holden). Zaleska burns the body she claims belongs to her father,[29] believing that it might free her of her own damned existence. Predictably, it does not, and another vampire roams the streets of England.

Dracula's Daughter paved the way to expand Universal's *Dracula* mythos even further – and gave audience members an encore performance from Van Sloan as Von[30] Helsing – though it would be another seven years before the next installment.

Interlude II

Dracula's Daughter was the last Universal Monster film for two years. Whale's aforementioned production of *Show Boat* was excessively lavish; because of that – coupled with Laemmle Jr.'s spending habits – stockholders demanded that the Laemmles take out a loan against their personal holdings to fund the picture. The picture went over budget and the loan was called in. Universal couldn't pay, and the lender – Standard Capital Corporation – foreclosed. Despite *Show Boat* actually being a financial success, the Laemmles were ousted on 2 April 1936.[31]

During that same time, the Production Code Administration (PCA), under the guidance of troubleshooter Joseph Breen, did what they could to discourage the production of horror films, which Breen felt were immoral. According to writer Jim Ivers:

> Breen began collecting numerous press reports which greatly overstated the restrictions on horror films in England. These reports were used to perpetuate a myth that the complex and confusing British censorship process constituted a virtual embargo on horror films. In 1935 and 1936 the Breen Office began issuing increasingly dire warnings that any horror film exported to England was bound to be flatly rejected or at least cut to

---

[29] Though whether he's her biological father or her vampiric father is uncertain; that being said, Von Helsing (that just looks so wrong, doesn't it?) puts Zaleska's age at a hundred years, which would lend far more credence to a vampiric relationship than a – ahem – blood one.

[30] It does. It looks wrong.

[31] Ellenberger, Allen R. "Universal Studios, the Laemmle years, 1912-1936." *Hollywoodland: A site about Hollywood and its history.* 2012. http://allanellenberger.com/universal-studios-the-laemmle-years-1912-1936/

pieces by the censors. Breen painted as bleak a picture as possible. In addition, he found much objectionable content in every horror-based script submitted to the PCA, miring films in long and troublesome negotiations. He constantly advised producers and studios not to make more horror films and to remove all horror content from projects in development.[32]

Rather than go through all the trouble, the new management at the beleaguered Universal Studios avoided the topic altogether.

Horror started to return from the grave, however, thanks to Emil Umann, manager of the Regina-Wilshire Theatre at Wilshire and La Cienega in Los Angeles, in August of 1938. Trying to avoid bankruptcy for the theater, Umann started what was originally supposed to be a four-day run for *Dracula*, *Frankenstein*, and *Son of Kong*. It became unexpectedly, wildly popular, and the theater started running the triple-feature for 21 hours a day. Umann, understanding exactly how much money was to be made from this, even hired Bela Lugosi – who had not worked in two years, had a newborn son, and was all but broke – to make nightly personal appearances at the theater.[33]

Universal quickly caught wind of the success at the Regina-Wilshire and rushed to capitalize on the phenomenon, striking 500 new prints of each film and distributing them across the United States. Lugosi began a tour along the West Coast promoting the films, saying "I owe it all to that little man at the Regina Theatre. I was dead, and he brought me back to life."[34]

More importantly, this craze over Dracula and Frankenstein's monster reignited Universal's interest in horror films, and the studio started to put together a return to the genre. As a writer for the Associated Press at the time put it:

> It seems to have dawned on somebody that what the public wanted, after all, was horror. Confronted with the playfully murderous cavorting of two movie monsters, the public – at least momentarily – could forget about war and dictators. Perhaps the reasoning was not so direct. Perhaps it could be boiled down to "Horror's making money this year, hm-m-m!" So again there's gold in them thar chills, and Hollywood is bogeyman-

---

[32] Ivers, Jim. "The Horror Film Hiatus of 1936-1938." *Spooky Isles*. 27 April 2014. https://www.spookyisles.com/the-horror-film-hiatus-of-1936-1938/
[33] Brooks, Andi. "The 1938 Dracula & Frankenstein Double-Bill." *The Bela Lugosi Blog*. 30 January 2012. https://beladraculalugosi.wordpress.com/the-1938-dracula-frankenstein-double-bill/
[34] Ibid.

conscious. [...] Universal, scanning its profit books, has lost no time in producing another modern sequel, *The Son of Frankenstein*.[35]

Son of Frankenstein (1939)

By 20 October 1938, just over two months after the meteoric resurgence that started at the Regina-Wilshire, Universal had a script completed for *Son of Frankenstein*, written by Willis Cooper. The final shooting script, 57 pages lighter than the 195-page first draft, was completed eight days later. Yet, director Rowland Lee largely eschewed the script, using it merely as a starting point and improvising the majority of the shoot once filming began on 9 November 1938.[36]

Perhaps more impressively, shooting wrapped on *Son of Frankenstein* at 1:15 a.m. on 5 January 1939. Scarcely 70 hours later, it previewed in front of audiences. It opened to the public on 13 January 1939, merely eight days after the film was completed, and it received rave reviews.[37] Part of that was due, no doubt, to the magnificent cast.

Karloff was back as the Monster for his third and final performance. "He was going downhill. We had exhausted his possibilities. He was becoming a clown," Karloff said of his most famous role.[38] Yet Karloff did have one more memorable performance in him with this film, which saw the Monster return to his previously inarticulate self and start to adopt the lumbering persona which would characterize him for the remainder of his cinematic life – at Universal, at any rate.

Lugosi's popularity with the double-bill touring also secured him a part in this picture as Ygor, which would come to be one of his greatest performances. Basil Rathbone entered the scene as Wolf, the titular son of Frankenstein, with Donnie Dunagan (perhaps best remembered as the voice of the title character in Disney's *Bambi*) as his son Peter. *Son of Frankenstein* also saw Lionel Atwill (as Inspector Krogh) in his first of four *Frankenstein* movies.

---

[35] AP. "Credit Beverly Hills Man For Horror Film Revival." *Rockford Register Republican*. 10 December 1938.
[36] Riley, Philip J. *Son of Frankenstein (Universal Filmscripts Series / Classic Horror Films, Vol. 3)*. MagicImage Filmbooks, 1990.
[37] Ibid.
[38] Ibid.

Here, Wolf von Frankenstein, son of Henry[39] and Elizabeth, is returning to the village named after his ancestors with his wife and son, after growing up in England, attending school, and opening a practice in America. The village of Frankenstein is understandably wary of his coming to live in his ancestral home, despite his assurances that he has no designs like those of his father.

Until, that is, he sees the Monster for himself.

It is with *Son of Frankenstein* that the writers start to take liberties with the mythos. Continuity was scarcely a concept that had been invented yet; this was decades before the invention of home video, and very few people could afford home projectors. Thus, if something didn't necessarily track from one film to another, the studio really didn't care.

For instance, in this film, Wolf's father's laboratory – ostensibly the one in which he did all of his experiments – is on the Frankenstein property and receives much of its power by a molten sulfur pit. This doesn't jibe with the previous two films, however, as Henry's lab was in a watchtower far off-property which is destroyed in an explosion by the Monster himself. (This sulfur pit, however, does play into the climax of the film.)

Son of Frankenstein was the last of the big-budget horror pictures Universal Pictures produced during that era. From there on out, the Universal Monsters were mostly B-movie residents.

Interlude III: Enter the Sequels

Following the success of *Son of Frankenstein*, Universal went back to its established stable of horror icons to mine for more gold. Its first venture, *The Invisible Man Returns*, was released on 12 January 1940, nearly a year to the day after *Son of Frankenstein*. This time, the title character is played by Vincent Price, though he is only visible onscreen for little more than a minute. The rest of the time, he is only heard as a disembodied voice. Price plays Sir Geoffrey Radcliffe, in prison and awaiting execution for a murder he didn't commit. Dr. Frank Griffith (John Sutton) – brother of the original Invisible Man – injects Radcliffe with the invisibility serum, allowing him to escape. He tracks down the actual killer, is eventually cleared, and has his visibility restored after a transfusion.

---

[39] Referred to in this movie as Heinrich von Frankenstein, in one of *many* mythos changes to come.

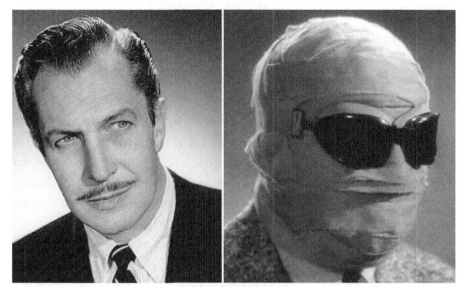

Horror-film legend Vincent Price as the Invisible Man.

The Invisible Man Returns is considered one of the better – if not the best – of the *Invisible Man* sequels. On top of that, it is also noteworthy in that it is the first horror role for the then-29-year-old Vincent Price, who would return to such a role – however briefly – eight years later. Additionally, this film was the first of two Universal horror appearances for Sir Cedrick Hardwicke (here as Inspector Richard Cobb) – though, interestingly, neither of his appearances warranted a mention in the actor's obituary.[40]

Universal hurried to capitalize on the film's success and released *The Invisible Woman* at the end of 1940. This one, a comedy starring Virginia Bruce as Kitty Carroll, has no seeming connection to the previous two beyond the theme of invisibility, and was not particularly well received, with one reviewer writing, "It is silly, banal and repetitious; it is essentially a two-reel comedy with elephantiasis and full of the trick disappearances and materializations that seemed new when *Topper* first came out."[41]

That being said, this film *does* hold the peculiar distinction of being the only Universal Monsters flick to unite John Barrymore (known to horror fans for his

---

[40] "Sir Cedric Hardwicke Is Dead; Actor on Stage and in Films, 71; Created Roles in Shaw Plays and Excelled in Character Parts for Many Years." *The New York Times*, 7 August 1964.

[41] Strauss, Theodore. "At the Rialto." *The New York Times*, 9 January 1941.

portrayal of both title characters in 1920's *Dr. Jekyll and Mr. Hyde*), Margaret Hamilton (the Wicked Witch of the West in 1939's *The Wizard of Oz*), and Shemp Howard (of The Three Stooges).

Universal also revisited another earlier smash in 1940, releasing *The Mummy's Hand* on 22 September. This film is not so much a sequel to the 1932 Karloff vehicle as it is a reboot of sorts, with an entirely new disgraced ancient Egyptian priest, Kharis (Tom Tyler). Kharis's backstory is virtually identical to that of Imhotep's – even down to footage from *The Mummy* being reused, but with Tyler replacing Karloff – with the only major difference being that, instead of stealing the Scroll of Thoth to resurrect his dead love, Kharis uses mystical, sacred tana leaves to get the job done and loses his tongue for his sacrilege. The rest – mummified alive, entombed alive, damned for all time, etc. – is virtually the same.

In this one, Kharis does not return from the dead to find his love reincarnated. Instead, the High Priests of Karnak watch over him, for he never truly died – the brew from three tana leaves, imbibed during the full moon, keeps him alive. If someone attempts to desecrate the tomb of his love, Princess Ananka, nine leaves will restore him to full power.[42]

Universal took a slight break from its sequels and reboots in 1941, introducing filmgoers to one of the most enduring, influential characters of all time – and the key to tying its various franchises together.

The Wolf Man (1941)

After delving into the lycanthrope genre with *Werewolf of London* to mixed success, Universal decided to walk into that thorny mythos once more, and it tapped Curt Siodmak – who had previously written *The Invisible Man Returns* – to write the project. According to Siodmak, he did a great deal of research for the screenplay, reading "books and books on lycanthropy,"[43] but much of the mythology that moviegoers take for granted surrounding werewolves was, in fact, the product of Siodmak's mind. Among Siodmak's contributions to the genre are the belief that only silver objects – not just bullets – can kill a werewolf, though there is some credence to the idea that Siodmak may have

---

[42] Which, of course, someone does.
[43] Weaver, Tom. *Return of the B Science Fiction and Horror Heroes: The Mutant Melding of Two Volumes of Classic Interviews.* McFarland, 2000.

been inspired by the Beast of Gévaudan, which terrorized that region of France from 1764-1767 and was supposedly killed by a bullet forged from silver.[44]

Siodmak was also responsible for the oft-quoted poem featured in this film, subsequent sequels, the 2004 *Van Helsing*, and even an episode of *Dark Shadows*: "Even a man who is pure of heart / And says his prayers by night / May become a wolf when the wolfbane blooms / And the autumn moon is bright." (Subsequent films change that last line to "...and the moon is full and bright," thereby cementing that change is brought about by the full moon, year-round, leaving no room for ambiguity). Siodmak happily copped to this poem's creation, telling Tom Weaver in a 1989 interview, "Nowadays, film historians think it's from German folklore. It isn't. I made it up."[45] He also acknowledged the staying power of the poem, noting, "That's how folk history is made."[46]

The Wolf Man starred Lon Chaney, Jr. as Lawrence Talbot, Claude Rains (last seen in a Universal horror flick in *The Invisible Man*) as his father, Sir John Talbot, Ralph Bellamy as Col. Montford, Maria Ouspenskaya as Maleva the Gypsy, Bela Lugosi as her son, also named Bela (the werewolf responsible for biting and turning Talbot), scream queen Evelyn Ankers as Gwen Conliffe, Patric Knowles as Frank Andrews... a veritable who's-who of stars and studio players, to be sure.

Chaney Jr.'s portrayal of a good-natured man driven by forces beyond his control to maim and kill struck a nerve with audience members, as well as with Chaney Jr. "He never wanted to hurt anyone. During his period of sanity, in between full moons, he begged to be confined, chained, even killed to avoid the horrible consequences of his curse. He was a classic product of misunderstanding," Chaney Jr. wrote.[47]

Like all movie monsters – and most tragic figures – Chaney Jr.'s Talbot dies at the end of *The Wolf Man*. And just like the good movie monsters, that didn't keep him down for long.

---

[44] Jackson, Robert. *Witchcraft and the Occult*. Devizes, Quintet Publishing, 1995.

[45] Weaver.

[46] Siodmak, Curt. *Wolf Man's Maker: Memoir of a Hollywood Writer*. Scarecrow Press, 1997.

[47] Oscars. "The Legacy of Lon Chaney, Jr. and *The Wolf Man*." Filmed 9 October 2012. YouTube video, 03:51. Posted 25 October 2012. https://www.youtube.com/watch?v=LnCh9Qujjkl

Interlude IV: But First, More Sequels

While still enjoying the success of *The Wolf Man*, Universal Studios returned to the saga of the Frankenstein family with *The Ghost of Frankenstein* (1942), this time with Ludwig Frankenstein, the *other* son of Henry (or is it Heinrich?) and Elizabeth Frankenstein (or is it Von Frankenstein?), who is a celebrated doctor working on diseases of the mind in the small Bavarian hamlet of Vasaria.

The film begins shortly after the end of *Son of Frankenstein*, with the villagers sick of all the trouble visited upon them by the Frankenstein family, and they agree to just blow up the family's castle and be done with the whole mess. Ygor (Lugosi) has somehow survived a seemingly fatal gunshot wound inflicted by Wolf in the last picture and, as he is fleeing the exploding manor, discovers that the Monster (Chaney Jr.) had been freed from the confines of the now-dried-up sulfur pit – and is alive and ambulatory, if a little worse for the wear (and probably smelling absolutely God-awful). The two flee the village of Frankenstein, making their way toward Vasaria to pay a call on Ludwig – hoping to make him heal his "brother"... by placing Ygor's brain in the Monster's body.

Universal started to recycle a few of its studio players here: besides Lugosi reprising his role as Ygor, Hardwick plays Ludwig, while Bellamy and Ankers are back (in completely different roles from *The Wolf Man*), and so is Lionel Atwill, whose character bears no relation to Krogh from *Son of Frankenstein*.[48] This represented the company's clear shift of their horror films into solid B-movie territory, with budgetary restrictions limiting the variety of actors and locations, and even – as evidenced in the *Mummy* films, and in some subsequent *Frankenstein* vehicles – reusing footage.

That year also saw a return to the Griffin family – of *Invisible Man* fame – with *Invisible Agent*. This focuses on Jack Griffin's grandson, Frank Raymond (John Hall), who owns a print shop in Manhattan. Axis spies try to steal the invisibility formula, but Raymond escapes and is soon sucked into a world of espionage and intrigue with double agents and treachery at every turn.

Hardwicke made his third entry in a Universal horror flick here – and his second in an *Invisible Man* film, though this time as Nazi Gestapo

---

[48] One can only imagine the outrage that might exist were these films produced today; the same actor playing different roles in the same universe? Different actors playing the same character? Hell you say.

Gruppenführer Conrad Stauffer. Peter Lorre also shows up, as Japanese Baron Ikito,[49] and Ilona Massey plays double-agent Maria Sorenson – and it wouldn't be long before she returned to Universal horror as another Bavarian native.

That year also saw Chaney Jr.'s first foray into the world of Kharis, playing that character in *The Mummy's Tomb*, which takes place 30 years after *The Mummy's Hand* – more on that in a minute. This film shifts the action to Massachusetts, where the archaeologists from the previous film and their descendants reside. The High Priests of Karnak revive Kharis to go and enact their revenge.

At the film's end, Dr. John Banning (John Hubbard) receives his draft notice and must leave to serve in World War II. That would, then, place this film firmly between 1941 and 1945, which is logical as it was made in 1942. The issue, of course, is that this takes place *30 years* after *The Mummy's Hand*, which would thus set that film in 1912. Nothing in that film – the clothes, the tech, the language, nothing – supports that placement at all.[50]

Chaney Jr. would, of course, return to the role of Kharis in the future – you can't keep a good, or even mediocre, monster down for long – but not before returning to the role for which he is still best-known.

Frankenstein Meets the Wolf Man (1943)

As the story goes, Curt Siodmak was having lunch in the Universal commissary when he joked to George Waggner (who had directed *The Wolf Man*) that he had a title for a great new film: *Frankenstein Wolfs the Meat Man*. Half-joked, actually, as Siodmak needed a down-payment for a new car. A short time later, Waggner called Siodmak into his office and told him, "Change the title to *Frankenstein Meets the Wolf Man* – and go ahead, buy the car."[51]

---

[49] Back in the days when this wasn't viewed as wildly racist – and even if it was, not many people seemed to care. *Action Comics* #58 from March of 1943, for instance, features Superman on its cover operating a printing press rolling out sheets that say "Superman says YOU can slap a Jap with war bonds and stamps!"

[50] This would not, of course, be the last time that Universal horror films asked its viewers to accept such leaps. One must suppose that, if one can believe in reanimated corpses, vampires, werewolves, and the like, then taking wonky time frames with the same grain of salt doesn't require suspending *that* much more disbelief.

[51] Weaver, Tom. *Interviews With B Science Fiction And Horror Movie Makers: Writers, Producers, Directors, Actors, Moguls and Makeup.* McFarland, 2006.

Team-ups like this weren't a new concept in and of themselves – the first major comic book team-up, for instance, had taken place three years prior[52] – but it *was* a new idea for motion pictures. In this case, the "Frankenstein" in question is Elsa Frankenstein (Massey), the daughter of Ludwig and the granddaughter of Henry (Heinrich? Oh, forget it) who made her first appearance in *The Ghost of Frankenstein*, to which this film is a direct sequel. This is also, of course, a direct sequel to *The Wolf Man*, and it starts four years after the end of that motion picture.

The shared cinematic universe is born, as Larry Talbot (Lon Chaney, Jr.) comes face to face with Frankenstein's monster (Bela Lugosi) in *Frankenstein Meets the Wolf Man*.

Grave robbers decide to burglarize the tomb of Lawrence Talbot (Chaney Jr.) during a full moon, and, once its rays hit Talbot's body, he is resurrected, much to the consternation of the robbers in question. As the Wolf Man, he manages to find his way to the city of Cardiff and is taken to the local hospital, where he is placed under the care of Dr. Frank Mannering (Knowles, playing a

---

[52] Everett, Bill. "The Human Torch and the Sub-Mariner Meet." *Marvel Mystery Comics*, vol. 1 no. 8. Timely Comics, June 1940.

different Frank than in *The Wolf Man*).

After terrorizing Cardiff for a moon cycle, Talbot leaves the hospital and goes on a search for Maleva (Ouspenskaya), looking for her help in ending the curse that won't let him die. Maleva can't help him, but she promises to take him to a place that she knows, where a great man who has healed the unhealable will surely know what to do.

That man's name? Dr. Frankenstein. And just like that, with the uttering of a single word by an old Gypsy woman, the shared cinematic universe was created.

The plot was, of course, a tad more complicated. Talbot finds his way into the bowels of what remained of Ludwig Frankenstein's castle, there uncovering the Monster (now played by Lugosi) in an ice cave. Together they search for Frankenstein's journal, but to no avail. Talbot later poses as a man named Taylor, who is interested in buying the property from Elsa. That evening is the Festival of the New Wine, to which the mayor (Atwill, in yet another role in the series) invites them both. They attend, Mannering shows up, as does the Monster, and somehow Mannering and Elsa agree to help Talbot die while destroying the Monster.

Neither of which, of course, actually happens.

When casting first began for the film, Universal originally wanted Chaney Jr. to play both Talbot – the role he had originated – and the Monster, which he had previously played in *The Ghost of Frankenstein*. Chaney Jr. ultimately decided against it, presumably due to the grueling hours of make-up required for both roles, and Karloff was done with the character, so the part went to Lugosi, who had originally been offered the role in 1931.[53]

Lugosi was a logical choice for the Monster. At the end of *The Ghost of Frankenstein*, Ygor's brain had been implanted into the Monster's body, and the Monster was able to speak – with Ygor's heavily accented voice. Thus, with the possibility of a speaking Monster – as was originally written in the screenplay, and the lack of speech was one of the factors that had chased Lugosi away in the first place – having Lugosi take up the role now made complete sense. the Monster had also gone blind due to differences in blood type between its brain

---

[53] Rhodes.

and Ygor's body,[54] and Lugosi incorporated that into his portrayal, often walking with arms outstretched because he couldn't see.

Unfortunately for Lugosi, a speaking Monster with Ygor's accent – which worked at the end of *The Ghost of Frankenstein* but didn't have the luxury of an entire movie's worth of build-up this time around – tested quite poorly with the studio, and they cut all of Lugosi's speaking scenes. The result is a grunting brute – exactly what Lugosi had wanted to avoid 12 years prior.[55] As such, Lugosi only saw about five minutes of screen time in *Frankenstein Meets the Wolf Man*, but it *was* enough time to give viewers what they had waited to see: a climactic battle between the Monster and the Wolf Man, and fans would only have to wait a year before seeing them again.

Interlude V: Another Reboot and More Sequels

Hot on the heels of *Frankenstein Meets the Wolf Man* came *Phantom of the Opera*, a lavish, full-color, musical extravaganza. At least, that's what Universal had hoped.

A remake of the 1925 Chaney Sr. classic had been in the works for a number of years and finally found its way to the screen in 1943, this time with Rains in the title role – though it often seems to be little more than a vehicle to showcase the talents of Nelson Eddy, who played opera baritone Anatole Carron... and received top billing.

If you're wondering who *that* is, you're not alone.

This movie takes a *wide* departure from the original source material – both Gaston Leroux's 1910 novel *Le Fantôme de l'Opéra* and the 1925 version – which isn't that unusual in cinema, and certainly not in the Universal Monsters catalogue. This difference, largely, is that previous adaptations tended to combine character traits into other characters, seldom simply creating new ones whole-hog. This film, however, has completely different characters, inexplicably; Erique Claudin (Rains) instead of Erik; Christine DuBois (Susanna Foster) instead of Christine Daaé; Raoul Dubert (Edgar Barrier) instead of

---

[54] Apparently, Henry had been able to find body parts from the various cadavers from which he had stolen body parts that all, miraculously, had the same blood type – presumably O-positive, as that *is* the most common, and the most compatible with others. Theoretically, then, Ygor's blood type might have been AB-negative, which is the rarest.

[55] Vieira.

Vicomte Raoul de Chagny; and Carron instead of... well, there's really not much of an analogue there.

Here, Claudin is a violinist with the Paris Opera House, and it is strongly suggested that he is DuBois's father. He has squandered his savings secretly paying for her vocal lessons – secret even from DuBois – but is certain that he will make money selling his concerto. The publisher doesn't seem interested, but composer Franz Liszt, who just happened to have stopped by that day, has been enamored with the concerto, fiddling with it on the piano.

Claudin thinks the publisher is trying to pull a fast one and strangles the publisher with his bare hands. The publisher's assistant tries to save her boss by throwing acid at Claudin, who ends up horribly scarred. Wanted for murder, he flees to the depths of the opera house.

Much of this version was filmed on the same sets as the Chaney Sr. version, though the lushness of color often makes them seem wholly unique. Unfortunately, that aspect, as well as the title and the falling chandelier – why the Phantom in this version decides to drop it is a mystery never fully explained – are about all that tie this version to its predecessor.

Or, as *New York Times* film critic Bosley Crowther put it:

> This remake of the old Lon Chaney film is bereft of much of the terror and macabre quality of the original. [...] the scenes in the catacombs beneath the opera, where the Phantom lives, receive a kid-glove treatment. It's a nice little spot the boy has there. To be sure, the production is elegant. Settings and costumes are superfine and, photographed in Technicolor, they all make a lavish display. But that richness of décor and music is precisely what gets in the way of the tale. Who is afraid of a Phantom that is billed beneath Mr. Eddy in the cast?[56]

That lavishness in design and music kept the film from being particularly scary,[57] but it resonated enough with audiences that a sequel was planned and written. However, Rains was unavailable, so it was repurposed with a new cast of characters and actors (Foster returned, but in a differently named role),

---

[56] Crowther, Bosley. "Nelson Eddy Much in Evidence in 'The Phantom of the Opera,' Wherein Claude Rains Also Appears, at the Capitol." *The New York Times*, 15 October 1943.

[57] Though it certainly set the stage – no pun intended – for the success of Andrew Lloyd Webber's interpretation of *The Phantom of the Opera* four decades later.

including Karloff, and was released as *The Climax* the following year.[58]

Universal once again returned to the *Dracula* bloodline in 1943 with *Son of Dracula*, this time with Chaney Jr. in the title role. Here, in a film directed by Siodmak's brother Robert, Dracula's descendent, Alucard (Chaney Jr.) finds his way to the United States – Louisiana, specifically – where he is in cahoots with an estate heiress. Exactly what he's in cahoots about is unclear, as he has already turned his bride, and the plantation – named Dark Oaks – appears to be theirs. Soon there are murders (of course), mysterious bite marks, a foreign professor who suspects vampires, and someone who has figured out that Alucard is "Dracula" spelled backwards.

That last bit, incidentally, may seem remarkably obvious to moviegoers now – and, presumably, moviegoers in 1943, as the word "Dracula" was right there in the title – but, story-wise, it's a decent deception. Unless Dark Oaks happens to be in a municipality where residents regularly try to make anagrams out of names, there was no reason – except to further the story – to use "Alucard" as a word scramble. Additionally, rearranging the letters in a vampire's name is not new in *Son of Dracula*; as vampire lore goes, it can be dated at least as far back as 1872.[59]

There has also, in recent years, been an ongoing debate as to whether Alucard was, in fact, Dracula's son or the Count himself. This is presumably based on the line in which the heiress, Katherine (Louise Allbritton), tells her former lover Frank (Robert Paige) that "he *is* Dracula." Of *course* he's Dracula, assuming that "Dracula" is a family name. But, to bury the debate once and for all, they are, indeed, two separate entities.

Ignoring the fact that the title of the film is *Son of Dracula* (which could just as easily have been *Dracula's Return* or *The New Adventures of Dracula – The Vampire Lives!* or some other such nonsense, but no, Universal specifically chose a title which incorporated "son" in the same vein as *Dracula's Daughter*[60]), press kits from the time quite clearly refer to Alucard as kin, stating that, "*Son of Dracula* deals with the ghoulish activities of a descendant

---

[58] MacQueen, Scott and Skal, David J. *The Opera Ghost: A Phantom Unmasked.* David J. Skal, dir. Universal Studios, 2000.

[59] Le Fanu, Sheridan. "Carmilla." *In a Glass Darkly.* Richard Bentley & Son, 1872.

[60] Interestingly, there has been no debate over whether or not Countess Zaleska was Dracula's daughter, other than speculation over biological or supernatural relation.

of the 'vampire' man"[61] and "In the new film, Chaney plays a descendant of Dracula, who is able to change himself into various forms, including a wisp of smoke."[62]

Contemporary reviewers knew it, too, as one wrote, "It all has to do with Count Alucard (Dracula spelled backward – see?), a descendant of that apparently indestructible and legendary vampire."[63] Additionally, an early draft of a later film, *The Brain of Frankenstein*, was set to feature both Dracula *and* Alucard, which would have been quite impossible if the two were the same individual. The only matter that could possibly be up for debate, then, is the same as with *Dracula's Daughter*: is it a blood relation, or a... well, *blood* relation?

In 1944, Universal returned to two other franchises with *The Invisible Man's Revenge* and *The Mummy's Ghost*. *The Invisible Man's Revenge* starred John Hall in the title role as yet *another* Griffin goes mad, turns invisible – this time at the hands of Dr. Peter Drury (John Carradine) – and seeks vengeance on those who wronged him. This rather unremarkable entry – which also takes place in South Africa, for some reason – effectively signaled the end of the franchise.

Meanwhile, Chaney Jr. returned as Kharis in *The Mummy's Ghost*, which continued the story from *The Mummy's Tomb*, still taking place in Mapleton, Massachusetts. Kharis's love is revived, and so Kharis is revived again, of course, but his lady friend has gotten a boyfriend, so Kharis carts her off and, through a series of misadventures, ends up sinking with her into a bog – because there are so many of them in Massachusetts. It was an ignoble end, but one which prompted one reviewer to write, "Oh! please, Universal, do not disturb their rest."[64]

Universal did not heed the warning, unfortunately, and returned for one

---

[61] Universal Studios Publicity Department. "*Son of Dracula* Brings Fearsome Horror Legend to Life on Screen." *Son of Dracula Pressbook*. 1943.
https://www.zomboscloset.com/zombos_closet_of_horror_b/2011/03/son-of-dracula-pressbook.html
[62] Universal Studios Publicity Department. "Chaney Describes Eerie Film Role." *Son of Dracula Pressbook*. 1943.
https://www.zomboscloset.com/zombos_closet_of_horror_b/2011/03/son-of-dracula-pressbook.html
[63] A.W. "At the Rialto." *The New York Times,* 6 November 1943.
[64] T.M.P. "At the Rialto." *The New York Times*, 1 July 1944.

more outing – just like their titular character – with *The Mummy's Curse*, in 1945. Somehow, the locale shifted from New England to Louisiana, featuring characters named Cajun Joe and Tante Berthe. Yet, miraculously, Kharis and Ananka (Virginia Christine) rise from presumably the same bog in which they "died" in the previous entry, with no explanation given. This was Chaney Jr.'s last role as Kharis, and it's not hard to see that Universal slapped this together in a quick cash grab. It recycles footage from both *The Mummy* (1932) and *The Mummy's Hand* (1940), even using footage with Tylr as Kharis instead of Chaney Jr. Universal did have more in mind with Chaney Jr., however, and the role for which he is most well known.

House of Frankenstein (1944)

With the success of *Frankenstein Meets the Wolf Man*, Universal made the logical conclusion that if two monsters did well in a single picture, then three or *more* would do even better. To that end, the studio released *House of Frankenstein*, with a story by Curt Siodmak and a screenplay by Edward T. Lowe. Promotional materials for the movie promised a cadre of movie monsters "All Together!," according to its movie posters, touting The Wolf Man, Frankenstein's monster, and Dracula, as well as "The Hunchback" and "The Mad Doctor."

For the Wolf Man, of course, Universal had Chaney Jr. reprise his role once more. For Dracula, the studio opted for John Carradine. Various sources indicate that there was a bit of bad blood between Lugosi and Universal; however, during filming of *House of Frankenstein*, Lugosi was bound by contract for a stage run of *Arsenic and Old Lace* and was thus unable to be in the film in the first place.[65] For Frankenstein's monster, Universal went with Glenn Strange, who was purportedly found by makeup master Pierce while working on another Universal picture.[66] Karloff was done with the character, and Chaney Jr. and Lugosi – the two actors to play the Monster previously – were not options.

The Hunchback in question was not Quasimodo, the titular character of *The Hunchback of Notre Dame*. Not only was there nothing supernatural about that character, but he had also (spoiler alert) died at the end of that film, which took

---

[65] Rhodes.
[66] https://www.imdb.com/name/nm0833363/bio?ref_=nm_dyk_trv_sm#trivia

place more than 500 years before *House of Frankenstein*. However, Universal must have thought that people suffering from angular kyphosis[67] were monsters, indeed, so they hired J. Carrol Naish – an otherwise handsome man – for the role. As for the Mad Doctor, since Boris Karloff wasn't playing the Monster and was otherwise available, he took the role after coincidentally coming off of a run of *Arsenic and Old Lace* himself.[68]

The movie made it seem like all of these characters would appear together, but it didn't quite work out that way. Karloff played Dr. Gustav Niemann, who had been imprisoned because of immoral experiments he'd conducted in Visaria (no explanation for the spelling differential from *Frankenstein Meets the Wolf Man*) involving humans and animals and whatnot. Naish plays Daniel, his friend from prison; when the opportunity presents itself for the two of them to escape, they do so, with Niemann promising to help cure Daniel of his affliction.

Along the way, they run into a travelling horror show run by Professor Lampini (George Zucco), who claims to have the body of Count Dracula in his caravan, after retrieving the staked corpse himself from the count's castle in Transylvania.[69] Niemann accidentally revives the Count, who promises to do Niemann's bidding in return for Niemann's servitude (...huh?), but ends up out of the picture before the 30-minute mark.

Niemann and Daniel end up rescuing a Gypsy girl, Ilonka (Elena Verdugo), who falls for Daniel before she notices his back, which completely kills the mood for her. They find their way to the ruins of Castle Frankenstein in the village of Frankenstein, which was destroyed during the Monster's fight with the Wolf Man. They also find the Monster and Talbot, both frozen in the same ice cave from the beginning of the last picture (which, by the way, took place in Vasaria, not Frankenstein) and revive them, in the hopes of finding where Dr.

---

[67] https://www.mayoclinic.org/diseases-conditions/kyphosis/symptoms-causes/syc-20374205

[68] Which makes more sense than Lugosi anyway, as the play utilizes self-referential humor in having the character in question, Jonathan Brewster, surgically altered to resemble Boris Karloff.

[69] Though Lugosi's Dracula was staked at Carfax Abbey, not in his Transylvanian home, and his son Alucard wasn't staked at all. This is either flagrant disregard for previous stories, or it's the introduction of a *third* male of the Dracula line; this author places his money on the latter.

Frankenstein hid his notes – which should have been washed away in the flood but, of course, were not.

Also (spoiler alert, again) – by the end of the film, everyone who has been mentioned here has died, most notably Dracula by sunlight, Talbot by a silver bullet, and the Monster by drowning in quicksand. There's a lot going on with this picture, and it's clear that the studio wasn't all that keen on continuity. Their goal was to pack people in seats and to throw as many monsters at them as they could, and that's what they did.

That's also what they would do in the next picture.

Theatrical posters for *House of Frankenstein* and *House of Dracula* promised a bevy of monsters together, but the movies didn't quite deliver.

House of Dracula (1945)

The monsters returned the next year, to the surprise of no one. Both Talbot and Dracula have risen from the dead – again – but this time without even so much as an attempt at an explanation. They both simply show up on the doorstep of Dr. Franz Edelmann (Onslow Stevens) – the "mad doctor" on the poster for this film – seeking a cure for their respective diseases.

Carradine returns as Dracula, who introduces himself here – and in the previous picture – as Baron Latos but soon tells Edelmann his true identity, as he is purportedly seeking a cure for his vampirism. Talbot (Chaney Jr.) also shows up – on the night of a full moon, naturally – seeking Edelmann's help to cure his lycanthropy. An attempted suicide attempt leads Talbot to a cavern below Edelmann's castle, where he and the doctor discover the body of the Frankenstein Monster (Strange), caked in mud and still holding Niemann's skeleton.[70]

There's a hunchback in this one, too: Nina, Edelmann's assistant (Jane Adams), who, like Daniel before her, is an incredibly attractive individual,[71] and whose only downfall seems to be kyphosis. It's a pity she and Daniel never met; they would have raised a beautiful (albeit stooped-over) family.[72]

Before long – but not before transfusing his blood into Edelmann's veins – Dracula once again perishes by sunlight. Edlemann turns evil, kills Nina, and is shot by Talbot, while the Monster gets trapped in a fire.

Again.

House of Dracula clocks in at 67 minutes, but they manage to pack a lot into it – except, of course, a fight between the three main movie monsters, which is what most audience members had paid to see. While, yes, they are technically in a movie together, complete with a mad scientist (shockingly common in that part of Europe) and another hunchback, neither this film nor *House of Frankenstein* really delivered on the spirit of the promise, particularly since at no point in either film do the three monsters appear all together at the same time.

---

[70] That quicksand must have had one hell of an undertow.

[71] Adams would later go on to have the first cinematic portrayal of Vicki Vale in the *Batman and Robin* serial from 1949.

[72] Interestingly, the 1943 serial predecessor, *Batman*, starred Naish as its villain. It seems the two actors kept missing each other.

For that, audiences would have to wait three more years.

Abbott and Costello Meet Frankenstein (1948

By 1946, Universal had become Universal-International Pictures via merger, and it was tanking financially. Studio head William Goetz decided to take a gamble with the declining returns of the studio's monster stable and couple it with the diminishing revenue from its most popular comedy duo. The result was a screenplay for a film originally titled *The Brain of Frankenstein*.[73]

Together at last: the monsters finally share screen time in *Abbott and Costello Meet Frankenstein*. Left to right: Chick Young (Bud Abbott), Wilbur Gray (Lou Costello), Frankenstein's monster (Glenn Strange), the Wolf Man (Lon Chaney, Jr.), and Count Dracula (Bela Lugosi).

The screenplay, written by Robert Lees, Frederic I. Rinaldo, and John Grant, was originally going to be the be-all, end-all monster rally picture – as Toho

---

[73] Picart, Caroline Joan S. *Remaking the Frankenstein Myth on Film: Between Laughter and Horror*. SUNY Press, 2003.

Studios would eventually do for the Godzilla franchise with *Destroy All Monsters* – with its earliest draft including Alucard,[74] Kharis, the Invisible Man, Dracula, Frankenstein's monster, and the Wolf Man.[75] However, by the time the film made it into production, only the big three remained – with the Invisible Man (voiced by Vincent Price) making an extremely effective cameo at the film's end. Strange and Chaney Jr. returned to their respective roles, but Carradine was replaced by none other than Lugosi, marking his second and final feature-film performance as Count Dracula.

The film centers around two shipping clerks, Chick Young and Wilbur Grey (Bud Abbott and Lou Costello, respectively), who, as part of their job, come across two crates bound for McDougal's House of Horrors. These crates allegedly contain the bodies of both Frankenstein's monster and the "original" Count Dracula, so naturally they actually do, despite that being impossible in each case.

Talbot, from London, attempts to warn Grey about the crates, trying to keep them at the shipping depot until his arrival, but is unsuccessful. He arrives in town several days later, and, after a series of misadventures – exactly what one would expect from an Abbott and Costello flick – he finds himself, and the comic duo, trying to stop Dracula (in disguise as the aristocratic Dr. Lejos) from enacting his nefarious plan: putting a new brain into the Monster's body.

Whose brain, incidentally? Grey's, of course.

Abbott and Costello Meet Frankenstein managed to provide a perfect blend of horror and comedy. At no point are the monsters treated with anything less than respect, cinematically; that, coupled with the dimwitted shenanigans of Abbott and Costello, actually helps to provide some of the more realistic moments in any of the monster movies. Often, the question is asked as to how "real" people would act in horror movies; one need only to look at this film to realize that *Abbott and Costello Meet Frankenstein* demonstrates such scenarios perfectly. Additionally, this movie *finally* delivers on the promise of its predecessors, by having Dracula, the Wolf Man, *and* Frankenstein's monster together in the same scene... even if it *is* for only a few seconds.

---

[74] Whose appearance separate from Dracula would have laid to rest that debate once and for all.

[75] Picart.

Aftermath

Abbott and Costello Meet Frankenstein marked the end of the classic movie monster cycle for Universal. However, the duo would later go on to meet both an invisible man (though not Price) in *Abbott and Costello Meet the Invisible Man* (1951) and a mummy named Klaris – changed from Kharis for some reason – in *Abbott and Costello Meet The Mummy* (1955).

Universal made several other pictures that now fall under the Universal Monsters banner, most notably the *Creature* trilogy: *Creature from the Black Lagoon* (1954), *Revenge of the Creature* (1955), and *The Creature Walks Among Us* (1956). These films, about a mysterious Gill-man living in South America – who really just wanted to be left alone and was fine until mankind interfered (a common theme in monster flicks, going back to RKO's *King Kong* in 1933) – are wonderful motion pictures, but they inhabit their own standalone universe, with no overlap to the previous shared one, much like two other films sometimes touted as Universal Monsters flicks, *This Island Earth* (1955) and *The Mole People* (1956)... sort of.

On 21 February 1954, Abbott and Costello hosted NBC's *Colgate Comedy Hour*, wherein they performed a live skit of the duo exploring Universal's prop department. During their excursion, they not only bump into Frankenstein's monster – played by Strange – but also come face to face with the Creature (Ben Chapman, who was one of two actors, along with Ricou Browning, to portray the Gill-man in the first *Black Lagoon* film). Given the performances of both Strange and Chapman, it is not outside the realm of believability for some to consider this completely and totally in-universe, thus tying in the *Creature* films to Universal's previous monster movies.[76]

This, however, did mark the true end of the Universal Monsters cycle.

The characters would experience a renaissance of sorts in the 1960s with the television series *The Munsters*, and the excellent 1998 novel *Return of the Wolf Man*, by Jeff Rovin, actually picks up right where *Abbott and Costello Meet Frankenstein* ended, bringing the classic monsters into the modern day. In 2004, Universal attempted to revive their creations via *Van Helsing*, an action-adventure film starring Hugh Jackman as the title character, and featuring

---

[76] And if that doesn't do it, then perhaps consider Gill-man's turn as Uncle Gilbert on the 22 April 1965 episode of *The Munsters* titled "Love Comes to Mockingbird Heights."

Dracula, Frankenstein's monster, and a werewolf, but that film did not live up to the expectations of either the studio or the audience.

Other reboots and remakes, of course, have come to pass, most notably the *Mummy* trilogy of the late 1990s and early 2000s starring Brendan Fraser (and the utterly forgettable 2017 remake starring Tom Cruise), Benicio del Toro's turn as Larry Talbot in 2010's *The Wolfman*, and a remake of *The Invisible Man* released on Amazon Prime in 2020. Universal also briefly tried to sell the public on a concept it called the "Dark Universe," which would have created a modern cinematic universe for its stable of classic monsters (Cruise's film was supposed to kickstart that endeavor, but its box office failure forced the studio to reconsider this position).

The enduring popularity of the Universal Monsters, however, almost certainly guarantees that Universal will continue to breathe new life into its classic monster stable. Whether or not the studio will be able to resurrect a successful cinematic universe as it did decades ago remains to be seen, but it also doesn't matter. New generations of filmgoers will be exposed to these characters, and all incarnations of them will continue to live on.

In any event, cinematic universes of every kind owe their existence to the Universal Monster films of the 1930s and 1940s, particularly *Frankenstein Meets the Wolf Man*. Without these films in general – and that film in particular – shared-universe film franchises as we know them might never have existed. If any of you feel that you do not care to subject your nerves to such a strain imagining such a horrifying prospect, just pull yourself together and remember that, after all, there *are* such things.

Boris and Bela: The Best of Fiends

by Greg Cox

October can be a galling month for us vintage horror-movie fans. Pretty much every newspaper, magazine, blog, and website feels obliged to run features and listicles on all things spooky, but as the years go by and the classic black-and-white horror flicks of the 1930s and '40s recede further into the past, such features often seem to be written by folks who are only vaguely aware that Boris Karloff and Bela Lugosi were not, in fact, the same person — or who may see them as interchangeable. In truth, however, they were each very distinctive performers with their own particular strengths and styles, as can be seen on those special occasions when the two iconic horror stars shared the screen with each other.

Karloff and Lugosi (and they were *always* billed in that order) co-starred in seven movies together after both men achieved stardom in 1931 with *Frankenstein* and *Dracula,* respectively. Right from the beginning, their signature roles as the man-made Monster and the vampire Count neatly demonstrate their contrasting gifts.

Lugosi practically exudes *sinister.* As Dracula, he has an unearthly quality that sets him apart from humanity. He may appear human, even well-groomed and cultured, but there's no trace of warmth or feeling in Lugosi's sublimely chilling performance. Oh, the script may occasionally have Dracula pay melancholy lip service to the burden of immortality ("To die, to be truly dead, that must be... glorious."), but, honestly, the Count seems perfectly content to prey on the blood of the living for all eternity. Devoid of conscience or remorse, he's not remotely sympathetic – and all the more frightening for that reason.

Boris Karloff and Bela Lugosi were always billed in the same order: Karloff first, Lugosi second.

By contrast, Karloff's Monster engages our compassion from his first appearance in *Frankenstein*, lumbering into view as he encounters sunlight for the first time like the innocent newborn he essentially is. As violent and dangerous as the Monster becomes, Karloff conveys the pathos in the creature's unhappy existence. One feels for the tormented Monster in a way one doesn't for Dracula.

At the risk of generalizing, these two performances neatly encapsulate the two stars' styles. Karloff had a gift for finding the humanity in his monsters and madmen, while Lugosi could make even mortal villains seem positively inhuman. Those were their singular talents – even if, as we'll see, their shared films didn't always take full advantage of those specialties.

The Black Cat (1934)

Universal Pictures didn't waste time pairing up their freshly minted new horror stars, both of whom had already been working overtime to frighten Depression-era moviegoers. By the time their first real collaborative effort, *The Black Cat,* was released, Karloff had previously starred in *The Old Dark House* (1932), *The Mummy* (1932), *The Mask of Fu Manchu* (1932), and *The Ghoul* (1933), while Lugosi had played human fiends, just as heartless as Dracula, in *Murders in the Rue Morgue* (1932) and *White Zombie* (1932). Although both actors' names had become synonymous with horror, Karloff was already eclipsing Lugosi[1] – as proven by the fact that he gets top billing (as simply "Karloff") in *The Black Cat,* a twisted tale of Devil worship and revenge only loosely "suggested" by the Edgar Allan Poe story of the same name, to which it bears utterly no resemblance.

Karloff plays Hjalmar Poelzig, a brilliant architect who is also the high priest of a satanic cult. Lugosi is Dr. Vitus Werdegast, an old comrade of Poelzig, who is now out for revenge – and with good reason. Some 15 years earlier, during the First World War, Poelzig had betrayed the troops under his command by selling out to the Russians, resulting in Werdegast being shipped off to a Siberian prison camp, "where the soul goes to die." In his absence, Poelzig stole Werdegast's wife, then his daughter, whom he married one after the other, after possibly killing the mother.[2] Needless to say, Werdegast has a score or

---

[1] Editors' Note: In Tim Burton's 1994 film *Ed Wood*, Lugosi (Martin Landau) seems to bitterly resent Karloff's success, though their supposed rivalry was just media hype. The two had a cordial, respectful relationship, and Lugosi's son denounced the depiction despite Landau winning an Academy Award. (Mitchell, Lisa. "'Wood' Tarnishes a Good Man – Lugosi." *L.A. Times*, 24 Oct. 1994: https://www.latimes.com/archives/la-xpm-1994-10-24-ca-54104-story.html.)

[2] Poelzig never actually confesses to the crime, but his guilt is strongly implied, especially after he murders the daughter as well.

two to settle with his old frenemy, though his mission of vengeance is complicated by a hapless pair of American honeymooners, Peter and Joan Alison, who inadvertently stumble into the tense reunion between the two.

With their names established, Karloff's and Lugosi's first real pairing in a film was in *The Black Cat.*

What's fascinating about this movie is that Boris and Bela are each cast in parts that, in theory, seem better suited to the other. Karloff portrays the suave, satanic seducer while Lugosi has the more sympathetic role, playing a man more sinned against than sinning – even if he does end up skinning Karloff alive with fiendish glee. It works, though; Karloff is coolly menacing as Poelzig, minus his usual pathos, while Lugosi still comes off as distinctly creepy despite his character's tragic backstory. It's no surprise that Werdegast ends up being shot to death by Peter, who fails to realize that the crazed physician is actually trying to save the innocent newlyweds. Oops!

You can't really blame Peter, though. Would *you* trust Bela Lugosi, of all people, while trying to escape from a spooky Hungarian fortress?

The Raven (1935)

Karloff and Lugosi are cast more to type in their next co-starring venture. Although "Karloff" again gets top billing, Lugosi is very much the dominant villain here, playing Dr. Richard Vollin, an arrogant surgeon so obsessed by the works of Edgar Allan Poe that he's built a secret torture chamber beneath his luxurious mansion, complete with a working recreation of the infamous swinging blade from Poe's "The Pit and the Pendulum." Unlike poor Vitus in the previous film, Vollin is as evil as Dracula — and Lugosi revels in the character's sadistic malevolence.

Echoes of Edgar Allan Poe are everywhere in *The Raven*, once again starring Karloff and Lugosi.

Granted, the plot has Vollin supposedly driven to homicidal madness by his unrequited love for a beautiful patient, one Jean Thatcher, but it's not as though he's remotely sympathetic to begin with. If anything, his romantic obsession comes off as just an excuse to put his dungeon to good use at last. "I love... torture," he cackles at one point, grinning diabolically, and we believe him.

Karloff, on the other hand, is back in Frankenstein mode, playing a reluctant brute who doesn't want to be a monster, but who just can't catch a break. Edmond Bateman is a dangerous fugitive, ashamed of his violent past, who comes to Vollin in search of a new face, partly to elude the police, but also in hopes of turning over a new leaf. "Maybe if a man is ugly... he does ugly things," he reasons, so he's praying a more handsome visage will make him a better person. Alas, Vollin double-crosses him by turning him into a disfigured monster instead, then extorts Bateman into doing his dirty work – until Bateman balks at harming Jean, who has been kind to him. He rebels against Vollin and the two men kill each other.

The Black Cat is arguably the better movie – weirder, kinkier, and more disturbing – but I'll admit that as a kid, I preferred *The Raven,* possibly because it's as close as the Boris-Bela two-handers ever came to pairing them up as Dracula and Frankenstein. Lugosi is suave and demonic, while Karloff is both heartbreaking and monstrous; it's just what you want from the two stars. Bateman even recycles some of the Monster's trademark grunts and gestures when angry and/or distraught, and it's easy to imagine Vollin as Dracula, forcing the Monster to do his bidding and then pushing the creature too far.

The Invisible Ray (1936)

The actors' next pairing is as much science fiction as horror, even if it begins in a remote castle in the Carpathian Mountains before heading off to Africa in search of an ancient meteorite with mysterious radioactive properties. Karloff is Dr. Janos Rukh, a brilliant but antisocial scientist with an asteroid-sized chip on his shoulder where his more mainstream colleagues are concerned. Rukh understands science better than people, and, no surprise, Karloff finds the poignancy in this fatal flaw, even after Rukh's reckless experiments cause him to become literally untouchable: suffused with radiation, he glows in the dark and can kill with a touch. Driven insane, possibly by an experimental serum, possibly by his own inner demons, he sets out to avenge himself on those he (unreasonably) believes to have wronged him.

Lugosi is Dr. Felix Benet, a fellow scientist, who, surprisingly, is an unqualified good guy this time around. Not only does Benet attempt to cure Rukh of his radiation poisoning, he also uses "Radium X" to heal the sick and handicapped. Although Rukh accuses Benet of stealing his discovery, the movie makes it clear that this is just Rukh's paranoia speaking; Benet is a healer and humanitarian, not a glory hog (not that this saves him from Rukh's deadly touch in the end).

Lugosi is perfectly fine as the shrewd, capable Benet, but while it's interesting to see him on the side of the angels for once, it also seems like a waste. What's the point of casting Karloff and Lugosi in the same movie if only one of them gets to bring the chills and gooseflesh? Lugosi is basically playing Van Helsing here, but I would have preferred a bit more Dracula.

Son of Frankenstein (1939)

Their next film makes better use of Lugosi, who comes close to stealing the movie as Ygor, a broken-necked grave robber herein retconned into Universal's Frankenstein lore as the original Dr. Frankenstein's former accomplice — never mind that he was nowhere to be seen in the previous two films in the series.

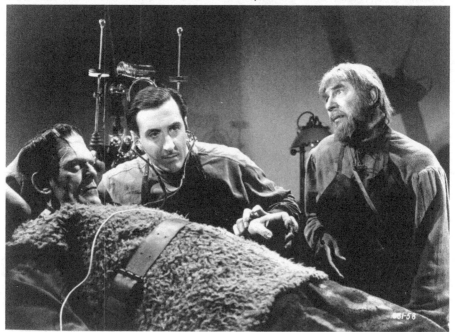

Lugosi showcases his versatility as the disheveled assistant Ygor in *Son of Frankenstein.*

Lugosi certainly demonstrates his versatility here; Ygor is as coarse and unkempt as Dracula is debonair, coughing and cackling through a shaggy beard and a mouthful of crooked teeth. Yet Lugosi again excels at portraying evil over pathos. Ygor may have an understandable grudge against the villagers who tried (and failed) to hang him to death years before, but he's too gleefully intent on using the Monster (played by Karloff for the third and final time) for revenge to engender any sympathy. Even his professed concern for the Monster's well-being comes off as suspect and self-serving, in that it's unclear whether he truly views the Monster as a friend and fellow outcast – or just as an unstoppable instrument of murder.

Karloff has less to do this time around, spending the first part of the movie in a coma, until Ygor finally persuades the titular son of Dr. Frankenstein (played by Basil Rathbone, who gets top billing over both Karloff and Lugosi) to restore the Monster to full strength. Still, Karloff finds opportunities to reveal the torment behind the Monster's murderous rages, as in a tragic scene in which the creature is dismayed by his reflection in a mirror. Similarly, his wail of anguish when he discovers Ygor's seemingly[3] lifeless body, after the duplicitous grave robber has been shot in self-defense by the junior Dr. Frankenstein, is obviously torn from his secondhand heart. This was Karloff's last performance as the Monster, who was never quite as poignant and soulful a figure again, despite the best efforts of such actors as Lon Chaney, Jr., Glenn Strange, and even Lugosi, who would eventually assay the role in *Frankenstein Meets the Wolf Man* (1943), two movies later.

Black Friday (1940)

The last and least of their pairings at Universal, *Black Friday* can best be described as a lost opportunity. The plot involves an obsessed scientist who gives a mild-mannered college professor the brain of a dead mobster, causing the poor academic to develop a Jekyll-and-Hyde-type personality as the gangster's personality gradually overwhelms his own.

Originally, the plan was for Lugosi to play the scientist, Dr. Ernest Sovac, and for Karloff to play the split personality, and this is obvious from the script, which features numerous tense encounters between the two characters – as

---

[3] "Seemingly" in that Lugosi would reprise the role of Ygor in the immediate sequel, *The Ghost of Frankenstein* (1942).

one would expect from a Boris vs. Bela movie. And yet, in the end, Karloff claimed the scientist role, while the showier part of the professor/gangster went to a character actor named Stanley Ridges, with Lugosi relegated to a minor role as a rival mobster who never even shares a scene with Karloff.

Come again?

The reasoning behind this switcheroo remains unclear. Some say Karloff balked at the dual role, uncertain about his ability to pull off the transformation from absent-minded professor to snarling hoodlum, while others theorize that it was the studio that worried Karloff would be unconvincing as a tough, big-city gangster.[4] The former theory strikes me as odd considering that Karloff had managed another dual role in *The Black Room* (1935) just a few years prior, playing good and evil twins. Then again, that was a Gothic melodrama, not a modern-day crime thriller, so it may have been more in the actor's comfort zone.

In any event, the result is a Boris-Bela movie in which the two actors never meet onscreen, even though posters and publicity still hyped the pairing for all it was worth, and the plum role went to another actor altogether. To be fair, Ridges is fine as both the increasingly confused professor *and* the ruthless gangster, but talk about a missed opportunity! Lugosi, in particular, is wasted in a nothing part as an ordinary mob boss, while one can't watch Karloff's confrontations with Ridges without wishing that he was facing off against Lugosi instead. It doesn't help that, aside from the brain-transplant gimmick, the movie plays more like a routine gangster flick than a classic Universal horror film. Instead of spooky laboratories or dungeons, we get urban hotels and nightclubs and mobsters intent on rubbing each other out, which is not exactly what one wants or expects from either a Karloff *or* a Lugosi movie.

Ultimately, *Black Friday* makes one pine for what might have been.

You'll Find Out (1940)

Among the pair's more obscure movies is this haunted-house comedy starring Kay Kyser, a popular bandleader and radio personality of the era. Karloff and Lugosi team up with Peter Lorre (who gets top billing over both of them) as they plot to dispose of a beautiful heiress before her 18th birthday.

---

[4] Both accounts are reported in *Boris Karloff & Bela Lugosi: The Expanded Story of a Haunting Collaboration*, by Gregory William Mank (McFarland & Co., 2009).

Lugosi is fun as a phony spiritualist, complete with a turban, while Karloff plays an avuncular friend of the family who is actually up to no good.

At this point in their careers, both Karloff and Lugosi (and Lorre, for that matter) had acquired so much creepy cred that all they really had to do was just lurk about ominously to get the job done. The plot is your usual "old dark house" shenanigans, complete with secret passages and séances, but the three horror icons get enough screen time to make it worth checking out if you're in the right frame of mind, especially since, as far as I know, it's the only time Karloff, Lugosi, *and* Lorre shared the screen together.

And speaking of comedies...

Gift of Gab (1934)

I would be remiss if I didn't mention that Boris and Bela had briefly cameoed together in an earlier comedy, albeit only for few minutes. Set at a radio station, this largely forgotten movie includes a sketch parodying murder mysteries, in which a pair of bumbling detectives, while searching for clues, stumble onto Lugosi lurking in a closet, then bump into Karloff as well.

Lugosi has only one line ("What time is it?"), while Karloff gets a *slightly* bigger part as "the Phantom," an ominous figure in a black top hat and cape who climbs in through a window and bums a light off one of the detectives before slipping back out the window with a diabolical laugh. It's worth noting that Karloff is already getting the choicer part here, but there's not much to the segment, which runs less than four minutes in length and can be found on YouTube if one is so inclined.[5]

The Body Snatcher (1945)

Make no mistake. *The Body Snatcher*, based on a story by Robert Louis Stevenson (and not to be confused with the science-fiction classic *Invasion of the Body Snatchers*), is Karloff's movie all the way – and it features one of his finest performances. As John Gray, a 19th-century Scottish grave robber who secretly provides fresh cadavers to a distinguished surgeon for medical research, before deciding that murder is a much less laborious way to get his hands on a corpse or two, Karloff is a marvel, sliding effortlessly from bluff congeniality to icy malevolence and back again, often in a single scene.

---

[5] https://www.youtube.com/watch?v=AY6oOgc12zU

Overtly obsequious to his social betters, Gray relishes the power he holds over his distinguished employer (played by Henry Daniels) by virtue of their shared guilt, and he delights in making the other man squirm. It's a nuanced, layered, Oscar-worthy performance. Gray is a rotter, no doubt, but a smart and astute one, even when it comes to his own motives and insecurities. "I am a small man, a humble man," he says. "Being poor, I have had to do much that I did not want to do. But so long as the great Dr. McFarlane comes to my whistle, that long am I a man..."

Lugosi, alas, has a much smaller role as Joseph, a sullen, slack-witted servant who makes the fatal mistake of trying to blackmail Gray, but the two stars have one last great scene together as Gray, feigning camaraderie, cozens the suspicious Joseph into lowering his guard long enough for Gray to suffocate him with his bare hands. Lugosi is convincing as Joseph, who lacks both scruples and cunning, but, like his character, Bela never stands a chance against Boris, who owns the scene and the movie.[6]

The Body Snatcher marked the last time the two stars appeared opposite each other. Lugosi lived another 11 years, finally passing away in 1956, while Karloff kept working until his death in 1969, but they were never paired together again – a shame, really. If only Lugosi had lived into the Sixties, he and Karloff might have been reunited in some hypothetical Roger Corman film alongside Vincent Price, and perhaps even their old comrades Lorre and Rathbone. (Hey, a horror fan can dream.)

Of the movies they *did* make together, *The Black Cat*, *The Raven*, and *Son of Frankenstein* best combine their talents, while *The Body Snatcher* provides a memorable epilogue to their collaborative efforts, which ultimately spanned more than a decade of classic black-and-white horror. Despite the films' ages, these and the other vintage movies discussed above provide a double dose of two iconic stars in their prime, as well as confirmation that they were each very distinctive performers in their own right, who can still captivate and chill fans of the monstrous and the macabre.

And not just in October.

---

[6] For the record, Karloff kills Lugosi in three of their movies, while Lugosi only kills Karloff twice.

The Tragic Heroism of Larry Talbot, the Wolf Man

by Robert B. Nejman

from an original idea by Jim Beard

Conventional wisdom, film criticism, and countless monster fans have it that Larry Talbot's story in Universal's 1941 classic, *The Wolf Man*, is a tragedy. Heck, it's even been compared to the classic Greek tragedies because (70+-year-old spoiler alert!) Larry Talbot's father, Sir John Talbot (royalty in a Welsh village) kills his own son, whom he does not recognize in wolf form. It is only after Larry turns back to his human self that Sir John realizes he has just committed filicide.

Poor doomed Larry Talbot: bitten by a werewolf and killed by his dad. Roll credits. Tragedy? Yes, the film is easy to read that way. However, a good part of the Wolf Man's appeal is that he can also be perceived as heroic. And in today's world, Larry Talbot is not only the hero we deserve, but the one that we need.

The film opens as Larry Talbot (Lon Chaney, Jr.) returns to Castle Talbot in Wales, following the death of his older brother in a hunting accident. Despite the tragic circumstance, Larry is happy to be home after having spent 18 years in California. The two are able to put aside their history as Sir John comments that the second son in a Talbot family is often neglected in favor of the future heir. Acknowledging that their family dynamic has been no different from those

Talbots who have come before, they move forward with a newfound closeness that both look forward to developing.

Father and son bond over the arrival of new glass for Sir John's telescope. Their personality differences show in how they perceive the device: John is the astronomer, while Larry is the mechanic. Sir John is eager to see the heavens, while Larry enjoys assembling the piece, and he comments about having developed those skills while living abroad. Once the telescope is ready, Larry discovers that he is even happier to turn the machine's eye upon the village, where he discovers Conliffe's Antique Shop.

Larry Talbot (Lon Chaney, Jr.) and Gwen Conliffe (Evelyn Ankers).

Larry tilts the scope up to the second-floor apartment and spies upon Gwen Conliffe (Evelyn Ankers) as she preens in front of her mirror and puts on her earrings. Liking what he sees, Larry decides to pay a visit to the shop in order to meet Gwen. He behaves much like an entitled, arrogant rich kid, and pretends to be shopping for earrings. Having an inside scoop based on his spying, Larry enjoys giving Gwen a hard time about the earrings. She shows him a pair or two, but Larry wants to see "something half-moon-shaped with spangles on it, golden." He seems to enjoy her discomfort when he tells her that he has seen such a pair in her room.

Gwen asks, "How did you know about the earrings in my room?"[1] Larry

[1] All quotes taken from *The Wolf Man* Complete Legacy Collection DVD (Universal Studios release, 2004).

continues to toy with her, replying, "Oh, I'm psychic. Every time I see a beautiful girl, I know all about her." He snaps his fingers for emphasis, adding, "Just like that." These days, we would call this type of behavior stalking. In 1941, however, Larry was playing the wolf hunting the prey of his immediate interest, and this type of male aggression – which, in the film, is a metaphor for what he will soon become – was perceived as normal and quite acceptable.

They engage in spirited banter while he pretends to shop. Sensing that she is somewhat shaken, Larry changes his approach and moves over to a display stand with multiple walking sticks. The ones topped with carvings of domesticated dogs are not his style. Big Bad Larry gravitates to the one with the large wolf head and pentagram: a stick that is much more appropriate for the rich playboy and man about town whom Larry seems to be, but also epitomizes the creature he is *destined* to be.

Gwen comments that the pentagram is the sign of the werewolf. Larry goes so far as to quote from *Little Red Riding Hood*, stating, "What big eyes you have, Grandma." She recognizes the quote from the fairy tale and identifies it as "a werewolf story." Larry agrees to buy the walking stick, despite its ominous connection to werewolf lore, and it's then that Gwen asks where Larry has seen her before. Sensing an opportunity, Larry goes in for the kill and asks for a date, saying, "We'll take a little walk tonight, then we'll talk it over." Since she's engaged to another man, Gwen refuses his repeated requests, but Larry will not take "no" for an answer. The heir to Talbot Castle, who has just returned to a more simplistic Welsh village lifestyle after the urban cosmopolitan of California, is indefatigable in his style:

"See you at eight."

"No."

"Let's go to the gypsies."

"No."

"I'll be here at eight."

Larry shows up on time. Gwen not only steps out to meet him, but is wearing the earrings that he liked. Larry takes this as a good sign that his roguish charm is working – then out steps another woman. Gwen introduces her friend and chaperone for the evening, Jenny Williams (Fay Helm). Larry's body slumps in defeat. Resigned to his destiny with both women, however, he extends his arms and they all go off together, laughing. Despite his predatorial tendencies, he is still respectful and modest enough to admit defeat and accept the situation for what it is.

It is easy to draw a parallel between Larry Talbot and contemporary bad boys, especially in terms of their behavior toward and treatment of women. It is also important to note a significant difference: despite his arrogance, Larry demonstrates respect by graciously accepting his defeat. He also shows respect for his father, whom he calls "Sir," and he's eager to befriend the locals in the town as he settles in to his role as the future Lord of Talbot Castle. A quick perusal of today's media shows that there is much less respect demonstrated by our pack of metaphorical wolf boys.

As wolfish as Larry Talbot behaves, though, he still acts like a gentleman in regard to his position and the people with whom he interacts. Larry seems concerned with how other people perceive him and is capable of empathy. Contemporary rogues appear lacking in respect and empathy, particularly with regard to women, as can be evidenced by the #MeToo movement and multiple comments made by politicians, business executives, and actors who could learn a thing or two from poor, doomed Larry.

Bela Lugosi plays a gypsy also named Bela in *The Wolf Man*.

While Jenny has her fortune read by Bela the gypsy (Bela Lugosi), Larry makes time with Gwen – and he's making some progress. There seems to be a definite connection among the young couple, and Gwen seems to have forgotten that she is engaged to be married to another man. It is only when they hear a woman scream that they break their embrace and realize that Jenny is missing.

Without a second thought, Larry runs out to the marsh to help Jenny. Coming across a wolf attacking her, he does not hesitate to act. He throws himself at the creature, engages the beast in fierce battle, and puts up a terrific fight. Larry knocks the beast down, then grabs his newly acquired cane and bashes the creature's skull until it dies. Catching his breath, he looks down at his wound and sees that he has been bitten. When other villagers arrive, Larry is stunned to find that the wolf's corpse has somehow transformed into the barefoot body of Bela the Gypsy.

Larry apologizes to Mr. Conliffe "about getting Gwen into this mess" after Jenny's mother and her friends berate Conliffe and accuse Gwen of abandoning Jenny to be with Larry. He then asks to see Gwen. When Conliffe does not permit such a visit, Larry apologizes about Jenny. Upset and showing concern, he very much wants to check on Gwen but he respects Conliffe's wishes and leaves. Again, Larry behaves respectfully and puts the feelings of others before his own desires.

After Larry meets with Bela's mother Maleva (Maria Ouspenskaya), who gives him a charm to protect him from the curse, he bumps into Gwen, left alone at the camp following a quarrel with her fiancé. He offers to take her home. On the way, Gwen asks Larry about the charm around his neck, and without hesitation, he takes it off and gives it to her for her protection in yet another selfless act by our entitled rich boy.

Gwen is reluctant to accept the charm and seems to find the whole thing ridiculous. "Protect me? From whom?" she asks. When Larry responds, "Me," she accepts the charm and they kiss. The romantic interlude is quickly interrupted as the gypsies break down their camp, because word has spread that a werewolf is on the prowl. Gwen suddenly runs away. Is she running from Larry, from the werewolf, or because the entire camp is in chaos? Let's assume it's all of the above – with the possibility that she's running from her own feelings as well.

About halfway through the film, we witness the first transformation of Larry Talbot into the Wolf Man. The monster goes out into the night and encounters Richardson, the grave digger (Tom Stevenson). The Wolf Man makes quick work of his first victim upon the foggy moor. The metaphorical wolf has now become a literal one.

Chaney's werewolf makeup took five to six hours to apply, but the results were worth the wait.

Before the bite, Larry had seemed to be enjoying *playing* the wolf. Now, however, he *is* a wolf, sees the true horror of his situation, and seems to understand that such behavior has dire consequences. The boy has grown into a man with the realization that giving in to one's animal nature and acting upon those impulses destroys lives. There is a tremendous difference between playing a role and living it. Post-bite, Larry must face himself in a way that most people do not: with a true, honest look in the mirror. Will he give in to the animal that wants to feed and indulge its passion, no matter the cost? Or will he fight against the curse to find a way out?

The next morning, we see the interior of Larry's room: there are muddy animal tracks leading from the open window to Larry's bed, where he wakes up barefoot and horrified. He looks down at his chest where the wolf's bite should be and sees only the pentagram, the mark of the werewolf. Then he notices the wolf tracks and starts to clean the room. For contemporary audiences, this scene plays out much like any crime show in which the killer sees the signs of what he or she has done and, in a panic, rushes to hide the evidence of the crime.

As much as he cleans the prints from his room, however, Larry cannot hide the trail left by the Wolf Man outside that leads right up to his bedroom window. What's more, a curious constable has had no trouble following the trail from Richardson's corpse directly to Castle Talbot. The policeman is beginning to suspect a connection between Larry Talbot and the murders of Richardson and Bela. Even Sir John is worried about his son's mental state. Larry's sudden interest in lycanthropy is not helping to calm his father's fears, or those of the community, that Larry may be unhinged and killing people as the result of his delusions.

At the film's one-hour mark, things are looking mighty grim for our man, Larry. Most viewers are thinking that all signs lead to tragedy. So, where is Larry Talbot, the hero? If you're waiting for him to become a super-werewolf who leaps in and saves the world from some kind of Nazi menace, then you're waiting for a different movie (one that probably went directly to streaming, did not pass Go, and did not collect $200 in gross receipts). What makes Larry Talbot a hero is that as he comes to understand his situation, he does not focus on laying blame on the gypsies, some vengeful god, the universe, or the Nazi menace facing the world in 1941. He owns it. Larry has come to accept his situation, the tragedy, the horror. Rather than focus on himself, he is more concerned about his father and the woman with whom he has fallen in love. He is willing to sacrifice everything to keep them safe, even when doing so goes against his own instinct for survival.

The villagers set bear traps to capture the wolf. Caught in one trap while in wolf form, Larry passes out and is rescued by Maleva. Returned to human form, and now fully understanding the horror that has become his life, Larry goes to Gwen, back at Conliffe's Antique Shop, and tells her, "I'm going away." She begs him to take her with him, but he refuses. His love for Gwen will not allow him to jeopardize her life, and he admits, "I killed Bela and I killed Richardson." Having confessed his sins, Larry then sees the pentagram appear on Gwen's hand, marking her as the Wolf Man's next victim. Despite Larry's admission, Gwen still wants to go away with him – but, rather than put the woman he loves in danger, he runs away.

Over at Castle Talbot, Larry confesses to his father. Showing Sir John the pentagram on his chest, he tells the elder Talbot that he also saw the mark on Gwen's hand. They decide that Larry should be restrained so that he cannot go out into the night to hunt. With Larry tied to a chair, Sir John bolts the door to prove that the whole matter is all in his son's mind. Of course, this is *The Wolf Man* and we all know better.

Sir John prepares to join the villagers out on the marsh to hunt the wolf. Before John leaves, Larry pleads with his father to take the silver wolf's head cane. Sir John pauses a moment, then does as his son asks. Knowing that silver can kill a werewolf and that regular bullets cannot, Larry hopes to give his father a fighting chance. He knows that the restraints will not hold his wolf self and that if he is not stopped, he will kill Gwen and maybe even his father. Larry has made his decision: he will not allow his animal self to ruin the lives of others. He must put an end to the curse.

Larry Talbot continually puts the safety of those he loves above his own well-being. While his fate as a monster may be sealed, his actions as a compassionate human being define his character, and he rises above his animal nature and the tragedy of his circumstance. The film's conclusion plays out not just as a tragedy but as Larry Talbot's finest moment. Having given his father the means to end the curse, Larry transforms, breaks free of his restraints, and goes out to hunt the woman he loves. Gwen, meanwhile, ignoring her own safety, has rushed out onto the marsh in search of the man she wants to help, the man she loves more than her fiancé. The Wolf Man finds Gwen and attacks her, and Sir John rushes to her rescue. Using the silver cane that his son had given him for protection, Sir John bludgeons the Wolf Man's head. The Wolf Man collapses, and when Sir John approaches the corpse, he is shocked to see his son's body, barefoot and dead, the same way they had found Bela the gypsy.

Back in 1941, the movie-going populace devoured *The Wolf Man*, and so Universal produced sequels to satisfy the cravings for more werewolf movies. While the Wolf Man remained popular, the studio initiated the mashup concept: putting many of its monster stars in the same movie to drive ticket sales. While the Talbot character remained the same – doomed Larry searches for release from his curse – the films added a bit of spin for each go-round in an effort to keep the franchise fresh.

In 1943, Universal released *Frankenstein Meets the Wolf Man*. Here, Larry is revived by two thieves, who open his grave to steal the jewelry with which he was buried. They remove the wolfsbane buried with Talbot, and when the light of the full moon shines on his uncovered body, Larry rises from the dead. He is found by police and taken to a hospital to be treated for a head wound. Escaping from the hospital, he teams up with Maleva. They then go in search of Dr. Ludwig Frankenstein, who may be able to help Larry die, thus freeing him from his curse. Still tormented, Larry is taking his efforts for release to the next level: a permanent death (perhaps one that is free from movie sequels). As the Wolf Man, he battles Frankenstein's monster until they are both swept away by a flood. The Universal Monster franchise would not leave him in peace for long, though.

House of Frankenstein was released in 1944, and this time we find Larry frozen in an ice cave, waiting to be released so he can resume his quest for freedom from his curse. A new love interest for Larry is introduced. His torment continues, and despite his best efforts, the curse still poisons his life until he is shot with a silver bullet at the end of the film, killing him yet again.

In 1945, World War II came to a close and Universal released *House of Dracula*, featuring our furry friend and his old pal Count Dracula, both searching for cures for their respective curses. While it may have been the finest hour for the Allies, audience interest in the classic monster movies was waning. With viewers already having seen Larry Talbot suffer in search of a cure yet again (despite having been dispatched in the previous films), the stage was set for the inevitable comedic monster mash-up.

Abbott and Costello Meet Frankenstein hit the screens in 1948, and while the classic monsters all look great, there is little attempt at serious horror. Larry is still our tormented hero, but his suffering is no match for Bud Abbott's and Lou Costello's zingers. When Talbot shares his story and deep misery with Costello, noting that "in a half an hour, the moon will rise and I'll turn into a wolf," Costello's response is to reduce Larry's suffering to an admittedly funny one-liner: "You and twenty million other guys!"

While the iconic special effects of Jack Pierce's Wolf Man design, the all-star cast, and the terrific atmosphere have kept the original *Wolf Man* alive in the hearts and minds of fans worldwide, we must not overlook the appeal of Lon Chaney, Jr.'s performance as Larry Talbot. Coming about two years after his landmark performance as Lennie Small in Lewis Milestone's adaptation of John Steinbeck's brilliant novel *Of Mice and Men*, Chaney makes Talbot a character whom audiences care about and can root for, even though we can all sense that Larry is doomed.

The Wolf Man (and, to a lesser extent, its sequels) provides a character arc that takes the leading man from being a wealthy, entitled son of the Lord of the Castle to someone willing to sacrifice his life for his family and the woman he loves. This is what truly makes Larry not just a tragic victim of circumstance, but someone we can respect and care about. As we are repeatedly told throughout the first film, "Even a man who is pure in heart and says his prayers by night may become a wolf when the wolfsbane blooms and the autumn moon is bright."

We may not be able to escape our destiny – our own personal, genetic, and familial histories. The Talbot family has its own non-lycanthropic curse: the exclusion of the younger son from inheriting the castle. How Larry Talbot faces these challenges makes his ending all the more epic. Yes, what happens to Larry is tragic. Through no fault of his own, his world is turned upside down and he turns into a monster. Yet his response to the tragedy throughout the original franchise films is heroic: he does not give in to the curse, nor does he allow the monster to win, run free, or kill regularly. Before he was bitten, Larry could look at himself in a mirror and be proud of his heritage, his history, and his accomplishments. After he is cursed, all he sees is horror. What sets him apart from so many is his response.

In today's world, there are too many examples of entitled children of wealthy parents behaving irrationally and not caring at all about those who are hurt by their actions. We see far too many people embracing the monster inside of them and letting it loose to slaughter. So it is inspiring to watch a character rise above his own weaknesses and put the needs and the lives of others ahead of his own.

Larry Talbot's growth as a character from the metaphoric wolf to creature to self-aware human being who owns his behavior, regardless of the cause, and who puts the welfare of those he loves above his own, is exactly the type of story we need to see more frequently. Too many people fail to realize that giving in to the monster, to the curse, to the horror is a choice. It is a conscious decision to avoid asking for help, to avoid shackling the impulse to run wild, to bare one's teeth – a metaphorical weapon – to shed blood and destroy lives. Larry Talbot shows us that just because we perceive a world of horror does not mean that we have to give in to it.

What's So Special About the Creature from the Black Lagoon?

by Lou Tambone

They call him the Gill-man. He's the creature that time had forgotten, existing happily in his Brazilian domicile that the locals called the Black Lagoon. No one knew how long he had lived there or how old he was. No one knew if there were others like him. Perhaps there still are. In any case, the Gill-man, also known as the Creature from the Black Lagoon, captured the attention of movie-goers at a time when the age of horror and monsters had already given way to more science fiction (or at least science-based) thrillers.

The Universal Classic Monsters shared film universe, the first of its kind, began in the 1920s when Lon Chaney personified such characters as Quasimodo in *The Hunchback of Notre Dame* (1923) and The Phantom in *The Phantom of the Opera* (1925). Universal released dozens of films from the 1920s through the 1950s, but one thing is clear: if you take a good look at the innumerable marketing materials pertaining to Universal's shared universe, there are a select few standouts that dominate the studio's marketing efforts, even to this day.

There are the usual suspects: Frankenstein's monster, Dracula, the Mummy, and, of course, the Wolf Man. The Invisible Man is often included when there's room on the posters, as are the Monster's Bride (of Frankenstein) and the Phantom of the Opera. But there's another easily recognizable regular who is lucky enough to make this prestigious list on a regular basis: the Gill-man from the Black Lagoon. Why is he habitually included with such heavy-hitters as Dracula and Frankenstein's monster? How is it that he can stand toe to webbed toe with the likes of the Mummy or the Wolf Man? What's so special about the Gill-man?

In the 1950s, it was clear that the cinematic landscape was changing. Space invasions and aliens had become all the rage and the world of monster films was waning. It seemed that audiences weren't ready to give up their monster flicks just yet, though. Universal was doing its best to keep monsters in the public eye, even if it had to do so in comedic ways, starting in the late 1940s with the beginning of its Abbott and Costello films, in which the comedic duo of Bud Abbott and Lou Costello would "meet" various monsters. The films were successful and are still highly regarded, but they only delayed the inevitable decline of the monster film genre. In 1960, Universal released a film called *The Leech Woman*, which anticlimactically ended its decades-long run of (mostly) successful monster, creature, and science-fiction films. It was the end of an era, to be sure.

Jack Arnold was one of the directors who helped to keep the monster films afloat throughout the 1950s by successfully merging the genres of horror and science fiction together. Instead of utilizing typical monstrous villains, like the Wolf Man or Dracula, the plots were more science-based. His first Universal film, *It Came from Outer Space* (1953), centered around an alien spaceship that crashed on Earth, as well as the ensuing chaos. His next film, *Creature from the Black Lagoon* (1954), was the one for which he'd be most remembered and the first time the world was introduced to the Gill-man. You might be hesitant to call it a science-fiction film, but if you think back to its opening moments, you'll remember that the movie starts with a literal bang – the Big Bang – and goes into a scientific, yet poetic, explanation of how the Earth was seemingly created:

> This is the planet Earth, newly born, and cooling rapidly from a temperature of 6,000 degrees to a few hundred in less than five billion years. The heat rises, meets the atmosphere, the clouds form, and rain pours down upon the hardening surface for countless centuries. The restless seas rise, find boundaries, are contained. Now, in their warm depths, the miracle of life begins. In infinite variety, living things appear, and change, and reach the land, leaving a record of their coming, of their struggle to survive, and of their eventual end. The record of life is written

on the land, where, 15 million years later, in the upper reaches of the Amazon, man is still trying to read it.

That's pretty scientific stuff for a monster film. Luckily for us, that's about as scientific as it gets. The rest of the story involves our friend the Gill-man and his eventual discovery by a group of scientists following a lead on a fossilized webbed hand found at an excavation site during the opening minutes of the film. A typical "Beauty and the Beast"[1] story plays out from there, with the expected results.

Today's science fiction is usually equated with space. When we think of modern science fiction, we recall films like *Star Wars*, *Alien*, and other epic space-fantasy tales. But back in the early 1950s, science fiction was also about science itself – the unknown and outlandish kind that could take an insect and blow it up to immense proportions. There were plenty of alien invasion films and the like, but it's important to note that science fiction wasn't always so focused on little green men.

The Gill-man was a definite product of the fusion of science fiction and horror. The science part isn't as evident, as it's never explained how the creature – assumed to be a direct link between land and sea beings from the Devonian period – has survived this long, or whether there are others like him out there. Those kinds of plot points and back story are generally not important to monster films; there's a monster, and that's all you need to know. The interesting thing about this monster, though, is that he came along relatively late in Universal's game, and yet he's immensely revered and repeatedly utilized as one of Universal's poster boys. I believe that the reason our fishy friend has endured for so long has less to do with science fiction or horror, and a lot more to do with aesthetics and appearances.

Let's face it: When it comes to movie monsters, they have to be frightening or else the effect is severely lessened. If the ants from the movie *Them!* (1954) were actual size, the film would be over in 30 seconds with a few well-timed stomps. Make them eight feet long, and now you've got terror! That's why we're so shocked when the Phantom of the Opera loses his mask and we see his horrific visage for the first time. Dracula is dressed in his classy outfit and cape when he's not taking the form of a bat. Frankenstein's monster has those iconic

---

[1] Referring to the fairy tale written by Gabrielle-Suzanne Barbot de Villeneuve, published in 1740 and made famous by countless adaptations since then, including recent versions by Disney.

bolts in his neck. The Wolf Man is covered in fur – a unique look for the monster family. Both the Invisible Man and the Mummy look properly frightening in their bandaged get-ups. Put them all together on a poster, and it's a hideously impressive sight to behold.

But wait, there's more. Add the Gill-man to the mix and now you've got something special: the *pièce de résistance.* Sure, the popular Universal monsters are all humanoid, but many of them have recognizable facial features: eyes, ears, noses, and such. The Gill-man looks like a humanoid fish, and that sets him apart from the others, while at the same time filling a gap that no one even knew existed. Removing him from the monster line-up now might result in someone asking, "Hey, where's the Creature from the Black Lagoon? You can't leave the Gill-man out!" This popularity, I maintain, is a function of the creature's design. He looks radically different from any monster that came before.

It's like seeing Godzilla for the first time, or a character like Darth Vader. In 1977, when Vader emerged from that spaceship doorway through a cloud of smoke, breathing *very* audibly, he was as frightening as any monster who had ever graced the silver screen. Had Vader come along in the 1950s, he might have been a regular force in Universal's marketing efforts. The point is, he was instantly unforgettable and is now etched into our collective long-term memories. His look, though based on earthly concepts like the Samurai, was so unusual that it cemented the character's place in film history within seconds. The same goes for *Star Trek*'s Mr. Spock, portrayed by Leonard Nimoy. One reason he's a standout character on the various television shows and movies (besides his being well-written and -acted) is his look. Those pointed ears and upturned eyebrows, along with his trademark bangs, are unmistakably Vulcan. I had known who Spock was before ever seeing an episode of *Star Trek*.

I grew up in the 1970s and '80s, and, as with Spock, I knew who the Gill-man was before I had ever watched *Creature from the Black Lagoon*. I can only assume countless others have had the same experience. If I may once again invoke Darth Vader, I'm sure children born in the 1980s and afterward grew up knowing who he was just from seeing that black helmet, and well before viewing a *Star Wars* film. You don't look at these characters and become confused as to who they are. You just *know*. That's popular culture at its apex. It's brand recognition. That's entertainment.

I believe something similar happened when *Creature from the Black Lagoon* was released. The creature's striking appearance and fluid motion in those aquatic scenes evoked a unique creepiness that the other monsters seemed to lack. The combination of human and fish was a stroke of genius at the time, and it demanded everyone's attention. Even when he was on land, he had a delightfully intense presence. We only saw his arms in his first few scenes, and that only added to the tension and excitement. When he walked on land, he lumbered slowly for dramatic effect, and the way his gills oscillated as he walked toward the camera and raised his webbed hands was hauntingly memorable – and most likely gave many a 1950s teenager some wicked nightmares.

Gill-man's distinctive fish-man hybrid appearance hasn't been replicated as much as his monstrous cohorts' aesthetics throughout the years, but his influence can be felt not only in comics like DC's *Swamp Thing*, but in films like *The Shape of Water* (2017). Beyond appearances, Steven Spielberg's *Jaws* certainly pays homage to *Creature from the Black Lagoon* in its opening sequence. Gill-man himself (or a slightly different version of him) shows up in 1987's kid-friendly adventure film *The Monster Squad*,[2] along with Dracula, Frankenstein's monster, the Mummy, and the Wolf Man. In fact, *The Shape of Water* was born out of director Guillermo del Toro's desire to remake *Creature from the Black Lagoon* from the creature's point of view, and possibly with the creature ending up with the girl in the end.[3]

Gill-man came back for two sequels, but he's remembered almost exclusively for his original film. I hadn't even viewed the sequels until shortly before writing this essay, and no one I'd ever spoken to about the creature had mentioned the sequels at all. The overwhelming popularity of that initial movie, along with its lasting first impression, seems to have rendered its sequels nearly irrelevant in hindsight. After seeing them, it's not hard to understand why.

The first sequel, *Revenge of the Creature* (1955), isn't remarkable by any stretch. If the first film is a different take on "Beauty and the Beast," this one is essentially *King Kong* (man captures creature, man displays creature for personal gain, creature escapes, creature falls in love with human woman), with

---

[2] See Greg Mitchell's essay, "Rock Until You Drop: The Enduring Legacy of Classic Monsters in *The Monster Squad*."

[3] Kit, Borys. "How Guillermo del Toro's 'Black Lagoon' Fantasy Inspired 'Shape of Water'." *The Hollywood Reporter*, 3 November 2017: https://www.hollywoodreporter.com/news/how-guillermo-del-toros-black-lagoon-fantasy-inspired-shape-water-1053206.

the bonus claim to fame of marking the film debut of a young Clint Eastwood. In the original film, Gill-man is smitten with the lovely Kay Lawrence (Julie Adams). In the sequel, it's Helen Dobson (Lori Nelson) who steals his heart away. He likes her so much, in fact, that even after escaping his aquatic prison at Florida's Ocean Harbor Oceanarium, he goes back to find her instead of counting his blessings and fleeing into the deep, apparently unaware that she won't be able to breathe under water and will die. But hey, there are other fish in the sea, am I right?

Clint Eastwood made his feature film debut as an uncredited lab technician in *Revenge of the Creature.*

Yet another sequel, *The Creature Walks Among Us* (1956), is definitely the most science-fiction-like of the three films, but at the same time the dullest. In a risky move, the filmmakers thought it wise to take the aquatic creature, alter his appearance, dress him in human clothing, and stick him in a caged area in the hope that he would, I guess, become more human. Partly through surgery and partly through some sort of unexplained mutation, the creature miraculously loses his gills and gains some rudimentary lungs, along with human-like skin. Movie science can be weird like that. Mostly, though, he walks around his fenced environment staring at the sea and looking rather glum and un-frightening. You get the feeling that Universal had decided it had done all it could do with the Gill-man in the previous film and wanted to try something new. Lesson learned.

These sequels certainly didn't hurt the Gill-man's popularity as an iconic Universal monster, as they kept the creature in the public eye. The fact that no one seems to care about them at all is nonthreatening. The creature found his little niche and there he stayed, thriving on the popularity of his debut film alone. When you see his image on any packaging or marketing materials, it's never the gill-less creature in human clothing from *The Creature Walks Among Us*, and it usually isn't the Creature trying to escape from the seaside restaurant in *Revenge of the Creature*. It's almost always something pertaining to *Creature from the Black Lagoon*. That's why we don't tend to refer to Gill-man as "the creature" when we see his scaly face. We say, "That's the Creature from the Black Lagoon!"

Universal tried to do something new with the Gill-man, both thematically and aesthetically, in the final film, *The Creature Walks Among Us*.

While a large part of the Gill-man's popularity has to do with his unique appearance, it's only a piece of the bigger picture. Unlike some other one-off monster films of the time, *Creature from the Black Lagoon* seems to have been well thought out, brilliantly shot, and even a bit clever. The Gill-man is smart enough to blockade the human characters' boat with logs and trap them in the lagoon, and the groundbreaking underwater scenes are still a thrill to view.

The fact that the Gill-man seems so real and isn't just a man in make-up (like Dracula, for instance) gives the underwater scenes a dark realism. Even now, the sight of his moving gills still gives me the heebie-jeebies, even though I know it's just a rubber suit. There has to be something more than just his appearance at work. The whole package has to be sold, and the film succeeds in selling it. The sequels unsuccessfully tried to recreate that initial shocking moment when we first saw the Gill-man in full, stalking Kay and apprehensively reaching out to touch her legs as she doggy-paddled in the water above him, but they never could pull it off. It had already been done. The thrill was gone.

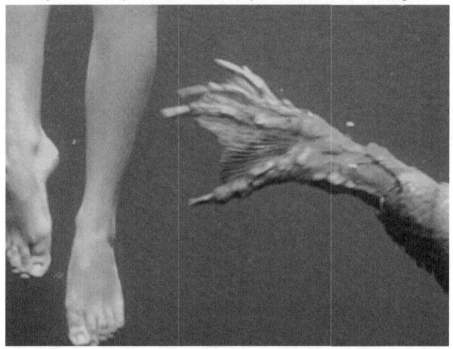

The Creature from the Black Lagoon includes some brilliant underwater cinematography.

Gill-man was very lucky to come along when he did. The other heavy-hitters had already worn out their welcomes by the time he debuted, wallowing in sequel after sequel and finally making comedic appearances with Abbott and Costello, which seemed to ring their individual death knells. Comedy was where the big Universal monsters went to die, apparently. Gill-man was not an exception, making a brief appearance with the duo on *The Colgate Comedy Hour* around the time that the first film was released in theaters, but before the two sequels.[4] His costume would even be reused as a character on *The Munsters*, Uncle Gilbert – though that iteration (a wealthy, treasure-seeking politician) could talk, unlike the original Gill-man.

In 2019, *Creature from the Black Lagoon* turned 65 years old. The fact that it's still revered is no small accomplishment, especially when you consider some of the other forgettable gems that came out of Universal at the time, like *Curucu, Beast of the Amazon*, and *The Deadly Mantis*. Compared to Universal's

---

[4] https://www.youtube.com/watch?v=EvrrYnagX3g

other monster-related releases from the 1950s, it's quite clear that no one can hold a candle to our friend the Gill-man. In a sea of mediocre science-fiction and giant monster films, *Creature from the Black Lagoon* somehow rose to the surface and persisted, drowning even its own two sequels.

Milicent Patrick was responsible for the design of the iconic Gill-man.

Though a remake of the original film seems inevitable, given Hollywood's penchant for remaking just about every movie that's ever been made since the dawn of cinema, a selfish part of me doesn't want that to happen. I think we've all grown so accustomed to the original Gill-man that seeing a computer-generated creature would be an enormous letdown. Even a physical actor in a suit would run the risk of bursting the bubble created back in 1954. It might be difficult to reconcile the two versions of the Gill-man.

Then again, Dracula and the other Universal Classic Monsters have been reimagined time and time again. Perhaps we need to finally face facts and let the Gill-man evolve, too. We can only hope that the right people with the right talent and the right amount of money will bring back the Creature from the Black Lagoon with the respect he deserves. We need him to maintain his prominence with his fellow monsters, after all.

If it all goes sideways, we'll always have the original film.[5]

---

[5] And its two sequels. What are they called again?

Frankenstein: Defining Monstrosity

by Kelli Fitzpatrick

"Draw a monster. Why is it a monster?"[1] So bids one of the enigmatic pages in Janice Lee's *Daughter* (2012), an abstract, visceral novel about the sand-stranded body of an octopus that may or may not be a god, and the woman who wrestles with boundaries of self as she encounters this being. On the cover of Lee's book, a spray of tentacles reaches from a pocket of abyss, either clutching in fury or flailing in confusion (it is not clear which from the drawing, nor from the text). "Are we talking about the octopus or me?" the narrator asks mid-book. "Am I becoming a blur or are you?...The long arms attached to a fleshy blob, the arms curl around my neck. But I just imagined that. I've imagined a lot of things." The uncertainty that slicks the surface of the omnipresent, repulsive-yet-tragic flesh makes for a story felt deep in the reader's cells. There is something monstrous here in these words, but it's difficult to pin it down to a definition or even a finite description.

In my English classroom, I use these lines from *Daughter* as a springboard into an 11th-grade unit on *Frankenstein* and personhood, and they effectively ignite student conversation about what it means to be monstrous. When asked to simply "draw a monster," most of my students sketch a three-eyed alien, a

---

[1] Lee, Janice. *Daughter*. Seattle: Jaded Ibis Press, 2012, p. 33, 67.

character from *Monsters, Inc.*, a ghost, or a creature with red eyes and fangs. The second question is harder: *why* is it a monster? After much debate, they respond with traits such as being scary, being different, harboring malevolent intent, hurting others, and even being misunderstood. The next instruction I give them is, "Draw a person. Why is it a person?" And instantly, their know-it-when-I-see-it understanding of what it means to be a person falls apart (in a philosophically constructive and educational way). What qualifies a person as a person, they ask each other. Certain appearance? Body structure? Brain function? Emotion, intelligence, logic? They are able to find reasonable counter-examples to all of these. Being "normal"? Being alive? Having a soul? The definition becomes increasingly nebulous the further they test it. What about people who act evilly, those who *behave* as monsters? What about monsters who are kind? What do these terms even mean, and who gets to determine their ascription?

As this exercise proves to me year after year, monster stories have considerable existential import and implications for essential ethical debate in an academic setting. While several stories could be used effectively in this manner as discussion touchstones, there is something captivating in Mary Shelley's seminal story of the mad scientist and the piteous plight of his creation. I would argue not only that *Frankenstein* launched the modern moral monster tale as a popular genre, but that Shelley's text remains timelessly relevant in its dramatic depiction of the humanity of monsters, and the monstrous in humanity.

Now celebrating two centuries as a lauded entry in the canon of classic Western literature, *Frankenstein* is a progenitor not just of the Gothic monster genre, but of science fiction as we know it. The first Gothic horror novel is generally noted to be *The Castle of Otranto* by Horace Walpole (1764), but many more familiar titles populate the genre, including *The Picture of Dorian Gray* (1890) by Oscar Wilde, *Dracula* (1897) by Bram Stoker, and the creepiest story I've ever encountered: *The Turn of the Screw* (1898) by Henry James. *Frankenstein*, however, broke the mold.

A page on The New York Public Library's website states that *Frankenstein* "marked a shift in gothic horror by changing the typical gothic villain from an evil man or supernatural creature into a physical embodiment of human folly, brought to life through the power of science."[2] Indeed, *Frankenstein* is oft-cited as the first science fiction novel – essayist Brian Stableford acknowledges it being referenced as the "foundation-stone of the modern genre of science fiction."[3] A fabulously intricate 2011 viral drawing by artist Ward Shelly titled "The History of Science Fiction" labels *Frankenstein* as the "First S.F. story" and depicts it as bubbling up from the influences of English Romantic poets and Enlightenment science, and tentacling off into scion successors Jules Verne and H.G. Wells.

But is there any real science in this first science fiction novel? Sort of. Mary Shelley was inspired by the galvanists,[4] a group of scientists in her era who were bent on bringing dead things back to life via electric current. Their experiments were based on Italian physicist Luigi Galvani's (1737-1798) idea of an animal electricity, a unique life force that supposedly flowed from the brain to power the rest of the body. Galvani's nephew, Giovanni Aldini (1764-1834), conducted experiments on the effect of current on the "animal machine," using freshly executed corpses of criminals obtained from the government, as he describes in his 1803 book *An Account of the Late Improvements in Galvanism.*"[5] His narration of his work rings chillingly similar to Victor Frankenstein's experimentation on corpses in chapter four of Shelley's novel. On the subject of obtaining decapitated bodies, Aldini writes, "The love of truth, and a desire to throw some light on the system of Galvanism, overcame all my repugnance, and I proceeded to the following experiments," one of which involved contorting the facial muscles of severed heads with electric shock. It's not a far jump to see how these accounts of galvanistic research sparked a horror story.

---

[2] Pagan, Amanda. "A Brief History of Gothic Horror." *New York Public Library*, The New York Public Library, 18 Oct. 2018, www.nypl.org/blog/2018/10/18/brief-history-gothic-horror.
[3] Stableford, Brian. "Frankenstein and the Origins of Science Fiction." *Anticipations: Essays on Early Science Fiction and its Precursors*, edited by David Seed, Syracuse, Syracuse University Press, 1995, pp. 46-57.
[4] Pilkington, Mark. "Sparks of Life." *The Guardian*, Guardian News and Media Limited, 6 Oct. 2004, www.theguardian.com/education/2004/oct/07/research.highereducation1. Accessed 14 Sept. 2019.
[5] Aldini, Giovanni. *An Account of the Late Improvements in Galvanism*. London, Cuthell and Martin, 1803, publicdomainreview.org/collections/an-account-of-the-late-improvements-in-galvanism-1803/. Accessed 14 Sept. 2019. "The love of truth" quote is from p. 68.

The tale of how the story was conceived is now legend. While staying in the Swiss Alps with Percy Shelley, Lord Byron, and other friends in June of 1816, Mary Shelley drank in the conversation as an evening of ghost stories evolved into debate about the "spark of life," and speculation on the possibility of reanimating lifeless matter.[6] Consumed with the wonder of it, Shelley's night was overtaken by a "waking nightmare" of the moment of the creature's awakening, and she based her book around it in such a way that, as Anne Mellor states, "gave birth to one of the most powerful horror stories of Western civilization."[7] Shelley wanted to write a story which would, in her own words, "speak to the mysterious fears of our nature, and awaken thrilling horror – one to make the reader dread to look round, to curdle the blood, and quicken the beatings of the heart,"[8] but I think the narrative's power, at least when looked at through a modern lens, emanates not from its spookiness, but from its depiction of how *not* to treat others. None of my teenage students has ever reported feeling afraid while reading the text, but there is plenty of *moral* horror rippling through the classroom as Victor's irresponsible choices exact a toll on the people around him, including his own creation.

Shelley's masterwork is not the first to mention monsters, but threads of influence, conscious or unconscious, can be drawn through subsequent stories from her contemporaries all the way through to works of today. There have, of course, been mysterious and vicious creatures appearing in human storytelling for as long as we've kept record, going all the way back to mysterious cave paintings,[9] epic poems like Homer's Cyclops-sporting *Odyssey*, and the Old English tale of Beowulf fighting Grendel,[10] to cite just a few examples. Following

---

[6] Dunn, Jane. *Moon in Eclipse: A Life of Mary Shelley*. New York, St. Martin's Press, 1978. p. 130.

[7] Mellor, Anne K. "Making a 'monster': an introduction to *Frankenstein*." *The Cambridge Companion to Mary Shelley,* edited by Esther Schor, New York, Cambridge University Press, 2003, p. 9.

[8] Spark, Muriel. "Frankenstein." *Modern Critical Views: Mary Shelley*, edited by Harold Bloom, New York, Chelsea House Publishers, 1985, p. 13.

[9] Sullivan, John Jeremiah. "America's Ancient Cave Paintings." *Slate*, The Slate Group, 20 Mar. 2011, slate.com/culture/2011/03/america-s-ancient-cave-art-mysterious-drawings-thousands-of-years-old-offer-a-glimpse-of-lost-native-american-cultures-and-traditions.html. Accessed 13 Sept. 2019.

[10] The "Beowulf and Grendel" section of Benjamin Bagby's Old English performance of *Beowulf* is a worthwhile watch. YouTube: www.youtube.com/watch?time_continue=3&v=o6tG9qdKKks.

Frankenstein's publication, some later Gothic books also employed questionably minded scientists and manufactured monsters, most notably Robert Louis Stevenson's *The Strange Case of Dr. Jekyll and Mr. Hyde* (1886). In the present, I see aspects of Shelley's creature in fantasy author Brandon Sanderson's Koloss characters, a race of engineered blue warriors who outgrow their skin,[11] as well as in the cobbled-together drones of the Borg from *Star Trek*.[12] In all these cases, the fictional maker's intent is to create something good, but the outcome is something ghastly and dangerous.[13]

Perhaps the most successful adaptations, though, in audience reach and impact, have been the films. Rebecca Laurence says in a BBC article, "Are there any characters more powerfully cemented in the popular imagination? The two archetypes Mary brought to life, the 'creature' and the overambitious or 'mad scientist', lurched and ranted their way off the page and on to stage and screen, electrifying theatre and filmgoers as two of the lynchpins, not just of the horror genre, but of cinema itself."[14] That cinema tradition started with Thomas Edison's 1910 silent-yet-horrifying *Frankenstein* Kinetogram,[15] in all its red-tinted glory. Clocking in at only 14 minutes long and relying on title slides and a lot of gratuitous fainting, it constitutes a wonder of special effects for its era, including reverse-played images of a burning mannequin to simulate the grotesquely growing flesh of the creature's inception. Since it's so short, it's only able to hit the highlights of the story, and the ending is modified considerably (for much less doom and death), but it is nonetheless a must-see curiosity for *Frankenstein* aficionados.[16]

---

[11] Sanderson, Brandon. *Mistborn: The Well of Ascension*. Tor, 2008. Print.

[12] That is to say nothing of the plethora of books that are modern adaptations or that draw heavily on the premise of *Frankenstein,* such as *This Monstrous Thing* (2015) by Mackenzie Lee and *Spare and Found Parts* (2016) by Sarah Maria Griffin.

[13] Dangerous, yet perhaps misunderstood, as evidenced by the Koloss, who calls himself "Human," and by the Borg drones Hugh, Seven of Nine, and Locutus, who are each separated from the collective and regain some measure of their humanity, though at great cost.

[14] Laurence, Rebecca. "Why *Frankenstein* is the Story That Defines Our Fears." *BBC*, BBC, 13 June 2018, www.bbc.com/culture/story/20180611-why-frankenstein-is-the-story-that-defined-our-fears. Accessed 21 Aug. 2019.

[15] *Frankenstein*. Produced by Thomas A. Edison, Edison Mfg. Co. Performances by Ogle, Charles, Augustus Phillips, Mary Fuller. 1910, www.loc.gov/item/2017600664/.

[16] At time of print, it is available to view on the website of the Library of Congress.

Charles Ogle as the monster in the 1910 Kinetogram version of *Frankenstein*.

The films that have enjoyed the most widespread impact on cultural awareness are the eight black-and-white Universal Pictures movies – starring Boris Karloff, Lon Chaney, Jr., Bela Lugosi, and Glenn Strange as the Monster – starting with *Frankenstein* in 1931.[17] A classic horror jaunt, it deviates from Shelley's tale in many ways, some of which make sense (such as giving the scientist an assistant so he has a reason to narrate his motives), and some of which do not, at least to me (such as changing Victor Frankenstein's name to Henry, his best friend in the book). This film introduced several tropes into the franchise that persist in cultural association with the story, including tropes of "Hulk-speak" for the Monster, the "Ygor" character, and townsfolk with "torches and pitchforks," none of which appear in the book.[18]

---

[17] The others were *Bride of Frankenstein* (1935), *Son of Frankenstein* (1939), *The Ghost of Frankenstein* (1942), *Frankenstein Meets the Wolf Man* (1943), *House of Frankenstein* (1944), *House of Dracula* (1945), and *Abbott and Costello Meet Frankenstein* (1948). Karloff later appeared in a non-Universal film titled *Frankenstein 1970* (1958), this time playing the scientist rather than his creation.
[18] "Frankenstein's Monster." *TV Tropes*, TVTropes.org, tvtropes.org/pmwiki/pmwiki.php/Main/FrankensteinsMonster. Accessed 1 Sept. 2019.

An angry mob seeks vengeance in the original *Frankenstein*.

The speech issue is the biggest difference, and always the aspect of the text that shocks my students when they get to chapter ten in the book and discover the creation can speak more intelligently and eloquently than his creator. His first words to Victor in the book are, "I expected this reception...All men hate the wretched; how, then, must I be hated, who am miserable beyond all living things!"[19] Of course, it took the Monster months of painstakingly observing human speech to get to that point,[20] but he is far from the groaning brute Karloff so successfully portrays. This language proves key to the opening of communication between Victor and his creation in the text,[21] though that communication is not able to avert the tragedy of the conclusion. The film, on

[19] Shelley, Mary. *Frankenstein*. 1818. Reprint. San Diego: Canterbury Classics, 2013, p. 82.
[20] The Monster learns language by eavesdropping on the cottagers, as described in *Frankenstein* chapters 12-15.
[21] As noted in: Brooks, Peter. "'Godlike Science / Unhallowed Arts': Language, Nature, and Monstrosity." *Modern Critical Views: Mary Shelley*. edited by Harold Bloom, New York, Chelsea House Publishers, 1985, p. 103.

the other hand, must work from almost zero communication skills on the creature's part, and never does establish a meaningful emotional connection between scientist and experiment.

Elsa Lanchester and Boris Karloff in *Bride of Frankenstein*.

As a sequel, the film *Bride of Frankenstein* (1935)[22] continues threads of the original storyline alongside some rather bizarre additions. The opening sequence is an amusingly jovial mock-up of the legendary gathering of Mary Shelley, her husband Percy, and friend Lord Byron, complete with a (rather forced and lengthy) rehashing of the plot of the first film. From there, we are afforded some comic relief in the form of villager Minnie (played by Una O'Connor), as well as some unsettlingly jarred miniature people created by sinister Doctor Pretorius, who blackmails Victor (still called Henry) into re-opening his efforts to generate life and, more specifically, to make a mate for the Monster (a nod to the creature demanding his own mate in the book). One crucial scene from the text makes it on screen: the encounter of the Monster with the blind cottager, in which he is shown some kindness and learns how to use language somewhat more effectively. After being rejected by the reanimated female, the Monster utters chillingly tragic words: "We belong dead." Even in this brutish portrayal of him (and even though preferring death over romantic rejection smacks of incel-like immaturity), the performance is bent toward garnering the sympathy of the audience for this being's tortured experience.

---

[22] *Bride of Frankenstein*. Directed by James Whale. Performances by Boris Karloff, Elsa Lanchester, Colin Clive. Universal Pictures, 1935.

The Internet Movie Database lists a total of 34 *Frankenstein* film adaptations, some of which are much more well-known than others. *The Illustrated Frankenstein Movie Guide* lists more than 400.[23] In addition to the popular Universal Pictures collection, some noteworthy titles include the incomparable *Young Frankenstein* (1974) starring Gene Wilder,[24] which milks and subverts established tropes of both Gothic literature and previous Frankenstein – ahem, *Fronk-en-steen* – films to hilarious comedic effect. Frankenstein's monster also makes an appearance in the 2004 urban fantasy film *Van Helsing*, also from Universal, though aside from the creature's anguished cries of *"Why?!"* in response to persecution, the original novel's themes are lost against the film's pantheon of supernatural characters and their shadowy deeds.

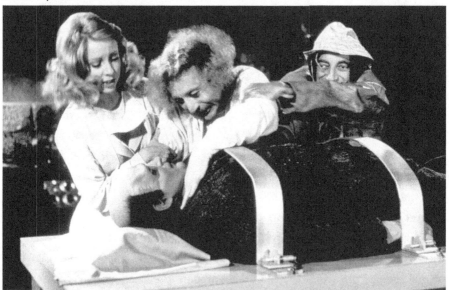

Gene Wilder as Dr. Frankenstein and Peter Boyle as his monster in *Young Frankenstein.*

[23] Bailey, Ronald. "Victor Frankenstein is the Real Monster." *Reason*, Reason Foundation, Apr. 2018, reason.com/2018/03/04/victor-frankenstein-is-the-rea/. Accessed 13 Sept. 2019.
[24] Wilder, Gene, Madeline Kahn, Mary Feldman, Peter Boyle, actor. *Young Frankenstein*. Directed by Mel Brooks, 1974. Twentieth Century Fox.

The 1994 movie *Mary Shelley's Frankenstein*,[25] starring Robert de Niro as the Monster and Kenneth Branagh as Victor, is a relatively faithful adaptation of the book, with a few interesting deviations. In this version, the Monster says that the skills he acquires, including speech, are "not things learned so much as things remembered," implying that he recalls fragments from the former lives of his body parts. "Who were these people of which I am comprised?" he asks Victor. "Good people? Bad people?" In typical form, Victor dodges the question, but this element of memory motivates Victor to later reanimate the dead body of his bride Elizabeth, who is so horrified at her new nature that she burns herself alive (along with the whole Frankenstein mansion). Earlier, the Monster challenges Victor: "Did you ever consider the consequences of your actions?" As we watch the scientist's flaming bride fly off a staircase, it's clear the answer is a resounding "no." While this film suffers from some pacing problems and incongruous shifts in tone, it successfully captures the dire result of Victor's choice to repeatedly place his own interests above everyone else's.

The most text-accurate film rendition is a 2004 Hallmark TV mini-series starring Alec Newman as Victor and Luke Goss as the Monster, later released on DVD.[26] Of the screen versions I have watched, this one follows the story of the text the closest, keeping the beginning and end essentially intact, although it does take some artistic liberties for heightened drama, such as allowing Victor's friend Henry Clerval to become aware of the Monster's existence, and letting the audience see some of Victor's romantic interludes with Elizabeth. The biggest difference is that this film paints the Monster in a somewhat more innocent and favorable light than either the Karloff films or the original text. Karloff's character has a supposedly "criminal" brain and is driven to murder and harm things by nature of his makeup, while the original text character is driven to violence out of desperation for Victor's attention, and vengeance for his neglect.[27] In the Goss film, the Monster's first murder – that of Victor's youngest brother, William – is portrayed as completely accidental, and the

[25] *Mary Shelley's Frankenstein*. Directed by Kenneth Branagh. Performances by Robert De Niro, Kenneth Branagh, and Helena Bonham Carter. TriStar Pictures, 1994.

[26] *Frankenstein*. Directed by Kevin Connor. Performances by Newman, Alec, and Luke Goss. Hallmark Entertainment, 2004.

[27] British-American television series *Penny Dreadful* (2014–2016) takes a similar approach to the Monster, played in this adaptation by actor Rory Kinnear.

Monster feels deep remorse for taking an innocent life. In the final scene of the film on Captain Walton's ship, as the creature laments Victor's death and the fatigue of his suffering, it is difficult to view him as anything but human.

Shelley's book has inspired many cultural artifacts outside of narratives. There have been toys, games, art, and of course the ubiquitous Halloween merchandise – everything from candy to costumes to confetti – sporting the iconic-yet-inaccurate image of the stocky green zombie with bolts in his neck. (Shelley's creature is described in the text as having yellow skin, pearly white teeth, and flowing, lustrous black hair[28] – he was intended to be the epitome of beauty). As Anne Mellor says in *The Cambridge Companion to Mary Shelley,* "*Frankenstein* can claim the status of a myth so profoundly resonant in its implications that it has become, at least in its barest outline, a trope of everyday life."[29] Likewise, Polish critic Barbara Braid calls it "one of the strongest memes of modernity."[30] However he's drawn or depicted, the creature known colloquially as "Frankenstein" is a fixture of American cultural consciousness.

It is no wonder, then, that my students (and much of the American populace) confuse the name of "Frankenstein" as belonging to the Monster, when it actually refers to Victor Frankenstein, the scientist. That might seem a moot point of trivia for literary nerds, but in the realm of meaning, names bear weighty significance. As Adam Alter discusses in an article in *The New Yorker,* "words carry hidden baggage that may play at least some role in shaping thought,"[31] meaning the name an object or person carries influences how we perceive it. But what if a being has no name? "What is the process by which

---

[28] Shelley, Mary. *Frankenstein*. 1818. Reprint. San Diego: Canterbury Classics, 2013, p. 43.

[29] Mellor, Anne K. "Making a 'Monster': An Introduction to *Frankenstein*." *The Cambridge Companion to Mary Shelley,* edited by Esther Schor, New York, Cambridge University Press, 2003, p. 9.

[30] Bailey, Ronald. "Victor Frankenstein is the Real Monster." *Reason*, Reason Foundation, Apr. 2018, reason.com/2018/03/04/victor-frankenstein-is-the-rea/. Accessed 13 Sept. 2019.

[31] Alter, Adam. "The Power of Names." *The New Yorker,* 29 May 2013, www.newyorker.com/tech/annals-of-technology/the-power-of-names. Accessed 14 Sept. 2019.

nameless dreads are named?" asks author Leo Brady.[32] For Frankenstein's monster, there is no such process; he is called "wretch," "daemon," and "devil" through the whole book – *but has no real name,* either given or chosen. This categorical labeling, absent of personal identity, contributes to his dehumanization and othering, especially by Victor.

Some may argue that the main themes of the story are that humanity should not play god,[33] or that technology is inherently dangerous and unnatural,[34] but those interpretations ignore Shelley's sympathetic depiction of the Monster as a person; the text is primarily, in my assessment, an unflinching treatise on compassion. In his article "*Frankenstein* and the Tradition of Realism," author George Levine states, "There is no evidence in the early stages [of the story] of anything essentially evil in the Monster,"[35] and indeed, Victor did not set out to make a "fiend," as he later calls him.[36] the Monster's motives are by no means wholly pure either, especially later in the book once he has become bitter and resentful (his request for a made-to-order mate that he can possess and manipulate[37] qualifies as selfish and creepy), but if asked to assign the title of "villain" to one character, most of my students choose Victor, and I would have to agree. They are always quick to point out that Victor's major flaw is not attempting to discover the "principle of life,"[38] but rather his total refusal to care for that life once he creates it. One of my students stated in discussion, "If Victor had just showed compassion to his fellow person, none of the suffering and pain in this book would exist. He just needed to *care* enough to do what was best for the creature, who had no power to help himself." It is Victor's

---

[32] Brady, Leo. *Haunted: On Ghosts, Witches, Vampires, Zombies, and Other Monsters of the Natural and Supernatural Worlds.* Yale University Press, 2016.

[33] Laurence, Rebecca. "Why *Frankenstein* is the Story That Defines Our Fears." *BBC,* BBC, 13 June 2018, www.bbc.com/culture/story/20180611-why-frankenstein-is-the-story-that-defined-our-fears. Accessed 21 Aug. 2019.

[34] Bailey, Ronald. "Victor Frankenstein is the Real Monster." *Reason,* Reason Foundation, Apr. 2018, reason.com/2018/03/04/victor-frankenstein-is-the-rea/. Accessed 13 Sept. 2019.

[35] Levine, George. "*Frankenstein* and the Tradition of Realism." *Modern Critical Views: Mary Shelley.* edited by Harold Bloom, New York, Chelsea House Publishers, 1985, p. 92.

[36] Shelley, Mary. *Frankenstein.* 1818. Reprint. San Diego: Canterbury Classics, 2013, p. 83.

[37] Ibid, p. 122.

[38] Ibid, p. 38.

negligence and self-centered cruelty, not his scientific ambition, that doom the story's cast to suffering and loss on an Oedipal scale.

It is in this analysis of the narrative's unflattering depiction of Victor's harshness toward his creation that my students frequently alight on a new definition of monstrosity: cruelty for cruelty's sake. Yes, they initially cringe at the grisly description of the lifeless corpse, as Mary Shelley intended,[39] and they start at the spookiness of that figure looming above Victor's bed, but as the tale unfolds, the word "monster" begins to carry less horror. In the context of the story, that term becomes desensitized as a descriptor in conversation, and instead comes to represent a specific person, with unique wants and needs, and eloquent, passionate self-awareness. Whatever messy new definition of personhood my students piece together from philosophical theories and their own conjectures, it almost always includes Frankenstein's monster. Once they have walked with him through neglect and abandonment, listened to him speak, and witnessed his yearning to understand the world, it is clear he is no different in his desires than most people. They do *not* excuse his violence or rationalize his rage, nor should they, but they believe that he, as an entity, deserves as much moral consideration as his creator or any other person.

Such inclusion is neither granted nor denied in a cultural vacuum: therefore, how do societal power structures surrounding identity and belonging play into those divisions? A group of my students came up with their own philosophy problem on this subject that turned into an involved debate: There is a planet on which live 20 scientists and one gorilla. The 20 scientists all agree, in their expert human opinions, that the gorilla is not a person, i.e. it is an animal not worthy of moral consideration or inclusion in the definition of "people." The gorilla, on the other hand, has one thought and one thought only for its entire life: "I am a person." Who is correct? Is the gorilla a person? One student said yes, because he believed "anything that thinks it's a person is one. All beings should be able to define themselves." Another student thought that the sum knowledge of human society should count for something when making these kinds of distinctions. The students called me over to show me the diagrams of their arguments and expected me to solve the problem for them. I told them that this is what philosophers do: they ask questions about existence

---

[39] Spark, Muriel. "Frankenstein." *Modern Critical Views: Mary Shelley*. edited by Harold Bloom, New York, Chelsea House Publishers, 1985, p. 13.

that rarely have easy answers. "It just leads to more questions," one of them said. "Does the gorilla need to be able to communicate its thought, or is thinking it enough? What if there were more gorillas than scientists? Who should count as an expert?" "Welcome to ethics," I said. He nodded, then replied, "It's very grey here."

In analyzing the grey – and there is no better example of greyness than Shelley's monster – we learn what versions of our own nature we can bear to live with. Because the *next* questions, the ones on the other side of that gorilla's fate, are terrifying: What does society do to people who are seen as *less* than people? What horrors are possible when personhood is ignored, when cruelty becomes a strategy for personal gain? What happens when evil people are running the show? In America in 2020, I would argue that we don't have to speculate. As a nation, as a culture, it is essential that we decide, in no uncertain terms, what basic human rights are owed to all people, and what the appropriate civic response is to sanctioned violation of those rights. Even though Frankenstein's monster is a fictional character, my students often say they wish that they could step in and show him kindness, to let him know that not all humans are horrible and that he has worth as an individual, separate from how he is treated or even from what he can contribute to society. They recognize that a lack of empathy and respect for others is the true "daemon" in the story, and I say we would do well to follow suit and hold public policy to that same standard of common dignity.

Mary Shelley's iconic and seminal tale has inspired countless interpretations, remakes, spinoffs, and memorable portrayals, and it remains crisply relevant today in its intimate look at the "other" who functions as a mirror to the worst workings of humanity. In analyzing monsters and our reactions to them, we probe our potential for behavior that can either enlighten or damn us. As author Brian Stableford points out,[40] Shelley was fully aware that it is not our monsters which can ruin the world, but we ourselves.

So: Draw a monster.

Then, learn from it.

---

[40] Stableford, Brian. "Frankenstein and the Origins of Science Fiction." *Anticipations: Essays on Early Science Fiction and its Precursors*, edited by David Seed, Syracuse, Syracuse University Press, 1995, p. 57.

Kharis: The Unsung Legend of Mummy Fiction

by Frank Schildiner

When filmgoers speak of mummies, one name rises above the rest: Imhotep. Boris Karloff's 1932 portrayal of the undead Egyptian in Universal's *The Mummy* changed the film world.[1] However, equaling Imhotep's influence upon monster movies, if not surpassing his metaphorical might, is the star of five other films – the terrifying, shambling, undead horror known as Kharis the Mummy.

Kharis, whose films include the B-quality Universal titles *The Mummy's Hand* (1940), *The Mummy's Tomb* (1942), *The Mummy's Ghost* (1944), and *The Mummy's Curse* (1944), as well as the A-quality Hammer Films movie *The Mummy* (1959), set the standard for this type of monster portrayal. Consider the methodology used regarding the typical depiction of mummies in film, television, literature, and comics: shambling, silent, bandaged beings who move slowly and with jerky actions, protecting tombs from foreign invaders.

---

[1] Decades later, Arnold Vosloo would assume the role of Imhotep in *The Mummy* (1999) and *The Mummy Returns* (2001), also starring Brendan Fraser and Rachel Weisz.

Imhotep? No, that is Kharis, the unsung, forgotten legend of the monster universe.

Imhotep may have started it all, but it was Kharis (pictured here) who laid the foundation for the rest of Universal's sequels.

Fictional mummies date back to *The Mummy!: Or a Tale of the Twenty-Second Century*, a three-volume novel series published in 1825 and written by 17-year-old Jane C. Loudon. Literary luminaries such as Edgar Allan Poe, Louisa May Alcott, Sir Arthur Conan Doyle, Bram Stoker, H.P. Lovecraft, and Robert Bloch each added tales to the canon of mummy-based fiction.

The first use of a mummy as a rampaging creature like Kharis appears to occur in Bram Stoker's short story "Lot No. 249" (1892). In this tale, Egyptology student Edward Bellingham uses a revived mummy as a weapon against his enemies. The story's protagonist burns the mummy, which could be an influence upon the Kharis series since that happens to the Kharis mummy more than once.

Who Is Kharis the Mummy?

Fortunately for viewers, the writers illuminated the details of Kharis's early life in a massive info dump in *The Mummy's Hand*. Kharis was a priest during the time of the Pharaoh Amenophis, approximately 3000 years ago. Amenophis is the Greek version of the Egyptian name Amenhotep, and we can approximately pinpoint the period in which Kharis must have lived.

The ruler, as shown in the pool of life, would have been a Pharaoh since he carried the royal symbols of the *heka* and *nekhakha* (crook and flail). These items were symbols of pharaonic authority in Egypt since pre-dynastic days. Additionally, he wore an Atef, a crown symbolizing the authority of the king over Upper and Lower Egypt.

Only four kings historically held the name of Amenhotep, all of whom were members of the Eighteenth Dynasty of Egypt. We can eliminate two from this list very easily, based on the historical record. Amenhotep I was the second king of the Eighteenth Dynasty and had no living heirs. His only child, a son, died young of unknown causes. It is possible that his successor, Thutmose I, was a cousin or a son by a lesser wife, but there is no evidence of any daughters in the records of Amenhotep I. Therefore, it is doubtful that this is the Pharaoh whom Kharis served.

Easily eliminated is Amenhotep IV (a.k.a. Akhenaten), because the details of that king's life are very well known. His children included Smenkhkare, Meritaten, Meketaten, Ankhesenamun, Neferneferuaten Tasherit, Neferneferure, Setepenre, Tutankhamun (better known to the world as King Tut), and Ankhesenpaaten Tasherit. Though the last king of the Eighteenth Dynasty, a general named Horemheb, sought the destruction of any records of Akhenaten's reign, many records survived. Akhenaten did not have a daughter named Ananka who died young. The best-known daughter of this period, Ankhesenamun, married Tutankhamun and outlived the boy king by some years. Additionally, Akhenaten's reign led to a religious change in which worship of the old gods was discouraged in favor of the sun symbol known as the Aten. Based on Kharis's story, this does not fit the king who imprisoned the high priest in his lonely tomb.

Amenhotep II appears improbable – though he fathered many children, his family members appear fully documented in history. This Pharaoh did have a wealth of sons, but few daughters, listed in the official records. This is important, since the daughters often married their fathers and brothers as a means of protecting the royal bloodlines.

The best choice for king is thus Amenhotep III, the father of Amenhotep IV. A powerful ruler during a period of great wealth and prosperity, he sired many children of both sexes. One of his daughters, Beketaten, vanished from the historical record without any trace. Her tomb appears lost – remarkably similar to the back stories of these Mummy films. Additionally, most members of the royal family held more than one name for religious purposes. The name "Ananka" could be another name for this almost unknown princess.

If this is when Kharis existed, then his life must have ended in approximately 1338 B.C., which, though more than "three thousand years" ago, does appear historically accurate. Obviously, in the world of fiction, this is a mere estimation based on the often-sketchy details presented in the film, but it is a good possibility.

Kharis's backstory has him as the high priest of Karnak (and later Arkam in *The Mummy's Ghost* and *The Mummy's Curse*). Karnak was not a god, but a temple complex created by Senusret I of the Twelfth Dynasty. As such — and given that the name inexplicably changed during the course of the films — the priests of this sect are probably using "Karnak" and "Arkam" as secret names for their god.

Based on the cult's devotion to protecting the dead, as well as the details of their temple as shown in *The Mummy's Hand*, they are probably devotees of a debased version of Anubis, the jackal-headed guardian of the dead and one of the oldest deities in the Egyptian pantheon. His images appear on massive statues of the secret temple inhabited by the high priests of Karnak. This also fits the story of Kharis in another way. Princess Ananka dies young and Kharis desires her return. He seeks the secret tana leaves, whose proper use can return the dead to a version of living. Who else but a priest of the guardian of the dead would know of the existence of such wonderous plants?

Imprisoned alive with his tongue removed, Kharis exists throughout the millennia as a unique form of undead. While not quite deceased, he definitely is not alive by our definition. His heart beats, thanks to the tana leaves, but this may be an artificial form of life under the control of the priests of Karnak. However, Kharis is not a mindless, shambling creature like a movie-conceived zombie. He understands more than most realize, especially whenever his protection of Ananka is threatened. Upon discovering Yousef Bey's plans to administer tana to the reincarnated form of Ananka as a means of keeping her alive for himself, Kharis reacts: he attacks the priest and violently kills Bey before leaving with the reincarnated princess in his arms.

The Mummy's Hand (1940)

The first Kharis-based Mummy movie establishes the character and the style of the films that will follow. The dying high priest of Karnak (portrayed by Eduardo Ciannelli) provides the back story of the monster through a vision pool. His successor, Andoheb (George Zucco), views the tale (detailed above) and learns the secret of the tana leaves: If one provides three leaves to the mummy, he will live again. Nine leaves make him an uncontrollable monster, and disaster is hinted to occur if Kharis receives more than nine. We never learn what would happen in such a situation, though, which is a missed opportunity.

After this setup, we meet the hero of the film, Steve Banning (Dick Foran), and his wisecracking Brooklyn sidekick, Babe Jenson (Wallace Ford). They convince a stage magician named the Great Solvani (Cecil Kellaway) to act as financier to their expedition. Also joining the trip are Solvani's attractive daughter, Marta Solvani (Peggy Moran), and an Egyptologist, Dr. Petrie (Charles Trowbridge). The mummified Kharis (Tom Tyler) rises at the behest of Andoheb, and some murders take place. Yet the intrepid hero, his silly sidekick, and the pretty girl continue in their quest as grave robbers and prevail by the story's end.

Loaded with far too much exposition and too little use of Kharis, *The Mummy's Hand* is a B picture that wastes much of its potential. The monster behaves like a drug addict, desperately seeking the tana solution in various locations and behaving violently when thwarted. His attacks demonstrate monstrous strength, but his shambling shuffle is so slow – anyone could outrun this mummy with ease.

The players in this tale – stalwart Steve Banning, wisecracking Babe Jenson, pretty Marta Solvani, stolid Dr. Petrie, and clever Great Solvani – are stock characters from B pictures of that period. Other than the stage magician, who is wasted after a promising beginning, there is not a lot to offer in terms of character development, mostly due to the hasty 66-minute running time of the film.

On the other hand, George Zucco's Andoheb sets the standard for conniving high priests who battle against despoilers of tombs. His influence in future mummy films is nearly as important as that of Kharis. In many of the films that use mummies as villains, such characters exist in both villainous and heroic roles. In the 1999 remake of *The Mummy*, for instance, Dr. Terrance Bay (Erick Avari) tries to prevent the expedition that could awaken the mummy, Imhotep. Like Andoheb, his intentions are protective, whereas in Bey's case the motive is positive. Andoheb, like most priests of this sect, desires the female protagonist of the film and decides to take her for himself. This appears to be a major issue for priests of Karnack/Arkam throughout the series.

What *The Mummy's Hand* does is provide us with the foundation of the series: Kharis, the protector of Ananka, possesses inhuman strength and near-invulnerability from harm. This silent sentinel acts as an attack dog and guardian of his lost love and is relentless in the face of any opposition. Empowered by tana leaves, Kharis is limited by his need for the drug and his undead ruin of a body.

The Mummy's Tomb (1942)

Set 30 years after *The Mummy's Hand*, the next entry sees Steve Banning (Dick Foran) relating the previous film's activities to his son John (John Hubbard) and future daughter-in-law, Isobel Evans (Elyse Knox). This would mean either that the first film's events had occurred around 1912 or that the current year in which *Tomb* takes place is 1970. Obviously, neither scenario works overly well – these are just explanations for the screenwriters not paying attention to such details. Banning's wife, Marta (from *Hand*), has passed away in the period between films and he now lives with his sister, Jane Banning (Mary Gordon), in the fictional town of Mapleton, Massachusetts. Herein, anything Egyptian in the series comes from stock footage.

Andoheb (George Zucco) somehow survived the previous film and is now the elderly high priest of Karnak. He assigns the task of murdering all those who robbed the tomb of Ananka and their descendants to Mehemet Bey (Turhan Bey). Mehemet's weapon is the mummy Kharis (now portrayed by Lon Chaney, Jr.), who looks none the worse for his previous adventure.

Mehemet Bey gets a job as a caretaker in a cemetery and sends Kharis after Banning. After Steve dies, the sheriff (Cliff Clark) and coroner (Emmett Vogan) search for a human killer. Babe Hanson (Wallace Ford) returns from New York and insists the killer was a mummy, which the coroner and sheriff ignore. Hanson (whose name was Jenson in the previous film) dies shortly afterwards, followed by Jane Banning.

Mehemet Bey falls in love with Isobel and orders her kidnapped by Kharis. The mummy resists briefly, then does as he's told, and the priest declares his plan to inject her with tana and make her his eternal bride. The mummy then carries Isobel back to the Banning mansion, followed by torch-wielding townspeople. John drops his torch while fighting Kharis, and the building is soon on fire. Isobel and John escape, but the inferno prevents Kharis from following.

The Mummy's Tomb is a little more effective a tale than its predecessor, since the motives of priest and mummy make sense. Their job is the protection of Princess Ananka's tomb, the contents of which Steve Banning had robbed and carried off to Mapleton. Lon Chaney. Jr. steps into the role of Kharis, a part he truly despised. The costume was painful and the makeup often cut open his face upon removal. For long-distance shots, the filmmakers created a rubber Kharis mask, which gave him some respite. Chaney is impressive physically and very imposing, and he makes do with his character's limitations.

Kharis (Lon Chaney, Jr.) carries Isobel Evans (Elyse Knox) to Mehemet Bey in *The Mummy's Tomb*.

Wallace Ford basically plays a different character in this film. Whereas Babe Jenson was previously a slow-witted, streetwise conman and wisecracker, Babe Hanson is now an imposing elderly man who resembles a retired banker. Other than the actor playing the part, there is no consistency to the character in these two films. John Hubbard and Elyse Knox are mere stock players, with nothing particularly interesting about them other than their movie-star good looks. Turhan Bey's acting skill rises above some of the weaker material, and his character's argument with John Hubbard is a very effective moment. His performance is only hampered by the short running time of the film (61 minutes).

The Mummy's Tomb is an enjoyable B-grade film, one that gives Kharis more screen time, even though a mummy in a small town in the United States does not work effectively. The low budget of the film does not harm the production, though small-town America will never be as interesting a setting as the dusty tombs of Egypt.

The Mummy's Ghost (1944)

Andoheb (George Zucco), the High Priest of Arkam (formerly Karnak), meets with his new underling, Yousef Bey (John Carradine), in Egypt's Temple of Arkam. He recites the tale of Kharis and Princess Ananka and charges Bey with the return of the mummy and his lost love. Bey travels to the United States and takes up residence in an abandoned mill with Kharis (Lon Chaney, Jr.). The mummy appears battered, but his return from the fire at the Banning home is unexplained.

John Carradine as Yousef Bey in *The Mummy's Ghost.*

Meanwhile, back in Mapleton, Professor Norman (Frank Reicher) teaches a class in Egyptology and shares his experiences with his skeptical students. One student, Tom Hervey (Robert Lowery), discusses the lecture with his girlfriend of Egyptian descent, Amina Mansori (Ramsay Ames). When she reacts poorly at the mention of ancient Egypt, he backs off. The professor deciphers a small chest containing tana leaves and boils nine of the plants under a full moon. Kharis shows up, kills the man, and drinks down the potion. Amina, in a trance, follows the mummy and passes out when she sees him walking. She cannot explain why she was outside in her nightgown, nor how a white streak ended up in her hair.

Hiding in the Scripps Museum after hours, the mummy reaches for the body of Ananka and it crumbles into dust. Bey explains that the spirit of Ananaka must inhabit a body, and that they will find her one immediately. In a rage, Kharis destroys the exhibit and murders an elderly security guard before leaving. The sheriff (Harry Shannon) decides he will trap the mummy and burns nine tana leaves near a hidden pit. Kharis follows the scent, but Amina walks to him in a trance. She is the reincarnated Princess Ananka, and he carries her back to the mill. Bey decides he wants her for himself, but Kharis learns of this and kills the priest.

Led by his dog, Hervey discovers Kharis and Amina and attacks the mummy. The monster strikes him down, but the young college student survives the battle. By the time the sheriff and townspeople arrive, Kharis has escaped by climbing down a ladder with Amina. As he walks into the nearby swamp, Amina ages into a mummy while Tom and the others watch. When Kharis and the reincarnated Ananka slip under the swamp waters, she is as aged as the undead Egyptian priest.

The Mummy's Ghost is often cited as the weakest of the Universal mummy films, and this is well-deserved. Though the running time is once again short (62 minutes), the film moves at a slow pace, and by the time Kharis and Ananka slip into the muddy waters, the end is welcomed. One bright spot is Lon Chaney, Jr. as Kharis. Though he is still silent, the script allows him greater action. When the mummy attacks Yousef Bey, the viewer understands the fear the man must feel. This Kharis possesses an inhuman strength and reacts to stimuli other than the high priest's orders.

Robert Lowery's Tom Hervey is the weakest hero in the series, and acts like he should be in a high school football comedy rather than a horror film. Despite Lowery's shortcomings, though, it is Ramsay Ames as Amina Mansori who drags every scene down like an anchor. The wooden sarcophagi demonstrate greater emotional range than this actor. Though a very attractive woman, she weakens an already poorly scripted film even further. Oddly enough, B-movie beauty Acquanetta originally had the part of Amina. On the first day of shooting, however, she struck her head on a rock that she thought was made of papier-mâché. Universal fired her in favor of Ames since they were shooting the entire film in nine days.

John Carradine's presence is minor, and that is too bad — though his blackface makeup is uncomfortable for many modern viewers, especially after the effective performance of the half-Turkish Turhan Bey. *The Mummy's Ghost* lives up to its reputation as the worst of the Kharis series, and one could assume that most viewers watch this film only for completion purposes.

The Mummy's Curse (1944)

For some reason, the swamps of Mapleton have relocated from Massachusetts to Louisiana. The employees and townspeople near the swamps speak and act like Cajuns while the Southern Engineering Company drains the region. A pair of academics from the Scripps Museum, Dr. James Halsey (Dennis Moore) and Dr. Ilzor Zandaab (Peter Coe), arrive on the scene and seek the bodies of the mummies who sank into the swamp years before. The site boss, Pat Walsh (Addison Richards), does not welcome the academics, while his beautiful niece Betty (Kay Harding) flirts with Halsey. A worker dies as they speak and the academics believe it is the work of Kharis.

We soon discover Zandaab is the high priest of Arkam, and he and his knife-wielding disciple Ragheb (Martin Kosleck) find the body of Kharis (still portrayed by Lon Chaney, Jr.). They bring the mummy to an abandoned monastery, where his tale is recounted. Ananka's body is unearthed and she rises as well, alive once more. Upon washing the mud from her face and body, she is now a beautiful, albeit amnesiac woman (portrayed by Virginia Christine). Soon Kharis arrives, Ananka flees, and Halsey and Betty Walsh find her. She has little memory save for a great knowledge of ancient Egypt.

Kharis follows and kills several men in his path before carrying Ananka away. Betty asks Ragheb for help in finding Halsey, and he takes her to the monastery. He wants her for himself and, when Zandaab objects, he stabs the high priest to death. The mummy attacks Ragheb, who hides in a locked room. Kharis destroys the building, killing Ragheb and destroying himself in the process, while the others discover the mummified remains of Ananka nearby.

The Mummy's Curse is the best of Universal's Kharis films, featuring a strong script with effective acting performances by all involved. Lon Chaney, Jr. is an imposing force of nature every time he appears onscreen. He is a true terror and viewers understand why people flee upon the sight of his bandaged body. Why the story suddenly switches from Massachusetts to Cajun country is completely unexplained, but this sort of thing is typical of the series.

Peter Coe as Zandaab is the most effective high priest we have viewed in the series, objecting to his underling's behavior toward Betty. Sadly, that does not work well for him in the end, but it is nice seeing that cliché put to rest. Virginia Christine, meanwhile, as the youth-restored Ananka, turns in a wonderful performance.[2]

---

[2] This lovely lady was best known to television viewers from her twenty-one-year run as the commercial spokesperson for Folgers Coffee. Her character, kindly

Lon Chaney, Jr. soaks up some sun on the set of Universal's *The Mummy's Curse*.

The Mummy's Curse works as a lightweight B-grade film, but at least the short runtime (62 minutes) prevents the movie from overstaying its welcome.

The Mummy (1959)

In 1895 Egypt, archaeologist Stephen Banning (Felix Aylmer), his brother-in-law Joseph Whemple (Raymond Huntley), and Stephen's injured son, John Banning (Peter Cushing), discover the hidden tomb of Princess Ananka. The high priest of Karnak, Mehemet Bey (George Pastell), warns that this act is considered desecration and that they will suffer if they proceed further. Joseph leaves, intent on updating John, who is stuck in his tent with a broken leg. Stephen discovers a small chest containing the famous Scroll of Life, and we soon hear him screaming with fear. The scroll is not in evidence and Stephen has fallen catatonic.

Three years later, at the Engerfield Home for the Mentally Disordered, Stephen comes out of his trance and demands to see John. He tells his son that he read from the scroll and inadvertently raised the mummy of Kharis. This

neighbor Mrs. Olson, offered advice to young couples through coffee from 1965 to 1986.

broke his mind then, and now he believes the monster will hunt them all down for desecrating Ananka's tomb.

A pair of drunken carters lose a chest of Egyptian artifacts in the swamps near the Engerfield Home. Mehemet Bey arrives and reveals he is now in the area. He later uses the scroll to raise Kharis (Christopher Lee), sending the mummy after Banning. Stephen, who was reacting with paranoia early, is in a padded cell at the hospital. Kharis rips through the metal bars and strangles the elderly archaeologist, and later breaks into the Banning home and murders Joseph Whemple. John shoots the mummy with a revolver, but to no affect.

John relates the tale of Kharis, who loved Ananka, and we later learn that John's wife Isobel (Yvonne Furneaux) resembles her. Kharis attacks John and is strangling him when Isobel arrives. She screams for Kharis to stop, and he stares at her and complies. Mehemet Bey believes John is dead and is shocked when the man arrives. Later, the mummy strangles John once again, until Isobel orders the monster to stop. Kharis initially does not comply, but after she loosens her hair, he does so and approaches her with slow steps. Bey orders Isobel's death and Kharis kills him instead, then carries her off toward the swamps, followed by John and the police. John yells to Isobel and she tells Kharis to release her. He does so, then the police and townspeople shoot the monster once she is clear. The mummy sinks into the swamp, the Scroll of Life in hand.

This version of *The Mummy* is a lavish production and arguably the best of the Kharis series. The script, by Hammer scribe Jimmy Sangster, does drag during the Egyptian history info dump, but in a film starring Peter Cushing and Christopher Lee, you cannot go wrong.

This is a highly recommended feature for all Mummy fans, one that will thrill and chill even jaded viewers. The story is a mixture of elements from two Universal productions, *The Mummy's Hand* and *The Mummy's Tomb*, while borrowing the Scroll of Life from Boris Karloff's *The Mummy* (1931) as a replacement for the tana leaves. The story flows well, and the scenes are visually impressive. This is also the longest Kharis movie (88 minutes), which helps the film's flow. The coincidental physical connection between Isobel and Ananka is a bit clumsy, but standard for this film style.

Christopher Lee is terrifying as Kharis, moving faster than Tom Tyler and Lon Chaney, Jr., as well as representing a greater danger to his enemies. His movements, though clearly inhuman, are powerful, sweeping attacks that destroy doors and walls and tear through metal bars with impressive ease.

When his all-too-human eyes slowly stare at his enemy, the viewers feel a chill of fear from this terrible monster.

Peter Cushing (John Banning) takes on Christopher Lee's Kharis in Hammer's *The Mummy.*

Likewise, Peter Cushing is excellent as the limping, intelligent John Banning. He adds a realistic quality to his role, especially when he risks his life antagonizing Mehemet Bey. Despite being a thin man of average height, Cushing somehow exudes an inner power that served him throughout his entire career. For more examples, I would suggest viewing *The Horror of Dracula*, *The Curse of Frankenstein,* and *Star Wars: A New Hope*.

There you have it: the history of Kharis the Mummy, the often-forgotten legend who changed the face of horror, and whose influence is still felt to this day.

A Monstrous Regiment of Draculas

by Charles R. Rutledge

Author Bram Stoker always wanted his novel *Dracula* made into a play. In fact, *Dracula* was actually "performed" before it was published. Stoker arranged a reading of a cut-down version of the novel at the Lyceum Theater in London, where he worked as the manager for many years, in order to secure copyrights to performance versions of his novel.

That reading took place on 18 May 1897, eight days before the novel *Dracula* was released, and it was as close as Stoker ever came to seeing his book dramatized. He probably would have been amazed to learn that not only did *Dracula* become a hit play, but the Count has since appeared in more than 200 films to date, making him the second most-filmed literary character, surpassed only by Sir Arthur Conan Doyle's Sherlock Holmes.

Of those many films, surprisingly few have been actual adaptations of the book, and few of those have followed the novel closely. The structure of *Dracula* makes it difficult to adapt. It has a large cast and is told through a series of letters, diary entries, newspaper articles, and the like. It also rambles around a great deal, from Transylvania to England and back to Transylvania. Prior to 1970, the novel was adapted three times with varying degrees of fidelity to the book.

The first film adaptation was unauthorized and used only the bare outlines of Stoker's novel. In 1922, *Nosferatu, a Symphony of Horror*, was released by a small German company called Prana-Film. According to the film program, the movie was "freely adapted" from *Dracula*, by Bram Stoker. In this case, "freely" takes on a dual meaning, as in not only was the film a loose adaptation, but the filmmakers hadn't bothered to pay for the rights from Stoker's widow, Florence.

The novel *Dracula* begins with a young British solicitor, Jonathan Harker, on his way to Transylvania to meet the reclusive Count Dracula, who wishes to buy property in England. *Nosferatu* starts with a character named Hutter saying goodbye to his wife Ellen before leaving the fictional city of Wisborg for the castle of nobleman Graf Orlok. Orlok wishes to purchase a house in Hutter's home town. The wife is the stand-in for Harker's fiancée, Mina Murray, in *Dracula*.

Nosferatu, starring Max Schreck as Graf Orlok, an ersatz Count Dracula, is technically the first film adaptation of Bram Stoker's classic novel.

Whereas Harker had to travel for some time on trains to get from London to Transylvania, Hutter takes a coach ride, stopping for one night at a gypsy inn, where he reads a book about vampires conveniently left in his room. The next day, Hutter is met by a coach with a driver whose face is mostly hidden by a hat and high-collared coat. This echoes a scene in *Dracula*, in which the disguised Count pretends to be his own driver and picks up Jonathan Harker at the Borgo Pass. Orlok, portrayed by actor Max Schreck, has weird eyes and a rat-like face, so his disguise isn't very effective. However, Hutter hasn't met him yet, so we'll let that pass.

The coach takes Hutter to Orlok's castle, where we get our first good look at Graf Orlok. Stoker's Dracula was an old man with white hair and mustache, hairy palms, sharp fingernails, and persistent bad breath. Orlok is even more repulsive, with a misshapen bald pate, glaring eyes, protruding teeth, and large, pointed ears.

During his initial discussion with Orlok, Hutter cuts himself, eliciting a frightening, predatory reaction from the vampire. A version of this scene occurs in the novel and will be repeated in almost all of the adaptations. Orlok also becomes the first movie Dracula to admire a picture of the hero's beloved, a scene that isn't in the book, but which will recur in later films as an important plot point.

Nosferatu was filmed in the German Expressionistic style and was directed by Friedrich Wilhelm Murnau. The movie will be a century old in 2022, yet it contains sequences that remain unsettling to this day. One is a sequence in which Hutter retires after his talk with Orlok, and then, later in the night, opens the door to his room and sees Orlok coming his way in full vampire mode: eyes glowing, long, claw-like fingers twitching, and moving in a weird, lurching gait.

Hutter attempts to bar his door but can find no way to keep Orlok out, and the rat-like vampire attacks him. Somehow, Hutter's wife "sees" this happening in her sleep and calls out her husband's name. Orlok flees the room.

Hutter manages to escape Orlok's castle while the vampire is traveling to Wisborg, and is hospitalized before returning home. He had "borrowed" the book on vampires from the inn and his wife reads it. She learns that a vampire can be killed if a virtuous woman can hold his attention until sunrise. That's pretty much what happens, as Ellen leaves her window open. Orlok, who has been watching from his house across the street, enters and attacks her. But he is so enthralled that morning catches him at Ellen's throat and he is vaporized by sunlight – the first time a vampire is dispatched this way on film, but hardly the last.

As mentioned earlier, the makers of *Nosferatu* didn't secure the rights to the novel *Dracula*. Florence Stoker was extremely protective of her husband's work, which was a major source of income for her, and she sued Prana-Film for plagiarism and copyright infringement. The courts decided in Florence's favor, ordering that all copies of the movie be destroyed. Luckily for film historians, this wasn't quite what happened, and the movie survived. Apparently, a copy would even find its way into the hands of the screenwriters for the 1931 Universal version of *Dracula*, as some scenes in that production aren't in the book or the play, but are in *Nosferatu*.

Dracula next moved to the stage, as Stoker had wished, but perhaps not in a form which would have met with his approval. Hamilton Deane, an Irish actor, director, and playwright, wrote the play with the cooperation of Florence Stoker. Deane took the sprawling novel and turned it into a more manageable "drawing room"-style play, eliminating many characters and scenes.

Bela Lugosi was virtually unknown when he starred in the stage adaptation of Bram Stoker's *Dracula*.

The play debuted in 1924 and became a hit, a real crowd-pleaser. This brought it to the attention of Horace Liveright, an American publisher and theatrical producer, who decided he could bring it successfully to Broadway. Liveright had the play rewritten for an American audience, keeping the basic structure, but very few lines from the original.

The names Lucy and Mina were switched for the stage adaptation, making Lucy the heroine. Presumably, Liveright thought Americans would find the name Mina a bit strange. The name switch would show up again throughout the years, most notably in the 1979 Universal remake of *Dracula*, starring Frank Langella, which was based more on the play than the novel.

Dracula premiered in New York in 1927. The role of Count Dracula went to a little-known Hungarian actor named Bela Lugosi, who was willing to work cheap. A representative of Universal Studios was in the theater on opening night. Universal would seek the film rights and the resulting movie would come to be considered a classic, with Lugosi reprising the title role.

Universal's 1931 *Dracula* begins, like the novel and like *Nosferatu*, with a young man – a solicitor named Renfield – on his way to Dracula's castle to sell him a house in England. In the novel, Renfield is a patient at the lunatic asylum operated by Dr. John Seward, one of the suitors for Mina's friend Lucy Westenra.

As in *Nosferatu*, Dracula arrives to pick up Renfield in disguise. Lugosi's disguise is a bit better than Graf Orlok's, but there's no mistaking the blazing eyes under the brim of his hat. In the novel, Count Dracula meets Harker at the front door, but in the film Renfield enters the castle and first encounters Dracula on a massive Gothic staircase. It's a very impressive set and Lugosi is a magnetic presence.

Dracula leads Renfield to a guest room, where a meal has been prepared. He tells Renfield that it is late and his servants are asleep. In the book, Stoker implies that Dracula has no servants and is handling all the household duties himself in secret. I find it difficult to picture the lord of the undead slaving over a hot stove, but that seems to be the case.

Dracula questions Renfield about his proposed property, Carfax Abbey. While flipping through his papers, Renfield cuts himself on a paperclip, drawing Dracula's bloodlust. As Renfield leans forward to inspect his wound, the crucifix around his neck falls into view and Dracula recoils. This scene is lifted almost entirely from *Nosferatu*. In the novel, a similar scene occurs, when Johnathan Harker, startled by Dracula, cuts himself while shaving, due to his not having seen the Count enter the room because the vampire's reflection didn't appear in Harker's shaving mirror.

Dracula tells Renfield he has arranged for a ship to take them to England the next day, then leaves his guest, ostensibly so Renfield can rest. During the night, Renfield is attacked by Dracula's three "brides." As the women gather around Renfield, Dracula appears and waves them away. This scene is right out of the novel, and was apparently important to Bram Stoker, as it appears in the earliest drafts. Dracula warns his brides away from Harker, telling them "This man belongs to me!"

Universal stakes the claim of the "world's greatest HOLD OVER picture" in this advertisement for ad mats.

Renfield and Dracula travel to England. Taking a page from Stoker's book, a newspaper account is shown to inform viewers that Renfield is hopelessly mad and has been sent to the asylum run by Dr. Seward. In the film, Seward's asylum and home is conveniently located next door to Carfax Abbey. In the novel, Dracula's new house is in the London suburb of Purfleet. This version of Seward is older and is also Mina's father, with Mina and Lucy switched back to their correct roles from the book.

Professor Van Helsing is introduced examining a sample of Renfield's blood. He brings up the subject of vampires, and even uses the word "Nosferatu." Van Helsing tries to protect Mina by putting wolfsbane at the doors and windows of her room, and a wreath of the plant around her neck, whereas garlic was used in the novel.

Dracula was a success for Universal and was followed by a sequel and several connected films. Oddly enough, Bela Lugosi wouldn't reprise the role of Dracula until 1948's *Abbott & Costello Meet Frankenstein*.

In 1957, the British studio Hammer Films had an unexpected and very lucrative hit with a new version of *Frankenstein*, starring Peter Cushing as Dr. Frankenstein and Christopher Lee as the Monster. The success of *The Curse of Frankenstein* made the studio look for other material to adapt. *Dracula* was the logical choice. Hammer's version, called *Horror of Dracula* in the United States to prevent confusion with the 1931 film, premiered in 1958. If the Universal film simplified things by moving the locations closer together, *Horror of Dracula* one-upped it by moving everything to one continent.

The Hammer version begins with yet another slightly altered version of Johnathan Harker arriving at Dracula's castle near the town of Klausenburg, somewhere in central Europe.[1] Harker has been employed by the Count to catalog his library. What Dracula doesn't know is that *this* Harker is fully aware his host is a vampire, and that the young man plans to kill him.

In Christopher Lee's initial scene as Dracula, he seems so friendly, urbane, and affable that one almost regrets he'll turn out to be a villain. He shows Harker to his room, where Dracula admires a photograph of Harker's fiancée, Lucy Holmwood. Arthur Holmwood is a character from the novel, and was yet another suitor of Lucy Westenra. In *Horror of Dracula,* they are siblings.

Van Helsing is played by Peter Cushing. This is the first time he is portrayed as an expert in vampires, and he is working with Harker toward Dracula's destruction. In the novel, he was simply a learned man who is aware of the legends of vampires. Cushing cuts a much more dashing figure than the more mature Edward Van Sloan of Universal's *Dracula.*

---

[1] There is an actual Klausenburg in Transylvania, but this doesn't seem to be it.

Christopher Lee's interpretation of Count Dracula took him to new and more violent levels.

Lee's version of Dracula has more limited powers than Stoker's vampire. He is not able to change his form to that of wolf or a bat, and sunlight will kill him. In the novel, Dracula could change to mist, dust, a wolf, or a bat. He could also move around in the day, though he loses most of his powers in sunlight.

In the movie, Van Helsing and Holmwood pursue Dracula back to his castle, making the trip by carriage in a single night, and a short night at that. In the book, the heroes travel mostly overland by train to try and overtake Dracula, who has again used a ship for transportation.

These were the three cinematic adaptations of Stoker's novel before 1970, and each in its own way is important to the history of horror films. *Nosferatu* is significant because it was the first adaptation and because its brooding atmosphere and creepy vampire lord were very influential to later films. Mr. Barlow, the vampire in Tobe Hooper's TV movie adaptation of Stephen King's *Salem's Lot*, was patterned after Orlok, while Petyr, the basement-dwelling vampire in the 2015 comedy film *What We Do in the Shadows,* was also an Orlok clone.

Nosferatu was remade in 1979. It starred Klaus Kinski as the vampire, now renamed Count Dracula since the book had fallen into the public domain. The folks at Prana-Film probably would have enjoyed that. As I'm writing this, there is talk of a new version of *Nosferatu*, to be directed by Robert Eggers, who directed *The Witch* (2015).

1931's *Dracula* was important for two main reasons. It was the first major Hollywood film with an actual supernatural menace. Up until then, monsters usually turned out to be people in disguise – shades of *Scooby-Doo*. Supernatural horror was suddenly a marketable genre on the big screen. Without *Dracula*, we likely wouldn't have seen Karloff's *Frankenstein* or the other Universal horror films.

Second, it was Bela Lugosi is his evening clothes (the clothes may make the man, but that's not meant to be taken literally) who established the idea of how a vampire should look and act for decades to come: the suave manner, the widow's peak, and the dramatic gestures. To this day, when most people think of Count Dracula, they think of Lugosi. He was portrayed as a romantic figure. Women loved him – and, in fact, the film was originally released in February (the same month as Valentine's Day) and was billed as "The story of the strangest passion the world has ever known."

Christopher Lee carried that passion even further in *Horror of Dracula*. The women in that film can't seem to wait for the sanguinary Count to put the bite on them. Lee's performance is important to the evolution of the vampire film because, in addition to making the link between vampires and sex more apparent, this is the first movie with vampires who snarl and hiss like cats when angered. They are animalistic and violently aggressive – a far cry from Bela in his top hat.

Later films would follow, more loyal to Bram Stoker's novel, but those earlier efforts on screen and stage had set the patterns that still influence new adaptations of *Dracula*, not only on film, but in books, video games, comic books, and other aspects of popular culture.

The Devil Has All the Best Films: Silver Screen Satans and Boob-Tube Beelzebubs

by Joe Bongiorno

> It has been written since the beginning of time that evil, supernatural creatures exist in a world of darkness, and it is also said man can call forth these powers of darkness...
> —*Night of the Demon*

> The TV set [is the] Satanic family altar.
> —Anton LaVey

Arguably the greatest monster in the history of film, television, and literature is the Devil, an entity shown to be utterly malevolent, intelligent, implacable, and nearly invulnerable – a shapeshifter who hides in the shadows, objects, your neighbors, and potentially even your own soul. With no one safe from his reach (or that of his demonic cohorts and human underlings), this figure remains the most terrifying and ubiquitous of villains, with a veritable cornucopia of films, books, and television shows featuring black magic, possession, hauntings, and evil cults.

But who really is this dark figure? Why is he such a popular villain? Why have Hollywood and television treated him in so many different ways? And what does it all portend?

Haunted History

The Devil pulls the strings which make us dance;
We find delight in the most loathsome things;
Some furtherance of Hell each new day brings,
And yet we feel no horror in that rank advance.
— Charles Baudelaire

Prior to the rise of the New Hollywood in the late 1960s, onscreen depictions of dark subject matter were considerably less common. Satan could be a subject of fun, but unlike the vampires, werewolves, and monsters of the 1930s – which were seemingly rooted in the fantastical – the Devil *might* just be real, making serious portrayals a bit much for mainstream audiences in the early 20th century.

Literature was the domain of supernatural horror at this time, owing a debt to Horace Walpole, William Thomas Beckford, and Matthew Gregory Lewis. Horror literature (then called Gothic romance) grew from the soil of the Bible and early fantasy literature, which, by way of George MacDonald, evolved into the forms we see today. Some were purely fantastical, as in the early works of Lord Dunsany (Edward Plunkett), while others lay just outside the periphery of our vision, as in the shadowy tales of Michel Ghelderode, Ambrose Bierce, and Robert W. Chambers; some belong to the night, as in the stories of M.R. James, Edgar Allen Poe, and E.T.A. Hoffman, or to the moldering ruins of ancient keeps and long-forgotten lands, as in the weird fiction of H.P. Lovecraft, Clark Ashton Smith, Robert E. Howard, and Manly Wade Wellman. Nor were the genres mutually exclusive, though it could be said that fantasy presents the otherworld as a hidden realm beyond our own, exhibiting dark, light, and neutral elements, whereas horror presents the incursion of the otherworld into our world, and is exclusively dark.

We've always been entertained by the things that go bump in the night, from the magic lantern shows of the 15th and 16th centuries that featured witches, ghosts, and fiends, to the French *Grand Guignol* and phantasmagoria shows of the 19th century, which utilized the newly developed techniques of rear projection, slides, superimposition, multiple projectors, actors, smoke, odors, sounds, and even electric shocks! Audiences' love for the spooky and supernatural led directly to the development of cinematography, providing a simpler and less expensive means to thrill audiences.[1]

Morbid Tales

> Searchers after horror haunt strange, far places.
> — H.P. Lovecraft

Where does interest in the dark side come from? Is it just sick or morbid people who are attracted to such faire? And isn't it psychologically harmful to society? Some would have us believe so, but the reality is quite different. Reverend Peter Laws, a Baptist minister and author of *The Frighteners: Why We Love Monsters, Ghosts, Death & Gore*,[2] argues that, contrary to conventional wisdom, interest in the macabre is not only the opposite of interest in real-world violence, but psychologically beneficial, channeling our dark sides in safe and healthy ways by relieving the tension, stress, and aggression that builds up from day-to-day life.[3]

We no longer gather at executions and gladiatorial arenas to gleefully watch real people kill and be killed. Emperor Trajan's military victory over the Dacians was horrifically celebrated by droves who watched and cheered the public slaughter of 11,000 wild animals throughout the course of a 120-day event, something that today would raise a vehement outcry from most horror fans!

There is a legitimate need for emotional stimulation and release. We want to be a little frightened because we need to feel courage, and confronting horror in art and entertainment provides that necessary rush, with viewers feeling shock (at the violence), empathy (for the victim), and a sense of empowerment (for having faced and overcome terror and fear). This is the very opposite of engagement in blood sports such as hunting, in which the adrenaline rush gives the participants thrill (at the violence), indifference (for the victim), and a sense of empowerment (at having killed a living creature). How ironic that western society has looked down on lovers of macabre fiction

---

[1] "History of Film," Wikipedia: https://en.wikipedia.org/wiki/History_of_film.
[2] *The Frighteners: Why We Love Monsters, Ghosts, Death & Gore*, by Peter Laws; Icon Books, 2018.
[3] This is true as well for darker music. See my book *Black Sabbath: The Illustrated Lyrics Vol 1: Supernatural Horror in Music*; The Royal Publisher of Oz (2016).

while celebrating the actual purveyors of horror and violence.

Another benefit is the intellectual need to understand evil. "Film scholar Søren Birkvard... thinks that our enjoyment of all things horror and attraction to the darker side of horror cinema could come from our need to understand the concept of what is evil... As religion has widely played less and less of a role in our understanding of how things work and our motivations, so too has the concept of evil diminished."[4]

Frank discussions of evil, morality, and death are all but nonexistent in modern times, leaving only three tools to help us process the horrors of the real world; thankfully, they're three of the best — and the most demonized: literature, film, and television.

Ironically, ultra-conservative groups who denounce such entertainment (as they do the genre of heavy metal) fail to discern that the vast majority of stories dealing with the demonic serve as admonitions *against* it, an approach utilized by the Bible itself — which, as Laws notes, "thoroughly explores the macabre... It acknowledges and ponders the dark side because it directly reflects the world we live in. A world filled with cruelty, fear and depravity. Through these dark stories, the Bible introduces radical, subversive and ultimately positive new ideas," utilizing morbid imagery because it "gets our attention... makes for a thrilling story" and because "the dark stuff allows us to see the light."[5] Such an informed view was, however, not shared by the puritanical powers-that-be in the early 20th century.

Breaking the Code

[The Code] had a very good effect because it made us think. If we wanted to get something across that was censorable... we had to do it deviously. We had to be clever. And it usually turned out to be much better than if we had done it straight.

— Edward Dmytryk

Named after Will H. Hays, then the president of the Motion Picture Association of America (MPAA), the Hays Code was set up as a self-regulatory board in 1930 to protect the industry from federal and state censorship sparked

---

[4] https://happiful.com/why-do-we-love-horror-the-psychology-behind-scary-entertainment/
[5] *The Frighteners: Why We Love Monsters, Ghosts, Death & Gore*, by Peter Laws; Icon Books, 2018.

by the outrage of religious, civic, and political groups over subject matter deemed morally questionable. To prevent having to issue multiple versions of films to different states with different censorship standards, the Hays Code adopted a wide array of criteria that often proved moralistic and arbitrary. After 1934, films were required to have a certificate of approval for distribution, giving the Production Code Association ultimate power over cinematic art, leading to an old saying that Golden Age Hollywood was "a Jewish-owned business selling Catholic theology to Protestant America."[6]

In the pre-Code era, serious supernatural chillers like *Dracula* and *Frankenstein* could be released to great success and acclaim. Four years later, the epilogue of the former would be cut out of fear of encouraging belief in the supernatural! This was not a mere domestic problem. Asia and the United Kingdom requested numerous cuts to *The Bride of Frankenstein*. Sweden demanded so many it was easier to just pull the film, while Hungary, Palestine, and Trinidad banned it altogether. Indeed, the Devil must have had a good laugh over the fact that while it was perfectly legal to kills one's fellow man in any number of ways in any number of wars, fictional violence perpetrated by a fictional monster was strictly prohibited!

In 1948, the U.S. Supreme Court removed the ability of the MPAA to enforce the Code, and in 1952 it gave films First Amendment protections as an artistic medium. By then, the state censorship boards were gone and the public was beginning to outgrow such stringent standards, allowing filmmakers and fans to delve into darker fare in dramas, thrillers, mysteries, and horror films.

As if unleashed in the summoning of diabolic entities by NASA rocket engineer Jack Parsons and L. Ron Hubbard's Crowley-inspired "Babalon Working" rituals, a new wave of monsters, aliens, ghosts, vampires, maniacs, mutants, mummies, voodoo priests, curses, zombies, shapeshifters, and evil spirits were ushered into A-list films and the new spate of low-budget B-films. In the early 1960s, when the MPAA tried to censor several European films that tackled subjects U.S. studios wouldn't touch, the attempt backfired. Finally, in 1965, the Supreme Court ended film censorship altogether, and new MPAA president Jack Valenti replaced the Code with the rating system still in use today.

---

[6] http://decentfilms.com/articles/hollywoodreligion

The Four Faces of Satan

Whether you call him Satan, Lucifer, or Mephistopheles, he's a beast with even more faces than he has names. Over the past five centuries, artists have variously depicted the devil as a fanged, horned demon; as an armored, Apollo-like army leader; and as a tailor of Nazi uniforms.

— Carey Dunn[7]

Who is Satan? The answer is more complex than it may seem, and given the figure's clandestine nature, it's not unsurprising that he's shrouded in contradictory narratives.

As cinema and television became unshackled from small-minded repression and austerity, they went on to incorporate four primary schools-of-thought on the subject of Satan: folkloric, mystical, skeptical, and theological. Although the Devil derives directly from the latter, a look at all four views will provide a better understanding of the interesting ways in which film and television have interwoven supernatural evil in the genres of comedy, drama, thriller, and horror.

The Folkloric View

Satan has become rather a figure of fun these days, or, at worst, a bogey-man with whom wicked old women sometimes frighten children; but all the same, he still remains our ultimate expression for the most concentrated form of Evil, and everything else must in a greater or lesser sense partake of his attributes.

— Dennis Wheatley

The folkloric view pertains to the ideas that circulate in popular imagination. Although it includes superstition, it isn't limited to that, drawing from a number of indigenous sources, spanning from region to region, era to era, and clan to clan. Founded on the worldview of pantheism, the folkloric view has mingled the myths and legends from ancient times with modern ideas from the other three views.

Awash in a world of magic and spirits, the folkloric view triggered the intelligentsia of the Enlightenment Age to seek to purge it. It persists, in large part, because myths have value in the binding of communities. Communities

---

[7] https://www.fastcompany.com/3034309/the-changing-face-of-satan-artistic-depictions-of-the-devil-1500-to-today

"share symbols and myths that provide meaning in their existence as a people and link them to some transcendent order," notes political theorist Donald Lutz, which "allow them to act as a people."[8] This can be seen in the folkloric view of the Devil.

The most commonly recognized imagery of the Devil, the horned, red-skinned, cloven-footed, pointy-tailed, pitchfork-wielding imp, was amalgamated in the Middle Ages from pagan, Arabic, and apocryphal sources, by way of Dante Alighieri's *Inferno* (e.g., horns from Pan and Cernunnos, cloven feet and tail from fauns and satyrs, trident from Hades/Pluto). What many do not know is that this comic imagery *was intentionally drawn ludicrous*. The medieval mystery plays were stories of scathing social criticism in which Satan was turned into a comedic stock character, made to appear repulsive, pathetic and ridiculous, in order to mock "the social and political hierarchy... the socially privileged," and serve as foil for the protagonists. "These plays suggest that the demonic destruction of community occurs in repeating the sin of Lucifer... in abuses of power by the powerful."[9]

Art and popular entertainment of this kind supported, at least tacitly, the peasant uprisings and revolts against the wealthy land owners, jurists, and magistrates of the era (1336 to 1525). This, in turn, led to a counterstrike, a political and class war against the peasantry. Subverting the very same imagery that had been used so effectively to caricature them, the land owners went on to demonize participants of the uprisings as traffickers with the Dark One, inaugurating the witch-hunts that spiraled out of control over the next three centuries.[10]

Failing to recognize the political machinations behind the scenes, intellectuals painted the entire era as an age of superstition and ignorance. Although demonstrably false, what *History for Atheists* author Tim O'Neill calls a "hysterical myth," it remains the prevailing narrative in popular and academic circles: "The Middle Ages as a benighted intellectual wasteland where humanity was shackled to superstition and oppressed by cackling minions of the Evil Old Catholic Church" comes from a "festering mélange of Enlightenment bigotry,

---

[8] *Colonial Origins of the American Constitution*, Donald Lutz; Liberty Fund, 1998.
[9] "The Devil and Society in the English Mystery Plays," by John D. Cox; *Comparative Drama, Vol. 28, No. 4* (Winter 1994-95).
[10] https://www.jacobinmag.com/2018/10/witch-hunt-class-struggle-women-autonomy

Protestant papism-bashing, French anti-clericism, and Classicist snobbery."[11]

This led to a significant change in artistic depictions of Satan: "By the 18th century, he's ennobled, almost looking like an Apollo," notes Stanford's Cantor Art Center curator, Bernard Barryte. Influenced more by John Milton's *Paradise Lost,* Barryte adds, "People interpreted the figure less as demonic creature and more as heroic rebel against the oppression of the paternal god."[12]

This was enlarged in the 19th century by Italian poet Giosuè Carducci's anti-papal "Hymn to Satan" and William Blake's *Paradise Lost* illustrations. "In his own book *The Marriage of Heaven and Hell*, Blake presented Satan as a messiah. Around the same time, Theosophical Society founder Madame Blavatsky wrote about Satan as a commendable insurgent offering humans wisdom."[13]

Left: *Satan Arousing the Rebel Angels*, from William Blake's illustrations to John Milton's *Paradise Lost*; right: a statue of the Devil on display in Lithuania's Šmuidzinavičius Museum.

---

[11] https://historyforatheists.com. See also https://www.quora.com/Why-did-science-make-little-real-progress-in-Europe-in-the-Middle-Ages-3/answer/Tim-ONeill-1?share=1.

[12] "The Changing Face of Satan: From 1500 to Today": https://www.fastcompany.com/3034309/the-changing-face-of-satan-artistic-depictions-of-the-devil-1500-to-today

[13] "Satanism": https://www.history.com/topics/1960s/satanism#section_2

Disparaged as nonsense by Enlightenment rationalists, denigrated as superstition by liberal theologians, and championed by Theosophists, the Devil had expanded his brand, and what started as a lark – the pointy-tailed, horned Devil as a way to mock the powerful wealthy – became codified into a symbol of folklorists' fears, skeptics' derision, and Luciferian idolatry! The storytellers of the macabre now had plenty of material upon which to terrify audiences at the dawn of the 20th century.

A Trip to Hell

The darkest places in hell are reserved for those who maintain their neutrality in times of moral crisis.
— Dante Alighieri

Georges Méliès' *Le Manoir du Diable, The Devil's Castle.*

It all begins with Georges Méliès' groundbreaking *Le Manoir du Diable, The Devil's Castle* (1896), the first film to feature the Devil, the first to use special effects to frighten viewers, and possibly the first vampire film (he initially appears as a bat and is scared off by a cross). With Satan conjuring up spooky beings to frighten an unlucky cavalier who stumbles upon his castle, this ambitious three-plus-minute film puts the Devil squarely in the folkloric – and comedic – role. One scene featuring a young temptress who creepily transforms into an old crone may have inspired a similar scene in Stanley Kubrick's adaptation of Stephen King's *The Shining*.

Famous for *A Trip to the Moon*, Méliès made 500 silent films (of which only 200 survive), from which it's clear he wasn't done with Old Scratch. *The Devil in a Convent* (1899) has Satan impersonating a priest to terrify nuns; *The Devil and the Statue* (1902) has him growing to giant size to frighten a woman; and *The Infernal Cakewalk* and *Faust in Hell* (1903) take place in the underworld, the latter of which utilizes multiple settings and a seemingly pre-Lovecraftian Cthulhu! In *Faust and Marguerite* (1904), Satan offers Faust youth in exchange for his soul; *The Black Imp* (1905) has him haunting a boarder, while in *The Merry Frolics of Satan* (1906), he takes his victims on a sky-ride to Hell! Finally, *Satan in Prison* (1907) has Lucifer conjuring up a young woman to keep him company in his cell!

Though modern cinema and television continue to utilize light, humorous, or bizarre approaches to the Devil,[14] things took a dark turn with the first full-length Italian feature film ever made. Based on Gustave Dore's illustrations of Dante's *Inferno*, the trailblazing *L'Inferno* (1911) took three years to make and remains an eerie and spectacular adaptation.

Faust and the Trickster Motif

> The devil doesn't come dressed in a red cape and pointy horns. He comes as everything you've ever wished for.
> — Tucker Max

Dramas tended toward more serious reflections of character and ethical dilemma, offering opportunities to pose questions about the human condition, morals, and role of society. This is seen in the multifaceted exploration of the Faust myth. While the "Deal with the Devil," or *trickster*, motif can be traced back to the temptation of Christ in the Synoptic Gospels, in which Satan offers Jesus rule of "all the kingdoms of the world" for an act of worship, the fantastical ways in which film and television have generally framed it is primarily folkloric, with an undercurrent of the theological.

---

[14] Such as Ricardo Freda's *The Witch's Curse* (1963), in which Hercules (Kirk Morris) tries to rescue peasants of the Middle Ages from the titular curse by descending into Dante's *Inferno*!

The 16th-century Faust story – based on Goethe's tragic play and the various legends of the real-life alchemist who sold his soul to the Devil – was first employed comically by Méliès, but was treated as a serious subject by German filmmakers Stellan Rye and Paul Wegener (who played the title role) in the 1913 silent film *The Student of Prague* (aka *A Bargain with Satan*). Loosely based on the Edgar Allen Poe story "William Wilson," about a poor man who makes a bargain with a sorcerer, it's the first of the German art films, and popular enough that it was remade with the talented Conrad Aiken in 1926, and again in 1935.

Not one to be outdone, German filmmaker F.W. Murnau, known for *Nosferatu* (1922), took on the Devil in *Satan* (1920). Played by Conrad Veidt, Satan travels the ages searching for one instance in which good came out of the evil he caused. The film is unfortunately lost, as is Veidt's earlier portrayal of the Devil in *Der nicht vom Weibe Geboren* (1918).

Yet it's Murnau's boldly imaginative *Faust* (1926) that set the pattern for the stories to follow. Barryte noted that in this tradition, "Instead of scaring people into sin and intimidating them, he now uses persuasion." No longer monstrous, Satan is "a sly, cunning, dandyish type of figure."[15] Emil Jannings played the satanic role, winning him the very first Best Acting Oscar in 1929 (which he went on to squander in various Nazi propaganda films, proving he didn't have much range after all). Faust becomes the subject of a trial between an archangel and the Devil regarding whether the latter can drive all goodness from him. *Faust* is the earliest cinematic example of the problem of evil countered by the power of love. Although the film starts and ends darkly, with iconic scenes of apocalyptic Horsemen and Satan hovering above a city, Murnau takes the comedic Satan to the point of outright camp – an odd choice, given that the film's second half deals with the suffering of Gretchen as her family is killed.

If portrayals of Satan as witty aristocrat are amusing on the surface, they nevertheless present a salient look at human dissatisfaction, greed, wish-fulfilment, and the price they exact – themes explored, as well, in Oscar Wilde's

---

[15] *The Changing Face of Satan, from 1500 to Today*, by Carey Dunne: https://www.fastcompany.com/3034309/the-changing-face-of-satan-artistic-depictions-of-the-devil-1500-to-today

The Picture of Dorian Gray, W.W. Jacobs' "The Monkey's Paw," and Richard Matheson's "Button, Button."

The Twilight Zone featured no fewer than six appearances by the Devil, four of which were based on the Faust myth. "Escape Clause" (1959) sees a miserable hypochondriac sign away his soul for immortality, only to discover he's no longer able to get enjoyment out of life. In "A Nice Place to Visit" (1960), a criminal ends up in a place that seems at first to be Heaven, only to realize that his "angelic" guide hasn't revealed the whole truth. And "The Howling Man" (1960) eschews the Faustian bargain for a different take on the trickster motif. When a storm drives a lost man to a monastery, he comes upon a prisoner who convinces him that the monks are madmen. The head monk tells him that the inmate is no ordinary convict, but rather Satan, and as a result of his incarceration, wars have ceased the world over. The skeptical protagonist ignores the warning and frees the prisoner, realizing his error too late when he transforms into the Devil before his eyes.

The six Devils of *The Twilight Zone* – top (left to right): Burgess Meredith, Julie Newmar, and Sebastian Cabot; bottom (left to right): Robin Hughes, Thomas Gomez, and Robert Foulk.

In "The Hunt" (1962), the Devil (or possibly just a demon – the Gatekeeper's identity is left a bit ambiguous) tries to trick a recently deceased old man into entering Hell instead of Heaven, but the hilbilly's faithful pooch can tell something isn't right and saves him from damnation. As an angel at the gates of

Heaven later explains, "You see, Mr. Simpson, a man, well, he'll walk right into Hell with both eyes open. But even the Devil can't fool a dog!" And in "Of Late I Think of Cliffordville" (1963), a wealthy industrialist believes his knowledge of the future will enable him to become even richer when the Devil offers to send him back in time to his home-town.

Finally, Burgess Meredith plays Satan in disguise in "The Printer's Devil" (1963), arriving just in time to turn a flagging local newspaper and its owner (Robert Sterling) into a success. Playing on the protagonist's skepticism and pride, he convinces him to sign away his soul on the basis that he'd look foolish otherwise: "As a sophisticated, intelligent, 20th-century man, you *know* that the Devil does *not* exist, true?" he asks. "If you don't sign, it'll be admitting fear and belief." Upon his hesitation, he exclaims, "Fancy that! A grown-up man who believes in the Devil!"

Boris Karloff's *Thriller* (1962) took a page from *The Twilight Zone* in "The Devil's Ticket," a Robert Bloch story in which John Emory plays the Satanic pawnbroker who purchases the soul of a starving artist (McDonald Carey), who's granted fortune and fame, but must paint the portrait of the Devil's next victim or lose his soul.

Rarely has the Faustian bargain been as effectively put to use as in Archie Mayo's *Angel on My Shoulder* (1946). When mobster Eddie (Paul Muni) is killed by his best friend, he descends into Hell. Mephistopheles, played by Claude Rains, sends Eddie back to Earth on the premise that if he corrupts a judge (who looks just like him), he'll be permitted to avenge himself on the man who betrayed him. But as Eddie comes to examine the decisions he'd made in life, he's tempted to make a different choice.

The popularity of this trope would continue into the modern era, in films such as *Needful Things* (1991), *Angel Heart* (1987), *The Witches of Eastwick* (1987), *The Devil's Advocate* (1997), and *The Messenger* (1999), seeing Max Von Sydow, Robert De Niro, Jack Nicholson, Al Pacino, and Dustin Hoffman donning the Satanic mantle respectively. Not all retellings of the trope were dark, as evidenced by the award-winning *The Devil and Daniel Webster* (1941), *Cabin in the Sky* (1943), a musical extravaganza starring an all-star African-American cast, and the whimsical and irreverent *Bedazzled* (1967), starring Peter Cook as the Devil and Dudley Moore as the Faust character (remade in 2000 with Brendan Fraser and Elizabeth Hurley), as well as *Oh God, You Devil* (1978), *Little*

Nicky (2000), *Deconstructing Harry* (2003), and the *Lucifer* television series (2015).[16]

The Mystical View

> The greatest trick the Devil ever pulled was convincing the world he didn't exist.
> — Charles Baudelaire

> The second greatest trick the Devil ever pulled was convincing the world he is the good guy.
> — Ken Ammi

Including theosophy and the popular New Age movement, the mystical view seeks to attain personal transcendence and world salvation in a Golden Age of Enlightenment through the "forgotten wisdom traditions of ancient cultures," such as divination, astral projection, channeling, and transcendental meditation, by which one can raise their consciousness to the level of self-divinity.[17] As defined by theosophy's founder, Helen Blavatsky, this approach is split into two categories, the "Left-Hand Path" of Satanism and black magic, and the "Right-Hand Path" of the New Age and various secret societies.

Hollywood has gotten much mileage from overt depictions of the Left-Hand Path, which itself is split into two factions. Popularized by Church of Satan founder Anton Lavey, atheistic Satanism draws from the philosophies of Ayn Rand, Friedrich Nietzsche, H. L. Mencken, and social Darwinism. Theistic Satanism was popularized by ceremonial magician Aleister Crowley, and is indistinguishable from theosophy, drawing from the same sources. Both present an overt repudiation of Christianity, with Satan as either the real or symbolic author of pleasure, wealth, and power. And in either Right or Left, the roles of God and Satan are reversed, with the former construed as an evil deity, and the latter as the wise Lucifer, "friend," "savior," and "lightbringer."[18]

---

[16] Though *Lucifer* was based on the darker and decidedly non-comedic same-named comic book series from DC Comics, written by Mike Carey as a spinoff of Neil Gaiman's *The Sandman*.

[17] https://intheriverblog.com/2019/07/23/new-age-or-christianity-defining-our-terms/

[18] "It is but natural... to view Satan, the Serpent of Genesis, as the real creator and benefactor, the Father of Spiritual mankind. For it is he who was the 'Harbinger of

The mystical view derives from gnosticism and hermeticism, which are:

> a blend of ancient Egyptian religion, philosophy, science and magic with elements of Greek Paganism, Alexandrian Judaism, ancient Sumerian religion and Chaldaean astrology/astronomy, and Zoroastrianism. It is associated with the philosophical schools of Platonism, Neo-Platonism, Stoicism and Pythagorianism... the Hermetic tradition was forced to the occult underground and permeates Western esoteric traditions. This includes secret societies such as the Freemasons, Rosicrucians, Hermetic Order of the Golden Dawn, Thelema, as well as modern Paganism, New Age, and Wicca. The Theosophical Society, the philosophy behind the Waldorf/Rudolf Steiner schools, is also influenced by Hermetic philosophy.[19]

The mystical view sees the folkloric view as limited by knowledge, the theological view by dogma, and the skeptical view by imagination. Enlightenment-era scientists may have striven to take science toward a strictly mechanistic approach to nature, yet the development of astronomy, chemistry, medicine, biology, and physics spring from the very same systems that the mystical view derives: "Hermeticism, Neoplatonic mysticism, and natural magic had a remarkable influence on the Scientific Revolution... Indeed, the fathers of the modern science and the scientific method were... alchemists and esotericists, traditions rooted in Hermeticism."[20] And with the advent of relativistic and quantum physics, science and mysticism have grown closer than ever. "In the Hermetic tradition, nature is investigated through observation, experiment and illumination. The purpose is to discover and detect that which is invisible and find the hidden linkages between things."[21]

With interest in the mystical view on the rise, films began to tackle it more frequently – albeit surreptitiously at first. In Val Lewton's noir thriller *The Seventh Victim* (1943), Kim Hunter's Mary travels to New York to find her missing sister, Jacqueline (Jean Brooks), who's joined a secret society called the Palladists, who are hunting her because she broke their vow of secrecy to her psychiatrist. A fascinating look at modern alienation and the ways in people are

---

Light,' bright radiant Lucifer, who opened the eyes of the automaton created by Jehovah..." *The Secret Doctrine, Vol 2*, p. 243, by Madame H.P. Blavatsky.

[19] https://spacedoutscientist.com/2015/06/01/hermeticism-the-nexus-between-science-philosophy-and-spirit/

[20] Hermeticism: the nexus between science, philosophy and spirit: https://spacedoutscientist.com/2015/06/01/hermeticism-the-nexus-between-science-philosophy-and-spirit/.

[21] Ibid.

driven to extremes, *The Seventh Victim* implicitly presents Jacqueline as a lesbian whose actions are motivated by the repression imposed on her by society. While the cult presents itself as the alternative to society's sanctimoniousness, by the film's conclusion, their hypocrisy as "a poor, wretched group of people who have taken the wrong turning" is exposed. The cult leader responds in a vein similarly to Pontius Pilate, positing the ancient sophists' view of moral nihilism: "Wrong? Who knows what is right or wrong?"

An even darker example is found in the eerie 1960 film *City of the Dead* (aka *Horror Hotel*). The iconic Christopher Lee plays a dissimulating professor who invites his student, Nan Barlow (Venetia Stevenson), to a misty Massachusetts town to write her thesis on the town's history of witchcraft. Nan's fiancé and brother scoff at the idea as nonsense, but she goes in spite of them, unaware that a very real cult awaits her as their sacrifice. The first known film in which the lead protagonist is killed partway into the story, it's also the first of many wherein a witch, earlier burned at the stake, exacts her revenge.

Satanic cults, witches, and warlocks became the province of Italian director Mario Bava, whose Gothic *Black Sunday* (1960) presented an effective and gory horror film rarely seen at the time. Other films looked at the more subtle manipulation of evil. In *The Devil's Partner* (1961), Ed Nelson plays the friendly Nick, who comes to town after his uncle Pete dies under mysterious circumstances. When other locals start dying, an insightful sheriff begins to unravel a sinister plot.

The Alfred Hitchcock Hour got into the act with "The Sign of Satan" (1961), a Robert Bloch tale, once more starring Christopher Lee, this time as a former Satanist hunted by his acolytes when he breaks rank and goes to Hollywood. In this renewed landscape of popular horror, older monster-movie actors tried to reestablish their relevance. Boris Karloff had the excellent *Thriller* (1960–1962), while Lon Chaney played Satan in Curt Siodmak's 1959 television series *13 Demon Street* (the film *The Devil's Messenger* links three of its episodes).

A minor masterpiece from 1968, *The Devil Rides Out*, adapted from Dennis Wheatley's best-selling 1934 novel of the same name, and directed by Terrence Fisher, pits the Right-Hand and Left-Hand Paths against each other. When cult-leader Mocata (Charles Grey) seeks to sacrifice Simon, a bored bourgeois, and Tanith, his terminally ill girlfriend, Nicholas de Richleau (Christopher Lee) tries to rescue both before the fateful night. Although *The Devil Rides Out* over-relies on arcane powers (Marvel Comics' Dr. Strange owes much to de Richleau), it's a fun horror romp with no fewer than two satanic rituals, including an effectively creepy summoning of Baphomet, the goat-like entity of Crowley's Gnostic Mass infamously worshiped by the Knights Templar.

Of course, they can't all be winners. Prior to *Star Trek*, William Shatner starred in *The Incubus* (1966), created by *Outer Limits* producer Leslie Stevens, who directed the entire cast to speak in Esperanto! A nearly lost film, it details the attempts of a succubus to seduce Shatner into sin, only to discover – after summoning the titular incubus to kill him – that she's fallen in love with him.

Hammer had their own misfire with *The Witches* (aka *The Devil's Own*, 1966) – not to be confused with the 1967 anthology (aka *La Strege*, with Clint Eastwood), the Italian *La Strega in Amore* (1966), about a man enchanted by the titular lovesick witch, or the enjoyable 1990 Roald Dahl adaptation. Joan Fontaine's discovery of a coven of witches in a seemingly quaint English countryside is tepid but gets points for being the first of many films in that vein. Another is Lance Comfort's *Devils of Darkness* (1965), which mixes vampires and Devil worshipers in a rather insipid stew.

While the mystical view is shown in a sinister light in these films, it's openly advocated by Kenneth Anger in his 1954 grotesquerie *Inauguration of the Pleasure Dome*, which he describes as "derived from one of Aleister Crowley's dramatic rituals where people in the cult assume the identity of a god or a goddess."[22] In 1969, he returned with *Invocation of My Demon Brother*, in which Satan was played by none other than Anton LaVey. The film is, for all intents and purposes, "a ritual... laid out in ritual form... meant to evoke a response out of the watcher, to cast a spell, if you will."[23] It features appearances from The Rolling Stones' Mick Jagger and Bobby Beausoleil, who went on to join the Manson family. Art imitating life imitating art... or perhaps something far darker?

Anger's films were the only ones in this era to actually advocate *for* Satanism. The rest were warnings against it. Despite the general antipathy Conservatives have expressed toward Hollywood, movie and television writers have expressed considerable hostility toward the mystical view, depicting it as a doorway to something pernicious and dark. "Older films exploring Gnostic, Cabbalistic, or alchemical themes tend to be cautionary tales on the dangers of

---

[22] *The Devil Notebooks*, by Laurence A. Rickels; University Of Minnesota Press, 2008.
[23] https://www.denofgeek.com/us/movies/top-37-classiest-satans-in-film-tv/88319/top-37-classiest-satans-in-films-or-tv-shows-ive-seen-in-the-past-two-weeks

heterodox speculations. Otto Rippert's *The Revenge of the Homunculus*, from 1916, depicts the horrific results of a failed alchemical experiment: an artificial man who cruelly conquers and controls the world. Paul Wegener's *The Golem*, released in 1920, shows the tragic results of Cabbalistic magic: an animated form of mud trying unsuccessfully to be a happy human. James Whale's 1931 *Frankenstein* features a Gnostic's failed attempt to transcend deathly matter, a mad scientist's creation of monstrosity instead of salvation."[24]

The Skeptical View

> Very few people believe in the devil these days, which suits the devil very well. He is always helping to circulate the news of his own death. The essence of God is existence, and He defines Himself as: "I am Who am." The essence of the devil is the lie, and he defines himself as: "I am who am not."
>
> — Fulton J. Sheen

The skeptical view, more accurately called "scientific skepticism," was the Enlightenment era's response to the folkloric view, serving as an important challenge to the numerous, unverified claims of superstition and Spiritism in the 19th century, which saw charlatans taking advantage of grieving parents and widows. The skeptical view became the rallying cry of the materialist looking to debunk *all* claims made in the realms outside of empiricism, including religious belief, alternative medicine, the paranormal, UFOs, cryptids, and conspiracy theories, all of which were disparaged and lumped in the category of pseudoscience.

Thus, the Devil is nothing more than a symbol for evil. Evil comes not from any external source, but internally, from people alone. Those who believe in the Devil, skeptics chide, are ignorant and backwards, deceived by the fairy tales of the Church who – wanting a scapegoat – stole him from older mythologies in order to keep people in fear and to demonize the competing Celtic, Slavic, and Teutonic gods.[25]

Although Enlightenment-era views came to be among the more common and prevalent perspectives in modern society, they produced a counter-

---

[24] *Secret Cinema: Gnostic Visions in Film*: https://voegelinview.com/secret-cinema-gnostic-film-pt-1/

[25] Contrary to popular belief, several ancient sacred Jewish texts demonstrate that Satan predates the Christian era by centuries.

reaction in the Romantic era, which birthed the supernatural fantasy and horror genres: "As the new liberal ideology expanded across the continent, celebrating the empirical, the rational, and the scientific as forces that would liberate humanity from the inequities and superstitions of the past, a growing number of thinkers, poets, philosophers, and conservative moralists began to question its spiritual implications."[26] The Age of Reason resulted in war, violence, industrialization, factories, and environmental degradation, all of "which had been justified by a rhetoric of dominance over the natural world enabled through reason."[27]

The first of the skeptical views on the subject was Danish writer-director Benjamin Christensen's landmark film *Häxan, Witchcraft through the Ages* (1922). Citing the belief in spirits, sorcery, and witchcraft as the result of "naïve notions about the mystery of the universe," it uses medieval art and chilling enactments of witches, demonic entities, and the Inquisition to make the point.[28] The film was banned in the United States until 1929 (when H.P. Lovecraft saw and was terrified by it), and perhaps not without justification; its disturbing depictions of torture, bestial sexuality, nudity, urination, sacrilege, and infant sacrifice are still arresting. Christensen's film remains a fascinating amalgam of pseudo-documentary, social commentary, and bawdy horror, kick-starting the cinematic debate on cosmic evil!

In most of the visual arts in which the skeptical view is present, rarely is the supernatural merely a product of the mind, such as it is in *Häxan*, as well as Val Lewton's *The Innocents* and *Cat People*. More often than not, the debunker is himself debunked and comes to discover firsthand the truth of Albert Einstein's maxim: "One thing I have learned in a long life: that all our science, measured against reality, is primitive and childlike..."

Perhaps no better example of this can be found than in the cinematic masterpiece *Night of the Demon* (1957). Masterfully directed by Val Lewton's protégé, Jacques Tourner, and adapted by Hal E. Chester and Alfred Hitchcock screenwriter Charles Bennet from the chilling M.R. James story "Casting the

---

[26] https://sfucmns.wordpress.com/2010/06/01/reacting-to-the-enlightenment-the-conservative-backlash/

[27] Ibid.

[28] The film makes several absurdly false statements, e.g. claiming eight million were burned alive for witchcraft. Historians figure around 50,000, horrific enough without the need for gross exaggeration.

Runes," *Night of the Demon* is the first film to present the partnership of skeptic and believer, which the television series *The X-Files* would later put to great use. As noted by editor-author Chris Fujiwara, Tourneur (like James) believed that "there is another layer of reality that intersects our own at certain times and places... *Night of the Demon* above all else is a film about knowledge and belief. Holden thinks he knows how the world works and he has to find out that he doesn't."[29]

The titular demon of *Night of the Demon* was created using an unconvincingly rubbery dog-like mask.

Like many skeptical film protagonists, psychologist John Holden is likeable and smart. His journey is that of the viewer, a rational man who has cast off belief in curses, witches, and demons as the bunk of children's stories. His antagonist is Dr. Julian Karswell (Niall MacGinnis), a black magician who, although patterned after Aleister Crowley, is given a sympathetic portrayal as a man desperate for significance only to fall down a slippery moral slope. Unable to contain the darkness he's unleashed, he serves as a warning against the

---

[29] Documentary special-feature on *Night of the Demon* Blu-ray; Powerhouse Studios, 2018.

temptations of power (essentially what magic is) and arrogance, the same Achilles heel of Holden who is convinced he understands reality.

Whereas later horror films would go for excess, Tourneur uses restraint. The terror, until the end, is mainly psychological, but borne from the shadows of the supernatural. The demon of the title is problematic due to the producer's insertion of three close-up shots of its rubbery, dog-like head (which belong in the tradition of *Godzilla* – entertaining, but not for the film Tourneur created). Seen from afar, however, the creature design is excellent and still manages to evoke chills.

Another good example can be found in *Diary of a Madman* (1963), an adaptation of Guy de Maupassant's story, "The Horla," an early possession film that involves an invisible demonic entity tormenting Vincent Price's Simon Cordier. When Simon goes to see his psychiatrist, who's even more of a skeptic than he is, he's rebuked: "They are all from your own imagination. Science doesn't accept gnomes, ghosts, demons, images of evil." This reassures Cordier but leaves him utterly unprepared for the Horla's psychological attacks.

A similar scenario occurs in the Amicus film *The Skull* (1965), in which demonologist Peter Cushing is thrilled to have purchased the skull of the Marquis de Sade, ignoring the advice of his "superstitious" friend (the inimitable Christopher Lee again), who warns him of its danger. In *The Witchmaker* (1969, aka *The Naked Witch*), Anthony Eisley plays a journalist asked to overcome his unbelief in order to save a woman from a Satanic cult in the Louisiana Bayou: "I don't want to believe in witchcraft," he complains. "It goes against everything I was taught to believe."

Although beyond the scope of this essay, more favorable endorsements of the skeptical view can be found in the science fiction genre, where it's oftentimes subtly intertwined with the mystical view. While fantasy and horror are products of theological and folkloric views, science fiction replaced the supernatural aspects of fantasy and space opera (a fantasy subgenre – the primary difference being the *otherworld* is set on other planets, and technology is used in tandem with magic[30]) with scientific-seeming explanations, an emphasis on process, and the addition of mystical elements palatable to materialists such as astral projection, alternate dimensions, transhumanism, and the ancient astronaut hypothesis founded on the works of Zechariah Sitchin

---

[30] The *Star Wars* franchise is a prime example of this.

and Erich Von Daniken (who borrowed it from H.P. Lovecraft and theosophy), reconceiving supernatural gods and angels for technologically advanced aliens.

The Theological View

> Man may have been made in the image of God, but human society was made in the image of His opposite number, and is always trying to get back home.
>
> — Stephen King, *The Stand*

It's primarily from the theological view that the world first derived its understanding of Satan, and his chief opponent, and from which Hollywood and television have long drawn inspiration, even if at times conflating and confusing it with the folkloric view. The theological view tends to be more commonly found in films that attempt to take the question of evil more seriously than salaciously, but even comedic approaches touch upon aspects of it.

Derived from the Bible, 1 Enoch, and other ancient works then considered sacred, the theological view not only differs from the prevalent views found in mainstream churches, but rejects the other views, the folkloric for its superstition (the *Catholic Encyclopedia* defines superstition as an "excess of religion," often linked with idolatry, divination, and occultism), the skeptical for its materialism and scientism, the mystical for its distortions of theology.

The most systematic of the four, the theological view sets the stage with a cosmic war between the opposing celestial offspring of a wise, all-powerful, and benevolent Maker, who objectively determines morality as defined by other-centered love and regard for Him as parent and rightful lawgiver. In opposition is a malevolent cabal of fallen sons who desire power on their own terms. It's outside the scope of this essay to explicate the sophisticated demarcation of celestial entities, called *Elohim*, save to say that the cute winged babies and sexy winged angels are products of the folkloric view and have no theological basis.

The fallen Elohim are led by *the* Satan, a title meaning "the adversary" — also referred to as the Devil by the Greek word *diabolos* ("slanderer"). More accurately, they are led by plural *Satans*, who succeed in corrupting the earliest humans.[31] Evil spread from the aftermath of a coup in which celestial "Watchers" take on human wives in an attempt to establish a royal dynasty

---

[31] Gen 3, 6; 1 Enoch 40:7 and 69:5-12.

upon the Earth with their hybrid children as god-kings. With the establishment of the political-economic-social hierarchy of elites over a working/slave class, the Watchers teach humans to manage, defend, and expand civilization through warfare, sexual exploitation, legalism, and occultism. The domination system grows even darker when their mutant *Nephilim* offspring come to power.[32] Although the reign of these entities is brought to an end, others take their place and the exploitative system is perpetuated under the imperial rule of self-proclaimed "sons of the gods," using violence, pageantry, and religious ceremony in order to maintain legitimacy in the eyes of the masses.

> Indeed, nearly every human race speaks in its legends of tall, wonderful strangers of amazing skill, who came to their land in ancient times and taught their great-ancestors everything they needed to know; virtually every useful invention still practiced by humanity has been attributed to these visitors. The modern trend is to attribute such influences to advanced alien civilizations, as in the books of von Daniken and others, but our many-great-grandmothers and fathers had no doubt that they had walked and spoken with gods and the children of gods.[33]

Evil is thus not only internal, arising from negative proclivities of our internal brokenness, but external, originating from malevolent gods and their demonic allies.[34] Yet, through a covert and unfolding plan of God's, redemption for mankind from evil is made possible through the substitutionary sacrifice of his loyal offspring Jesus Christ, for which reason the theological view opposes philosophical individualism, folkloric fables, and occultic alterations. It's also why vampires are shown to fear crosses and the self-sacrificial love of a grief-stricken priest saves a demon-possessed girl.

One theological portrayal of Satan can be found in the Gothic soap opera *Dark Shadows*, in the form of the demonic entity Diabolos (a Greek word often translated as "devil"). Appearing in two 1968 episodes (#628 and #629 out of a whopping 1,225!), Diabolos presents himself as a mysterious human whose entire body, including his head, is cloaked in darkness. The entity is said to have dispatched witches to kill the Puritans in 1692, and he thrice attempts to bring an Antichrist to power – first his son Judah Zachery, and later Gerard Stiles and

---

[32] Enoch 7: 1-15.

[33] "Leviathan Chained: The Legend of the Nephilim and the Cthulhu Mythos," by Paula O'Keefe: http://www.chezbrodeur.net/erb/nephilim/leviathan/lev_p1.html. See also *Last Clash of the Titans*, by Derek P. Gilbert; Defender Publishing, 2018.

[34] For an in-depth discussion of these topics, see *The Unseen Realm* and *Reversing Hermon*, by Dr. Michael S. Heiser; Lexham Press.

Jeb Hawkes – in order to usher in the Apocalypse. The demon also gives rise to a Lovecraftian race called the Leviathans, which plague the main characters, including reluctant vampire Barnabas Collins, in one of *Dark Shadows'* creepier storylines. Despite only appearing in two episodes, Diabolos is vital to the show's mythology, for without his devilish influence, the fates of not only Barnabas, Stiles, and Hawkes, but also sorcerer Nicholas Blair and vampiric witch Angelique Bouchard, would be quite different.

Dark Shadows' Diabolos and his bewitching servant, Angelique Bouchard.

The Horror

> I wouldn't dare attempt to sanitize the actions of the Devil. Either IT is the most abominable creature set upon us to endure, or IT is not. There is no in between.
>
> — A.K. Kuykendall, *The Possession*

One does not need to necessarily believe in the Christian "myth" to see the value in it. Nor does Satan merely provide a context for what is morally bad, but rather a complex range of evils that society and the individual can recognize as morally repugnant. Society's failure to fully embrace this so-called myth has allowed it to continually perpetuate its greatest evils – war, greed, domination, deception, and hate – all of which can be seen in the various portrayals of the Devil.

Yet many of our contemporaries – a bizarre combination of those who have embraced secular modernity as well as those who abhor it, the Christian fundamentalists – have rejected the importance of myth... To the modernist, "myth," like religion, merely signifies a comfortable and entrenched lie. For the postmodernist, myth simply represents one story, one narrative among many... purely subjective, certainly signifying nothing of transcendent or any other kind of importance.[35]

The origins of Satan have, by and large, been forgotten. Rabbinic Judaism and Liberal Christianity went on to eschew most of the supernatural worldview for a skeptical one, while Fundamentalists replaced the theological view with the folkloric one: "There are some Christian leaders who never talk about Satan, and others who talk incessantly about him.... In the case of the latter, every time the toast burns or something doesn't go their way, Satan is behind it and it's time for an exorcism. Neither extreme is particularly helpful."[36]

It's rather interesting that it's mainly in the horror film – so frequently attacked by the religious and nonreligious alike – that one can find supernatural evil presented in ways that more closely match its earliest conception.[37] Timothy Milinovich, associate professor of theology at Dominican University, noted that "there's definite thematic overlap between horror fiction and religion," with both seeking to address "what is outside of us that is a threat, but also what is within us: rage and anger and jealousy and all these other things that are also corruptions – even the concept of guilt (and) the need for redemption."[38]

Prior to the horror film, it was in religious films that the darkest supernatural tales were told.

> Casting out demons goes back to the ministry of Jesus, and in the movies it goes back to the Jesus films of cinema's silent origins. The 1912 film *From the Manger to the Cross* depicts Jesus healing a demoniac. Cecil B.

[35] https://theimaginativeconservative.org/2019/10/j-r-r-tolkien-sanctifying-myth-bradley-birzer.html
[36] Carey Nieuwhof, "The Devil's 5 Favourite Strategies."
[37] There appears to be a sea-change in that regard with more religious thinkers embracing formerly reviled forms of art. See notes #2 and 3.
[38] https://www.usatoday.com/story/life/movies/2018/09/04/why-unholy-horror-films-have-creepy-appeal-nun-exorcist/1161880002/

DeMille's 1927 silent *The King of Kings* opens with Jesus dramatically delivering Mary Magdalene of her seven demons, here representing the seven deadly sins... Edward Dmytryk's 1962 biopic *The Reluctant Saint* climaxes with a dramatic extended exorcism scene featuring Ricardo Montalban as a Franciscan friar – an exorcism that fails because the exorcee, St. Joseph of Cupertino, isn't possessed![39]

One of the earliest human-possession scenarios in a non-religious film is *Back from the Dead* (1957). When a young newlywed becomes possessed by her husband's ex-wife, her sister begins to investigate and discovers she'd been part of a Satanic cult. The Polish art film *Mother Joan of the Angels* (1961), directed by Jerzy Kawalerowicz, and loosely based on the 1634 incident at a French convent in Loudun, deals with a conflicted priest who goes to exorcise eight possessed nuns, only to realize that he must take on the demons himself to free them. This motif would be echoed years later in William Friedkin's masterpiece *The Exorcist*.

The possessed doll trope was put to great use in *The Twilight Zone,* which featured three takes on the subject: "Living Doll," featuring the ever-eerie Talking Tina; "The Dummy," in which the titular object, named Jerry, decides his partner (Cliff Robertson) has to go; and "Caesar and Me," in which the doll from the previous episode trades in his bungling partner for a younger human!

The best of the possessed ventriloquist dummy tales, however, remains the earliest. *Dead of Night* (1945) is a British horror anthology that is far more than the sum of its parts. An architect arrives at a house where he reluctantly reveals he's had recurring dreams of each of the guests there, believing it will culminate in something terrible. Fascinated, the guests in turn tell of some supernatural occurrence from their past: a premonition of doom, a haunted room, an enchanted mirror, even a comedic ghost. A skeptical psychiatrist attempts to debunk each of these before adding his own tale of a possessed dummy and its owner.

Not all films dealing with Satan involve cults, dolls, or Faustian bargains. In the Amicus anthology *The Torture Garden* (1967), another Robert Bloch story, Satan appears merely to revel in the evil of man. The showrunner of a fairground sideshow, Burgess Meredith promises to really scare his four customers if they'll pay extra. When they agree, a facsimile of the goddess Atropos shows each one their future. The first man hastens his uncle's death to

---

[39] http://decentfilms.com/articles/exorcism

get his hidden gold, only to discover he'd been hiding the witch Balthasar, now in the form of a cat, who compels him to kill so she can eat her victims' heads! The young American woman of the second tale, meanwhile, will do anything to attain the status of the Hollywood elites, until she discovers the secret truth they share.

In the third story, a dominating English woman ignores the warnings of her boyfriend, a concert pianist, who reveals that the piano his dead mother gave him will stand no rivals for his attention (amusingly, you root for the piano). The final tale provides a rather prescient commentary on modern-day fandom, as an ardent Edgar Allen Poe fan (Jack Palance) discovers a treasure trove of Poe collectibles in the home of Peter Cushing, including unpublished manuscripts – and Poe himself, brought back from the dead by a necromancer who made a deal with the Devil. Yet, for Poe to be released, someone must take his place!

Here we leave off prior to the trifecta of diabolical horror that terrified audiences utterly unprepared for what was to come – Ira Levin's *Rosemary's Baby* (adapted by Roman Polanski in 1968), William Peter Blatty's *The Exorcist* (adapted by William Friedkin in 1973), and Richard Donner's *The Omen* (1976) – all three of which deal with the corruption of innocent youth by satanic entities in three different ways: conception, possession, and infiltration. From these descended a locust swarm of demonic novels and films that continues unabated to this day.

Chink in the Armor

> There are two equal and opposite errors into which our race can fall about the devils. One is to disbelieve in their existence. The other is to believe, and to feel an excessive and unhealthy interest in them. They themselves are equally pleased by both errors, and hail a materialist and a magician with the same delight.
>
> — C.S. Lewis

Cinematic history began with the Devil, and if the success of the demonic on screen is anything to go by, so too it may end there. Yet, as terrifying a monster as Satan is, from the theological perspective, at least, he "is a creature... finite and limited... stronger than men but no match for God. He has no divine attributes. His knowledge may exceed ours, but he is not omniscient.

His strength may be greater than ours, but he is not omnipotent. He may have a wider sphere of influence than we have, but he is not omnipresent."[40]

Some view him as a creature of the night, a monster for which crosses and charms might keep him at bay. Others see him as the ultimate outcast and rebel – for which reason they gravitate to him. Ironically, he's also considered the ultimate insider, the wealthiest, most handsome and powerful of the elites – for which reason the upper classes hobnob with him. All of this demonstrates how the Devil's various portrayals and approaches are interesting and appropriate in their own ways, including the skeptical view, which underscores Satan's ability to use subterfuge and disguise so well that many brush aside his existence as unreal.

However one approaches the subject, one thing is clear: for all the terror he inspires, Satan ultimately proves to be banal, loathsome, and false, a con-artist and counterfeiter in an ever-changing mask behind which stares a void, an emptiness born of things petty, greedy, and hateful. His entire modus operandi is centered on lies and dissimulation, convincing others he doesn't exist or, conversely, that he's worthy of their fear and adulation.

The greatest monster in history is also the greatest fraud. If there is a positive aspect to be found here, it lies in the idea that if there is a supernatural evil at work in the world, causing harm or tempting us to commit evil, then it is likely that there is also supernatural good, and hope beyond a world ruled by evil. Either way, one thing is certain: the Devil has all the best films.

---

[40] https://www.ligonier.org/blog/satan-proud-and-powerful-part-1/

Continuity of Terror: The Horror Comics of Warren Publishing

by Sam Agro

Men in their dotage, as I now find myself, spend an inordinate amount of time fondly recollecting our boyhood "firsts." We reminisce, wistfully, about the little joys and apprehensions which surrounded our first shave, our first time behind the wheel of a car, our first date, and all the little rites of passage that marked our transition from innocence to maturity. When numbering such heady milestones, it would be impossible to exclude one's first glimpse of a girly magazine.

The Treehouse of Horror

My premiere peek took place in the fall of 1969, about a month before my ninth birthday. My mother had seasonal work in the tobacco harvest, and I was dragged along each day to hang out with the farmer's two comparably aged sons. It was hot and humid, and each day was a war against monotony.

We played Crazy Eights, checkers, and Milton Bradley's *Operation*. We raced through the tobacco fields, fencing with tobacco slats and getting splinters in our fingers for our trouble. One fateful afternoon, we were offered respite from the tedium. The scion of a neighboring farm, a portly lad of 13, deigned to allow us entry to his sanctum sanctorum: a slapdash treehouse in the woods. It was there I had my inevitable first collision with the female nude.

This being rural Canada in 1969, the content of the lad's magazines was laughably tame. These outdoorsy "health and beauty" publications featured topless and tanned young women playing badminton, hiking, and sunning themselves on rocks in the great outdoors. Bottoms and bosoms were bared without shame, but the ubiquitous black bars of censorship marred all frontal angles. While there was a certain titillating sense of the forbidden about the photos, I confess I was a bit too young to fully appreciate their erotic intent.

However, it wasn't my only "first" that day. It was also the day I read my first horror comic. Amidst the stack of magazines was a single issue of *Creepy*, and the instant I clapped eyes on it, all interest in bare-naked ladies was (temporarily) eclipsed. Bill Hughes' beautifully painted cover, a lurid variation on the classic patchwork man, became so unequivocally seared into my memory that I was easily able to track it down many years later. It was *Creepy* #30, the final issue to be published in the 1960s – and, coincidentally, the termination point for the content of this essay.

In a satisfying twist of symmetry, one of Jim Warren's earliest publishing efforts was the erstwhile men's magazine *After Hours*. It was one among Warren's many abortive attempts to forge a publishing empire, which included far-out '60s music-scene periodicals, kid's comics, and humor magazines. Notably, however, it was during production on *After Hours* that Jim Warren first met Forest J. "Forry" Ackerman, who eventually guided him to his true publishing vocation: horror.

Midnight Monster Mania

In the late 1950s and early 1960s, as television programming continued to expand, the networks began broadcasting a lot of older black-and-white films. Among them were the great (and not so great) Universal monster movies. In an interview with TwoMorrows editor Jon B. Cooke,[1] Jim Warren described it thusly:

> Universal Pictures had collected all their classic horror films, packaged them for TV syndication, and was selling this "shock theatre" package to TV stations throughout this great land of ours. These old movies

---

[1] Cooke, Jon B. "Wrightson's Warren Days: The James Warren Interview." *Comic Book Artist* #4, Winter 1999:
http://twomorrows.com/comicbookartist/articles/04warren.html.

(*Frankenstein, Dracula, The Mummy, The Wolf Man,* etc.) were being shown usually late on Friday nights. Each TV station had its own "ghoul-like" host or hostess, who generally spoofed the film being shown and provided some live, low budget, comedy relief. Kids were watching these shows, not adults; and these kids were rooting for the monster – not for the townspeople with the pitchforks and the crude torches. A switch had taken place. When these films had been shown in the movie theatres during the 30s and 40s, the monster was the bad guy. Now it was reversed. These 10-year-old kids saw the monster on their TV sets and embraced him as the protagonist.

Warren, along with his pun-slinging new partner Forry Ackerman, capitalized on this trend of monsters-as-heroes and launched *Famous Monsters of Filmland*. This lighthearted ode to all things cinematically ghastly was an instant success and ran for nearly 25 years. This glorious resurgence of the classic monsters of film spawned a generation of beastly boys and ghoulish girls. Marketing companies capitalized upon this trend with avaricious abandon, and among those who jumped on the bandwagon was Jim Warren, who could pander with the best of them. With his mail-order arm, Captain Company, Warren hawked all manner of movies, models, masks, and memorabilia, and he made an absolute killing. With some of the profits from these successes, Warren returned to his first great love, comics. Seeing no reason to deviate from the subject matter that made *Famous Monsters* such a winner, he stuck with the "fear formula." In late 1964, along with editor Russ Jones, Warren launched *Creepy* and instantly made the world a more petrifying place.

The first issue of *Creepy* is, by any criteria, a home run. The cover, by the great Jack Davis, is somewhat sillier in tone than the contents, but it's a beautifully limned piece. It's there we first meet "Uncle Creepy," the rancid raconteur of the terrifying proceedings. The *Creepy* logo, too, seems more cartoony than one might expect, but at this point, who cares? It's time to open the cover and dig into the delicious gory center of this uncanny confection.

Inside, we get a veritable "who's who" of classic monsters: zombies, vampires, werewolves, witches, and the vengeful dead. The art is by some of the best in the business. It had been about a decade since the demise of the EC Comics horror line by this point, but Jones and Warren were somehow able to corral a great number of their finest artists. Joe Orlando is there, along with Reed Crandal, Frank Frazetta, and Al Williamson, not to mention Roy Krenkel, Angelo Torres, and the eternally underrated Gray Morrow. It was a smorgasbord of classic artists drawing classic monsters, and more great artists and marvelous monsters would appear in the issues to follow.

The stories themselves are somewhat uneven (the eternal curse of all anthologies), but several embrace the new trend of monsters as protagonists. "Vampires Fly at Dusk," by Archie Goodwin and Crandall, features the murderous Count Orsini, who kills for love. In "Werewolf," by Larry Ivey and Frazetta, a coarse and abusive big-game hunter, Demmon, is rewarded for killing the titular beast by becoming the beast in turn, and the witches get the upper hand in Ivey's and Morrow's "Bewitched." In the sharpest story in the issue, "The Success Story," Goodwin and Williamson recount the tale of con-man cartoonist Baldo Smudge, who uses hired guns for every element of his comic strip and contributes nothing to its success. When his employees get wise, he shoots them and dumps them in the river. The vengeful dead return, of course, and destroy the true villain of the piece in heroic fashion.

Warren's monsters would continue to triumph, and mete out rough justice of a sort, for most of the publisher's 1960s run. A few years after *Creepy*'s launch, *Eerie* was added to the roster, and finally, near the end of our target decade, the sexy blood-sucker Vampirella would join the fun.

Horrible Hosts and Pernicious Puns

There's no denying that Warren's use of Uncle Creepy and Cousin Eerie follows in the terrible tradition of EC's Crypt Keeper, Vault-Keeper, and Old Witch. It also harkens back to anthology films like *Twice Told Tales*, with voice-over introductions by Vincent Price; Mario Bava's *Black Sabbath*, which casts Boris Karloff in the role of a quippy master of ceremonies; and Hitch's wry intros to *Alfred Hitchcock Presents*.

I came to know the EC comics after the Warren line, so it may be a function of timing, but I must confess that I always identified more closely with Uncle Creepy and Cousin Eerie than with EC's hosts. Perhaps it was the implication that they were long-lost relatives, some murky offshoot of my own bloodline with hidden malevolent proclivities. These repulsive relations would reel off gory gags and delight in the unsettling little ironies of their fearful fables. This grim joy, particularly when the monster of the tale gained the upper hand, was infectious. I found myself longing to live in their world of the monstrous, malevolent, and mystical.

How to Judge a Book

When it comes to comics publishing, the cover is the first salvo in the battle of the magazine rack. On that score, the Warren line was handily winning the war for the horror market. Its covers were consistently impressive, and even after competitors began to invade the newsstands, they remained hard to beat. With issue #2 of *Creepy*, the cartoony logo is MIA, replaced by the classic blood-dripping letters readers had come to know and love. Gone, too, is the lighthearted art of Jack Davis, replaced with the lurid hues and deep shadows of Frank Frazetta.

The covers of the Warren line embraced the idea of the monster as protagonist. While EC's covers frequently featured monsters, they were more frightful, more threatening. At Warren, the creatures were rendered more lovingly, more lyrically, and were usually featured front and center in the composition. They were visually dominant, looming triumphantly over any puny humans who might happen to be cowering nearby. On some covers, in fact, the humans were absent altogether.

Many talented artists created outstanding cover art for the line, but there's simply no denying that the major story here is Frank Frazetta. Of the 56 issues of *Eerie*, *Creepy*, and *Vampirella* that hit the market during the '60s, Frazetta painted a whopping 20 covers! Vic Prezio comes in second with a respectable ten, while Gray Morrow brings up third place with seven frightful façades.

With occasional inspiration from long-time friend and collaborator Roy Krenkel, Frazetta brings all the classic monsters to life, offering his compelling take on ghosts, witches, werewolves, vampires, demons, and many more monsters. Just to shake things up, he also throws in the occasional wild card: the chilling winged beasts of *Creepy* #9, for instance, or the stalking Neanderthals of issue #15. All are rendered with typical Frazetta energy and power, in colors rich and brilliant or muted and misty, but always with an eye for maximum impact.

The truly staggering thing about Frazetta's Warren covers is that they continued to improve throughout the run. The early covers, perhaps due to the Krenkel sketches upon which they were sometimes based, seem more presentational than his later Warren offerings. The composition, color, and posing of each successive effort becomes ever more vigorous. His rendering, too, becomes more refined and confident. It was during this period that Frazetta began painting his paperback covers for the reissuing of Robert E. Howard's Conan stories, which caused his popularity to explode. Unfortunately for Warren, Frazetta was soon priced out of the magazine market, depriving the line of one of its greatest assets.

Ars Gratia Artis

In a visual sense, a direct link can be drawn between the exceptional art of Warren's comic magazines and the great horror films. They're both in black and white, of course, which I still contend is the ideal choice for horror stories of any kind. More than that, the sensibility of the art is evocative of a similar compositional style and atmosphere.

Reed Crandall's woodcut-style pen work, or the ink washes of Joe Orlando and Gray Morrow, seem a spiritual kin to James Whale's moody, formalist compositions. The lush blacks and shadowy renderings of Al Williamson, Angelo Torres, and Gene Colan recall the eerie styling of a Val Lewton thriller. Steve Ditko, Jerry Grandinetti, and Alex Toth, meanwhile, with their psychological use of page and panel design, harken back to the unsettling metaphorical imagery of German expressionist film. These are exceptional artists at the top of their game, and I contend that many of them did the best work of their careers in those pages. That's no doubt a contentious statement in the case of the EC alumni, but I stand by it.

The grid-based production techniques William M. Gaines and Al Feldstein used to maintain their house style were, I believe, overly restrictive for some artists. In the case of Joe Orlando, for instance, you can see that his early Warren work retains the formal layouts of the EC style, but soon his page design opens up to great effect. The same might be said for Al Williamson, John Severin, Wally Wood, and Reed Crandall. Only Johnny Craig, drawing for a time under the *nom de guerre* "Jay Taycee," seems to fall short of the unassailable quality of his EC pages. His page designs for Warren are generally more staid than the bold work he once created for Gaines.[2] Then again, the performance of talents like these is so confident at every stage of their careers that trying to assign superiority to one era over another is probably futile. Let's just agree it's top-drawer work and leave it at that.

As for talents who weren't part of the EC phenomenon, there's little doubt in my mind that they did their best work for Warren Publishing. While Steve Ditko's horror work can never match the pop-culture impact of Spider-Man, I have no doubt that he did his most compelling pages for Warren. Writer-editor Archie Goodwin cast him for any story involving weird alternate dimensions and

---

[2] An exception can be found in the marvelous "Eye of the Beholder," published in *Creepy* #19.

wizards, of course, to capitalize on that Dr. Strange flair, but Ditko was particularly adept at tales with an Edgar Allan Poe-like psychological angle. Take, for instance, "Beast Man," published in *Creepy* #11, wherein a boxer, falsely convinced he received a gorilla heart during a transplant, goes on a killing spree. There's also "Fly," in *Eerie* #7, which features a hit man recovering from identity-altering plastic surgery. A deadly combination of guilt, sedatives, and a fly lodged in his ear leads to an unfortunate psychotic break.

Dan Adkins, allowed a rare opportunity to both pencil and ink, delivers what is doubtless some of his finest art. "The Doorway," presented in *Creepy* #11, is a personal favorite of mine. I believe Angelo Torres created his best art for Warren, his humor strips for *MAD* magazine notwithstanding. Torres's exceptional layouts, with lavish blacks and delicate line-work in the Alex Raymond tradition, are irresistible. In the case of Gray Morrow, the colors and smaller reproduction size of regular comics made his dense, photo-referenced style appear quite muddy. In the pages of *Eerie* and *Creepy*, Morrow's art positively sings in glorious black and white. It was a rare inker who could properly interpret the mysterious chiaroscuro of the great Gene Colan's pencils. At Warren, he was able to complete the job himself and perfectly echo his tonal approach in ink washes.

As talented a stylist as Alex Toth was, I'm convinced that the work he did for *Eerie* and *Creepy* represents his most creative and unfettered page design. If one were only to consider "The Stalkers," which appeared in *Creepy* #6, I think my argument would still hold up. With its oppressive light and shadow, forced perspective, and claustrophobically cramped panels, the reader can't help but feel the crushing paranoia of the beleaguered protagonist. This was only the beginning, of course. In the very next issue, Toth managed another graphic masterpiece with "Rude Awakening." Page four of this story is arguably the finest page of suspense comics ever drawn.

Neal Adams was predictably great wherever he worked, but there's no denying he did some top-drawer stories for Warren. "Curse of the Vampire," published in *Creepy* #14, is an exceptional piece, for instance. While not every story Neal did for Warren represents his absolute best, there are several outstanding examples of his unique style of exaggerated photo-realist illustration.

Warren was also a proving ground for new talent. Jeffery (later Catherine) Jones, Billy Graham, Ernie Colón, and Tom Sutton all appeared during the '60s

This page from "Rude Awakening" showcases Alex Toth's psychological use of panel design.

run, and though they were not yet doing their finest work, their great potential was clear from the very beginning.

I believe the hands-off editorial style at Warren Publishing, as well as freedom from the constraints of the four-color process, allowed the Warren artists to experiment freely. The pages are laden with intense blacks, delicate cross-hatching, moody gray washes, deep zip-a-tone and duo-shade tinting, and unconstrained possibilities for page and panel design. These artists were having fun, pushing the limits of the form, and their lucky readers reaped the rewards of their unfettered liberty.

Big Win for Goodwin

There's no doubt the Warren artists were doing amazing work, but they'd have had little to draw if not for one remarkable individual: Archie Goodwin.

Goodwin went from contributing a few stories in *Creepy* #1 to serving as story editor in issues #2 and #3, and then as editor by issue #4. Based on all available evidence, one might conclude that the editor's job at Warren was basically writing 90 percent of the stories. There were other contributing authors, of course, including Russ Jones, Larry Ivie, Joe Orlando, Ron Parker, Otto Binder, Bob Stewart, Carl Wessler, and many others. I've no doubt that story ideas were bandied about by all and sundry to feed the writing machine that was Archie Goodwin, but it is no less an incredible feat, for all that.

While it's true that not every one of Goodwin's tales was a work of genius, I don't think it's fair to say that *any* of them were truly bad. Even at his worst, Goodwin was able to create characters and situations intriguing enough to keep the reader rolling along with the narrative, compulsively rushing toward whatever sardonic twist might be lurking at the end.

Goodwin's work is directly descended from both the classic horror movies and the great EC comics. While EC's horror comics certainly included their share of monsters, they frequently featured horrible people getting their just desserts for the unspeakably evil acts they perpetrated on their fellow man. Goodwin adheres much more stringently to the idea of monster as leading man. A few of his tales are more about suspense than horror, and he occasionally drifts into science fiction and fantasy, but he keeps the bulk of the narratives persistently monstrous. Mutants, vampires, ghouls, ghosts, and demons of all breeds take their bloody bows in the pages of *Eerie* and *Creepy*.

It would be impossible to cover all the terrific tales Goodwin wrote during his time at Warren, but in addition to some of the stories mentioned earlier, a few of my personal favorites are "Ogre's Castle," appearing in *Creepy* #2, which features superb artwork by Angelo Torres, and "Collector's Edition," in *Creepy* #10, which is cleverly visualized by Steve Ditko. Don't miss Jerry Grandenetti's terrifyingly rendered "Typecast" in *Eerie* #8, or "Fair Exchange" in *Eerie* #9, one of Neal Adams' finest Warren jobs.

Unfortunately, the prolific Goodwin stepped down as editor with *Creepy* #17 and *Eerie* #11, which soon led to dark days for the company. It is not within the purview of this essay to detail this decline, but if you want to know more, I highly recommend TwoMorrows' comprehensive volume *The Warren Companion*, by David A. Roach and Jon B. Cooke. For now, let it suffice to say that with Goodwin and many of the experienced artists taking their leave, the quality began to suffer. Moving forward, Jim Warren began to rely on less experienced staff, augmenting these shakier efforts with unrestrained use of reprints. Fans took notice of the uneven quality and quickly tired of the "reruns."

This brings us neatly back to my treehouse introduction to both horror comics and Warren's magazine line.

Creepy issue #30, featuring cover art by Bill Hughes.

Out On a Limb

It's difficult to reconcile the striking impact *Creepy* #30 had on my nine-year-old brainpan with the fact that it was smack in the middle of a fallow period for the publisher. I'm sure there are few who would declare Bill Hughes the equal of Frank Frazetta or Gray Morrow, but the cover to that issue is still a fine piece of work by a talented professional. The worn trope of the mad scientist and patchwork man is given an intriguing twist, in that the monster has fur and claws, a disturbing hybrid between Frankenstein's creature and vivisectionist Dr. Moreau's beast-men. The face of the creature, twisted horribly by the electricity animating it, tongue distended, eyes rolling back, is truly disturbing.

Many interior panels are equally haunting: Ernie Colón's depiction of a three-headed monster-mutant, Roger Brand's devout rendering of a Lockheed A-12 aircraft, and Tom Sutton's feverish vision of Los Angeles falling into Hell. Most disturbing of all, for me, was Carlos Prunes' axe-wielding hell-spawn in "To Be or Not To Be a Witch." The last panel of page five, with its off-frame beheading and unsettling "SWWWWWWIIISSSSSHHHH... CHUNK" sound effect, still springs unbidden to my mind from time to time, and it never fails to raise goose bumps.

In "To Be or Not to Be a Witch" from Carlos Prunes, a hairy demon performs an unspeakable act with a hair-raising sound effect.

It's true that half the stories were reprints, and that some of the new art wasn't quite the equal of the older stuff, but it was still good horror comics. The primitive thrill that the undraped female form failed to deliver that day in the treehouse was dispensed in abundance by these frightening, fascinating, unforgettable images. A few years later, I became a dyed-in-the-wool comic collector, and it wasn't long before I started following the Warren magazine line myself.

Vampi Leads the Way

For a time, the classic black-and-white monster movies reigned supreme, but it wasn't long before the next wave of horror films began to appear in grindhouses and drive-ins. This new style of horror, spearheaded by the fine people at Hammer Films, mined the same tropes as the Universal movies, only with more gore and heaving cleavage, and this time it was all in lurid, living-dead color. The classic creatures were all there, but with a harsher edge, more explicit carnage, and, perhaps most importantly, amplified sex appeal. Vampirella, the last Warren host to appear, feels like a direct response to the popularity of these films, with an additional nod to the sexy sci-fi vixen Barbarella.

Frazetta's cover of *Vampirella* #1 personifies the change in tenor. Vampi, decked out in her skimpy bathing suit and go-go boots, her lush body posed insouciantly before a full moon with one foot resting on a human skull, alludes to more titillating content than usual. The interior instantly delivers on the promise of the cover, depicting a nude Vampirella taking a literal blood-bath! When it came to sex, the earlier Warren tales were relatively chaste. There was the occasional hint of lustful impetus, and the odd glimpse of cleavage, but generally it was centered on the monsters and the evil machinations of men. There are more buxom ladies, per capita, in the first issue of *Vampirella* than in any ten issues of *Eerie* or *Creepy* from the 1960s.

While there are a few well-drawn stories in the first issue, particularly "Goddess from the Sea," by Neal Adams and Donald F. Glut, the general quality is inconsistent. The second issue is yet more uneven, and it would be some time before the magazine would reach its full potential.

Vampirella's sexy new style, however, would soon infect *Eerie* and *Creepy*, and, with an influx of new talent from Spain, the Philippines, and the United States, Warren's magazines enjoyed a wretched renaissance in the mid-1970s. By this time, I was a much more worldly 14 years of age, and I was right there at the beginning of this new wave of excellence. These later efforts soon led me to the 1960s back issues – including, of course, that never-forgotten copy of *Creepy* #30. I tracked it down in a used bookstore in London, Ontario, in 1979, and it has been scaring the bejeezus out of me ever since.

Modern Mythology on a Micro-Budget: Reinventing Classic Monsters on *Dark Shadows*

by Ross Johnson

Though some consider them exemplars of schlocky entertainment, it bears remembering that many of our most popular and beloved monsters began life as prestige projects. *Frankenstein*, the novel, was born on a stormy night when, bored by bad weather, three of the most significant literary minds of the 19th century dared each other to come up with scary tales. By any measure, Mary Shelley won that competition. The 1931 film version, from which so many of our ideas about the story come, was both critically acclaimed and wildly successful, establishing the reputations of both star Boris Karloff and director James Whale (who would similarly bring his light touch to *The Old Dark House*, *The Invisible Man*, and *Bride of Frankenstein*). Likewise, Bram Stoker's *Dracula* was a literary sensation in 1897 and an even bigger success at the box office in 1931, winning acclaim and almost singlehandedly kicking off a pop-culture love affair with monsters that has persisted to the present. Though decades of uneven sequels, remakes, and out-and-out cash-ins have dulled the impact of those early efforts, there's no doubt that many modern monsters were born with lofty pedigrees.

By the 1960s, however, the movies had, to many eyes, eclipsed the literary source material, and were themselves viewed as either kid stuff or late-night viewing for insomniacs. Filtered through the lens of 1950s creature features, monsters had, perhaps, never been more disreputable. For about a decade, the British Hammer Film Productions had been offering up brilliantly revisionist takes on Count Dracula, Frankenstein's monster, the Mummy, and other members of the old Universal horror pantheon, but with an eye toward lurid gore that hadn't done much to burnish the reputations of those aging creatures. In other words, Dracula and company were due for a bit of a polish. What they got instead was *Dark Shadows*, a live-to-tape[1] daytime soap opera with an inconceivably tight budget. It was a show known as much for dangling boom mics and flubbed lines as for its juicy supernatural storylines. The end product might have been a forgotten curiosity, but instead, the show still has cultural currency more than a half-century later. The name Barnabas Collins is still spoken, and he's not alone: he brought many classic monsters along with him.

As loyal fans know, *Dark Shadows* began as a more prosaically gothic soap opera from producer Dan Curtis. It was Charlotte Brontë's *Jane Eyre* set among the proprietors of a New England fish cannery. Victoria Winters (Alexandra Moltke) is a would-be governess with a *mysterious* past – her constant references to an upbringing at "the foundling home" and her own confusion regarding her origins serve, for a time, as her only discernible character trait. She's taken in by Elizabeth Collins Stoddard (Joan Bennett), shut-in and matriarch of a long-established family trying to maintain a sense of grandeur in a crumbling mansion and a struggling fish business run by her brother, day-drinker and functional alcoholic Roger (Louis Edmonds). His young son David (David Henesy) is sometimes charming, often contentious, and murderous on at least one occasion. Luckily, Vicki arrives in time to help out with the kid and to

---

[1] While the show wasn't broadcast live, it was filmed and performed as though it were. Budgetary constraints made editing cost-prohibitive, and so retakes were exceedingly rare. Flubbed lines, dangling boom mics, and even small set fires weren't deemed much of a problem because, after all, no one would be watching closely and episodes would never be viewed more than once (or so they thought). It made sense at the time.

serve as a buffer between the Collins family and their old frenemy, Burke Devlin (Mitchell Ryan) – recently out of prison and hungry for revenge, in a storyline based on Alexandre Dumas's novel *The Count of Monte Cristo*.

The main cast of *Dark Shadows*, with Barnabas at center.

In the days before content streaming, the early episodes (a couple hundred of them) were largely unavailable. That's unfortunate, because there's some solidly juicy daytime drama there, as well as a few strong hints about what was to come. It was, in many ways, a typical soap opera of the era, full of tortured romances, dubious lineages, misapprehensions, and double-crosses, but the unique New England-gothic atmosphere lent itself to the supernatural fairly readily – the series bible even suggested that there might be unseen ghosts hanging about the property.[2] Throughout the first several months' worth of episodes, it feels as though the show is straining to *avoid* anything overtly supernatural, even as the indelibly gloomy Collinwood Mansion set seems designed to hide specters in every... dark shadow.

Ghosts were almost a given, and the show was quick to suggest that the halls of Collinwood might indeed be haunted, though ambiguously. There wasn't much room for doubt that the mysterious cries in the night were spectral in origin, but, for a time, the show retained some deniability. The estate would become home to any number of squatters and long-term, non-paying guests throughout the show's run, so it's possible that Elizabeth just

---

[2] Wallace, Art. *Shadows on the Wall*. Dan Curtis Productions, 1995.

forgot about some distant relatives who'd taken up residence in the closed-up west wing. Only for a time, though.

The 30 September 1967 episode provides something a bit more concrete. David, not the most reliable witness, has been warning Vicki about the spirit who haunts the Old House on the Collins land – ill-fated ancestor Josette du Pres Collins, one of the victims of popular murder/suicide spot Widows' Hill. The audience suspects it might all be in David's imagination, until everyone leaves and Josette (Kathryn Leigh Scott) steps from her portrait and takes a stroll around the property.[3] It's perhaps not as definitive as it sounds, though; at this point, the ghost hasn't really interacted with any of the cast in a meaningful way, and it's entirely possible that the show could've moved forward as before, leaving Josette behind as an early Halloween flourish.

It also, inadvertently, sets the stage for another of the show's most beloved tropes: casting lead actors in multiple roles. Kathryn Leigh Scott, who had played waitress and perpetual voice of reason Maggie Evans, happened to be available when the script required an earthly body for Josette. Donning a gauzy wedding dress, she played the part then and for the rest of the series, a doubling which the writers worked into multiple storylines.

Just a couple of weeks later, though, Dark Shadows' 85th episode drew a clear line between the show that was and the show that would be. Cannery manager Bill Molloy, a major character for a time, had been murdered just several episodes prior for reasons that, in proud soap tradition, wouldn't be revealed for many installments to come. Here, though, he reaches out to a trapped Vicki – not in the flesh, but as a ghost who appears via the dark magic of early optical compositing special effects. The sudden shift to the overtly supernatural surprised even long-time series director Lela Swift in a way that the ghostly appearance of Josette had not.[4]

He's not exactly the Creature from the Black Lagoon, but Molloy stands in for more than just a garden-variety ghost. He appears covered in seaweed, reminding viewers that his body was found washed up at the base of Widows' Hill. Stories of nautical spirits abound in New England (think of John Carpenter's pirate-themed horror movie, The Fog), and among many cultures based around

---

[3] Voger, Mark. Monster Mash: The Creepy, Kooky Monster Craze in America 1957-1972. TwoMorrows Publishing, 2015.

[4] Scott, K. L., Pierson, J., & Frid, J. (2012). Dark Shadows: Return to Collinwood. New York: Pomegranate Press, Ltd., 63.

the water. The Japanese Funayūrei, for example, are the vengeful spirits of drowning victims, so there are a few tropes at play when it comes to old Bill Malloy. He's moderately vengeful, but mostly offers up overly vague warnings rather too late – that fecklessness, though, is itself a tried-and-true ghost trope. How many scary stories would be over way too quickly if the ghost just got to the point?

Despite the borrowed elements, there are some distinctly *Dark Shadows* elements in his appearance. First, there are strips of faux seaweed dangled generously about the actor in order to create a (fairly effective) mood in the quickest, most efficient way possible. Second, the character is tied strongly to a musical cue – in this case, Bill's favorite sea shanty, "What Do You Do With a Drunken Sailor?" There's a silliness to the use of that particular tune in signaling the coming of an angry spirit, and *Dark Shadows* would dance along the line between camp and horror for years to come.

With the audience primed, the time was ripe for the show's first full-blown supernatural storyline beyond those relatively subdued hauntings. The show went in a direction that was slightly more unique, offbeat, and cerebral than might have been expected from a ratings-hungry daytime soap opera. It was impressively and deeply weird, as the show's first big monster wasn't a vampire or a werewolf, but rather a phoenix, the bird from ancient Greek mythology that regenerates itself from its own ashes. Rather than resolving the mysteries of Victoria's past in any meaningful way, *Dark Shadows* sidestepped that plotline entirely.

Dan Curtis had originally intended for Vicki to be the daughter of Paul Stoddard (Elizabeth's husband, portrayed by Dennis Patrick) and Betty Hanscombe, according to *Shadows on the Wall*, the series' bible, but despite early hints, including a painting of Betty that resembled Vicki, that storyline was dropped. The *Dark Shadows* audio plays *Return to Collinwood* and *Haunting Memories: A Face from the Past* would later indicate that Vicki was Elizabeth's illegitimate daughter, which makes sense given the resemblance between Joan Bennett and Alexandra Moltke, though it ignores the Hanscombe painting, as well as several mentions of Vicki looking just like Josette Collins. (Her father wasn't named, but Ned Calder, the cannery's manager and Liz's former lover, seems a likely candidate.) On the other hand, novelist Dan "Marilyn" Ross had planned to reveal her parents to be Liz's best friend Rose Barlow and a man named Nathan Moore – who, as crazy as it sounds, was actually Barnabas Collins, and who (thanks to time travel) had fathered Vicki in the 1940s while free of the vampire curse.[5] Given Barnabas's onscreen romantic interest in Vicki, that scenario would have been odd, to say the least.

Vicki's story was dropped, however, in favor of focusing on the similarly mysterious backstory of Collinwood heir David Collins. Having been institutionalized ten years prior, David's mother Laura (Diana Millay) shows up in town – in fact, she's just in from (big hint) Phoenix, where a woman matching her description has recently died in a fire. She claims she's there to take custody of David, though the ghost of Josette leads Vicki to a 200-year-old painting of a woman identical to the modern-day Laura, while local painter Sam Evans (Maggie's self-medicating father, played by David Ford) can't stop himself from painting the visitor engulfed in flames beside her son. The foreshadowing is unmistakable, a virtue for a show meant to be watched over light ironing.

It soon becomes clear that Laura has returned for not just *custody* of David, but *his life* as well. This being just the latest of the phoenix's many cycles of death and regeneration, she plans to take David with her this time, in the hope that they'll be reborn together. It's a wildly audacious and disturbing plotline for a show that had only dipped its toe in the occult. The storyline's concluding episodes see Laura and David trapped together in a burning building while Vicki, Roger, and the rest of the Collinwood gang try to convince the phoenix to spare her son from burning alive in her embrace. It sounds like a budget-busting proposition, but the show manages to carry it all off with suggestion and images of flame superimposed over the actors.

Though it's unlikely that anyone had a long-term game plan at this point, much of what would make the show a phenomenon is already present here, and there's something utterly brilliant about the idea of putting an ancient legend in the body of a (then) modern woman struggling with alcoholism and in the middle of a custody battle. When *Dark Shadows* really worked, it was in that ability to drop old or outdated monsters and mythology into New England of the 1960s and imagine what, say, a phoenix would do among the drawing room crowd in a backwater town. Even before the ghosts and witches showed up, that was part of the show's spine – the whole Collins family, from the beginning, feel like they've been plucked out of time and are slightly uncomfortable in the modern era. Of course, the show would eventually pull them all out of time quite literally, but not before a game-changing

---

[5] http://www.darkshadowsonline.com/victoria/secret_story.html

introduction.

To even the most casual fan, *Dark Shadows* is synonymous with vampires, and with one bloodsucker in particular: Barnabas Collins. Polite and always immaculately dressed, the classically trained Jonathan Frid crafted a vampire equally at home skulking among the tombstones at Eagle Hill Cemetery as he was among the (relatively) polite society of the Collinwood drawing room set. He was also a deeply unlikely sex symbol: the thoroughly middle-aged Frid became incredibly popular among the then-common soap opera audience of female homemakers, with fan mail frequently tending toward the risqué.[6] He certainly wasn't the first vampire with erotic overtones, however. Although variations of vamp folklore go back millennia, the 19th century saw a marked improvement in the social standing of the night-walkers. Inspired by his patient Lord Byron, Dr. John William Polidori crafted the seductive Lord Ruthven for his short story "The Vampyre" in 1819, and it's been pretty much all sex, all the time, for vamps ever since.

If Bram Stoker's game-changing 1897 novel *Dracula* only teased erotic elements, most of the movie versions haven't been so coy. Though decades of camp parodies, bad Halloween costumes, and second-rate imitators have left the appeal of Bela Lugosi somewhat obscure to modern eyes, it's undoubtedly the elegance and Eastern European exoticism of the actor that cemented vamps as creatures to be both feared *and* lusted after, particularly by sexually repressed women of the British 19th century or, in the case of Barnabas, the not-entirely-unrepressed American 1960s. That transgressiveness hasn't always been entirely heteronormative, either – Joseph Sheridan Le Fanu's 1872 novel *Carmilla* introduced a distinctly lesbian vampire, inspiring a whole sub-genre that includes 1936's *Dracula's Daughter*, the direct sequel to the Bela Lugosi movie.

Sadly, while 1960s daytime television might have been happy to tease the idea of marriage-free erotic pairings with a murderous walking corpse, queer overtones were perhaps a bridge too far – Barnabas's bloodsucking was generally confined to women, at least onscreen. When nosy Dr. Woodard learns of Barnabas's true nature and thereby becomes a threat, the vampire comes up with an elaborate scheme to force his co-conspirator, Julia Hoffman (Grayson

---

[6] Benshoff, H. M. (2011). *Dark Shadows (TV Milestones)*. Wayne State University Press, 78.

Hall), to murder the doctor via an injection of lethal chemicals. When Julia demurs, Barnabas injects the doctor himself, demonstrating the great lengths to which he'd go to avoid putting his lips on the neck of a man.

Though later adaptations have offered any number of explanations for Dracula's powers, Bram Stoker avoided offering much in the way of an origin story in his original novel. Frid was initially contracted for a limited run, but once Barnabas was established as an important, ongoing character, the nature of serialized storytelling required that we learn everything that there was to know about Collinsport's[7] newest resident. A five-day-a-week schedule eats up storylines, after all, and there was plenty of time to dig deep into the show's most popular character, going backward, forward, and (almost literally) sideways in time to uncover his complete résumé. Much vampire folklore assumes that the creatures spring from the graves of witches, suicide victims, and other cursed or unfortunate souls, whereas modern vampire mythology focuses on the transmission of blood from one person to another, assuming a nearly unending line going back into deep history. Barnabas's story, we learn, is an extended take on the former version – a witch's curse from a jilted lover.

A young Barnabas Collins had traveled to Martinique circa 1790, where he met both Josette du Pres (Kathryn Leigh Scott) and her maidservant, Angelique Bouchard (Lara Parker). In love with the former but infatuated with the latter, he carried on a brief affair with Angelique before seeking Josette's hand in marriage. Angelique, the reincarnation of a powerful witch (as well as, in brilliant soap opera fashion, Josette's secret half-sister) used her powers to make Josette fall in love with Barnabas's uncle. Eventually, Barnabas discovered her deceit and – well, quite a bit happens. They kill each other, though neither murder takes, and Angelique makes Barnabas a vampire rather than see him die. (Clearly, mistakes were made on both sides.) The origin story also demands, perhaps, the show's most brazen suspension of disbelief: the idea that the fortysomething Frid is portraying a character who's perpetually 25.

It's a wonderfully heightened bit of melodrama with hints of moral ambiguity and very-nearly believable motives from both of the doomed lovers, though, perhaps predictably, Angelique is presented as the villain. With the bewitching Angelique portrayed as both a sexually voracious woman and the

---

[7] For those new to *Dark Shadows*, Collinsport is the fictional town where the show takes place, while Collinwood is the name of the affluent family's mansion.

foil to the show's most popular character, it was perhaps inevitable that she would take the fuller measure of the television camera's moral judgement. It's a tribute to Parker, who is clearly having fun with her juicy role, that she and the character would become almost as integral to *Dark Shadows* as Barnabas following her introduction during the time-traveling origin storyline. She would also, for a time, become a vampire in her own right, due to the machinations of her master, the demon-summoning warlock Nicholas Blair (Humbert Allen Astredo). Much later, Parker wrote the novel *Angelique's Descent*, which tells the story from the witch's point of view, offering a bit more balance to our view of the events that led to the birth of TV's favorite vampire.

Lara Parker as the breathtaking vampiric witch Angelique Bouchard.

Of course, it was all done through suggestion – the show's special effects budget being functionally nil, there were no grand onscreen transformations. Frid and Parker, the show's primary vampire characters, would generally slip in fangs while the camera focused on another actor. Bats dangled on strings through window shades, and attacks were generally implied via a musical swell and dramatic cutaway – none of which rob the show of the offbeat, low-budget grandeur for which it became famous once Barnabas arrived.

So there were ghosts, witches, and vampires – and Barnabas even had his own personal Renfield in the form of Willie Loomis, played briefly by James Hall, then far more effectively by John Karlen. The next step was perhaps obvious: the show clearly needed a Dr. Frankenstein and his monster.

Dr. Eric Lang, portrayed by Addison Powell, arrives in time to help out with the, by then, long-running subplot around Barnabas's desire to find a cure for his vampirism with Dr. Hoffman at his side. Lang has a very particular field of study, but one that would have been entirely familiar to classic monster fans (or, really, just about anyone): he's looking to create artificial life. Though a noble motivation, it's made questionable by his willingness to build bodies out of corpses. We've been down that particular road many times in pop culture, and there's rarely anything good at the end. Because this is *Dark Shadows*, there are numerous twists and romantic complications. Naturally, everyone's looking for a scientific cure for Barnabas's vampirism, so a thoroughly scientific solution is postulated: they'll build an undead creature out of dead bodies and transfer the vampire curse into it. Of course, there's every reason to believe that the unfortunate creature would be immune to vampirism, so there would be no harm.

Dark Shadows talks a good game about expertise and methodologies, but the scientific method made a U-turn *long* before it ever got to Collinwood.

The creature, named Adam, is born as planned, a bit of makeup being enough to suggest that he's been stitched together into an otherwise thoroughly appealing man. (The name Adam was itself inspired by Shelley's monster, who'd proclaimed "I ought to be thy Adam" to his creator.) Even though standards may have changed a bit with time, *Dark Shadows* never wasted an opportunity to make even its most gruesome monsters thoroughly hot. As in the original *Frankenstein* movie, Adam (Robert Rodan) is initially a raving beast (albeit a sexy one), taking Carolyn Stoddard (Nancy Barrett) hostage in his rage. Before long (à la *Beauty and the Beast*), she's able to see the soul behind his gruff exterior and develops an affection for him.

Right before he's driven off a cliff by local law enforcement.

Adam survives the fall from Widows' Hill, eventually developing the ability to communicate. He once again takes up with Carolyn, who loves him but sees their relationship as doomed – what with her being a fish cannery heiress and him being an undead monster. Anyone who's watched *Bride of Frankenstein* knows that there's only one possible solution: Frankenstein's monster – that is to say Adam – needs a mate! Convincing Barnabas and Hoffman (a scientist) to help him (by kidnapping perpetual kidnapping victim Vicki), Adam gets his wish: his very own Eve, a murderer played with relish by Marie Wallace.

Robert Rodan (left) as Adam, *Dark Shadows'* handsome analogue to Frankenstein's monster, and Alex Stevens as the werewolf; Don Briscoe played lycanthrope Chris Jennings in his human form.

There's actually quite a bit of *Bride of Frankenstein* here: the idea of the Bride and the more thoroughly sympathetic creature are all callbacks to that sequel, and Adam's fall from the hill before being discovered alive is reminiscent of the entire Universal Monsters oeuvre – a monster would "die" at the end of one film, only for the subsequent movie to reveal that all wasn't as it seemed. It's worth remembering, as well, that the grunting beast of the first 1931 *Frankenstein* film was less reflective of Mary Shelley's vision than the sensitive, talking monster of the second. In Adam's ability to communicate, he's more faithful still. Well, more or less.

Again, here was *Dark Shadows* taking a classic monster, stripping it down to its most beloved and fundamental elements, and then dropping it like a bomb on a sleepy, but spooky New England town.

Carolyn was unlucky in love once again when Chris Jennings (Don Briscoe) arrived in Collinsport with his younger sister, Amy (Denise Nickerson[8]), and investigating the death of their brother, Tom. Naturally, Chris has a secret: he's a werewolf, in the traditional mold, and certainly inspired by the 1941 Lon Chaney, Jr. movie *The Wolf Man* and its sequels. Like the Larry Talbot character in those films, Jennings is returning to his hometown following the death of a sibling. In the movie, the brother's death is just a means to set the plot in motion but, Collinsport being Collinsport, Tom had been a vampire.

Chris begins a relationship with Carolyn just as people are dying mysteriously around town (again). Chaining himself to a radiator apparently isn't quite cutting it for the tortured lycanthrope, so he gets some support from Barnabas, who locks him away beneath the Old House, making him just the latest guest to get a rent-free room at Collinwood. Other than allowing *Dark Shadows* to place its own stamp on werewolf mythology, the Jennings storyline is most notable for segueing into one of the show's most convoluted re-imaginings, and for introducing a character who would come to rival Barnabas himself in popularity: David Selby's Quentin Collins.

Though the show still had some time yet in its run, Quentin feels like a character meant to check off as many boxes as possible: he's a ghost at first, and a particularly powerful one, at that. Unlike earlier ghosts who had mostly hung around and made grim pronouncements, this family ghost is vengeful and impossible to exorcise. He quickly goes from scaring the kids to taking over the mansion, forcing the living family out entirely. He's not *just* a ghost, though. Traveling back in time, Barnabas meets the living Quentin: a playboy with a *Jane Eyre*-inspired wife locked in a tower room. When he accidentally kills her, he's subject to a curse that makes him into a werewolf, not at all unlike his descendent Chris Jennings. Fortunately, following a visit to a parallel timeline and a battle with the ancient Leviathans, Quentin is alive in the present thanks to a magical portrait that has absorbed his werewolf curse, aging so he doesn't have to.

That bit is, of course, inspired by Oscar Wilde's *The Picture of Dorian Gray*, but more specifically by the 1945 film version. While the novel was a dark social satire, that movie played up the horror elements. Quentin's story was inspired

---

[8] Who would later become famous as the bubblegum-chewing Violet Beauregarde in 1971's *Willy Wonka & the Chocolate Factory*.

as well by Henry James's gothic novel *The Turn of the Screw*, with many parallels to that book's ghostly character Peter Quint. He's also someone who was murdered and then reanimated as a zombie before being restored to life – and he's a warlock, to boot. While the show had done monsters piecemeal up to that point, Quentin gobbles up monster references and serves as a brilliant amalgam of tropes (ghost, zombie, werewolf, non-aging warlock) that have no business working together, and as proof that *Dark Shadows* is at its best when it's swinging for the fences.

Dark Shadows' reluctant monsters: Jonathan Frid as vampire-turned-hero Barnabas Collins (left) and David Selby as ageless ghost-zombie-werewolf-warlock Quentin Collins.

Though the show ended rather abruptly in 1971, and so never got to fulfill all of its classic monster ambitions,[9] there were others, all suggesting that the show's creatives nurtured a literary interest in monsters – a willingness to dive

---

[9] *Master of Dark Shadows*. Dir. David Gregory. MPI, 2019. Film.

into the source material or, put another way, to crib from the best. In the Parallel Time[10] of 1970, Quentin's good friend Cyrus Longworth (Christopher Pennock) was a scientist (another one) searching for the secret to mankind's evil, specifically looking for a way to separate out humankind's very worst impulses. It's a noble motive, though apparently Robert Louis Stevenson's 1886 classic shocker *Strange Case of Dr Jekyll and Mr Hyde* had never been published in that particular alternate universe – otherwise, Longworth might have known better. After mysterious visitor John Yaeger begins a spree of murder and mayhem in town, it takes quite some time for residents to suspect the mild-mannered scientist, but it eventually becomes clear that the potion has split the doctor in two: good and evil portions of his soul sharing time in a single body. Yaeger murders Longworth's fiancée and falls in love with Maggie (who, like Victoria, is not infrequently kidnapped by thoroughly toxic male characters).

Christopher Pennock in dual Jekyll-Hyde roles as Cyrus Longworth and John Yaeger.

Stevenson's novel ends with just a bit of ambiguity: Jekyll pens something akin to a suicide note, really just an acknowledgement that Hyde is soon to take over entirely and forever. Longworth's fate is somewhat more pat: he's killed by Barnabas in a struggle over Maggie, at which point his friends bemoan his tragic split. The novel that inspired the character emphasizes the duality in all of us; the show, instead, leans into its most successful trope: the conflicted monster. Longworth's hubris is punished, but he earns forgiveness from his old friends in

---

[10] The show's term for alternate timelines, which it explored in a pair of storylines.

death. His story gets a bit of a sequel in the 2013 audio drama *The Enemy Within*, in which we meet, for the first time, the version of Cyrus from the series' primary timeline (once again played by Christopher Pennock). This Cyrus, it turns out... isn't much luckier than his alt-universe version. Instead of resulting from a pseudo-scientific personality split, his John persona exists within Cyrus as a demon, the son of the perfectly named Dark Lord, Diabolos. One simply can't catch a break in Collinsport.[11]

Diabolos, on TV, was an oft-mentioned demonic entity at the heart of *Dark Shadows'* preoccupation with witches and warlocks. The black-hooded figure only appears a couple of times, but he has an influence that begins at least as far back as 1692, when he sends witches under his power to torment the Puritans of Massachusetts. Of course, witches are very real in the show's mythology, and are generally evil (or at least with dark leanings). Given the historical, real-life persecution of "witches," it's more than a bit problematic now to find the show suggesting that, perhaps, they were such dark creatures who might have deserved their fates.

Of course, *Dark Shadows* didn't pioneer that idea: the list of books and movies involving evil witches is extensive, going back at least to the Torah, but works like Nathaniel Hawthorne's *The House of the Seven Gables* were painting a more accurate portrait of the New England witch trials of the late 17th century as far back as 1851. A decade and a half before Diabolos sent his TV witches to wreak havoc, Arthur Miller's play *The Crucible* compared the Salem trials to modern-day McCarthyism, finding neither of them representing humanity at its best. All that having been said, the witches of *Dark Shadows* were some of the show's most powerful, and most fun, female characters.

Diabolos brought forth a warlock to command his not-easily-led witches: Judah Zachery (Michael McGuire), who was executed in 1692, but not before putting the curse on the Collins family without which there would hardly be a show. Around 1840, the spirit of Judah possesses Collins family friend Gerard Stiles (James Storm), who instigates a convoluted, decades-long plot to destroy Collinwood, literally: Barnabas and Julia Hoffman travel to the distant future of 1995 to discover that Stiles had, via his army of zombies, destroyed Collinwood, the culmination of a plan begun 130 years earlier. Fortunately, time travel being

---

[11] The Jekyll and Hyde story would also inspire the plot of the *Dark Shadows* novel *Barnabas, Quentin and Dr. Jekyll's Son*, published in 1971.

what it is, the two were able to revisit the disaster and prevent it. If the show's gender politics often place it firmly in its era and genre, the cross-dimensional, time-traveling vampires and devil-spawned warlocks are a reminder of its overall inventiveness.

Giant sea monsters have literary and religious antecedents going back at least as far as ancient Mesopotamia, with one variety of such creature, called "leviathan" in the Hebrew Bible, serving as a stand-in for then-global power Babylon. Likely inspired by stories of sea gods and demons from the Bible and beyond, writer H. P. Lovecraft created an entire horror mythology in the 1920s and '30s (developed further by later authors like August Derleth) involving impossibly powerful, heavily tentacled creatures from other worlds and dimensions to whom we mere humans are not even ants. Survival, in many Lovecraft stories, depends entirely upon avoiding their notice.

Dark Shadows drew from Lovecraft's short story "The Dunwich Horror" in telling its own tale of the Leviathans, beings who, for budgetary purposes, appeared almost entirely human – though their true forms were meant to be rather different (only the looks of horror on the faces of their victims hinted at their actual shapes). The serpent imagery with which the show frequently associates them doesn't line up neatly with either the mythological leviathans or their Lovecraftian inspirations, though snake creatures do feature elsewhere in Lovecraft's work.

The symbology is thus a little muddled, especially given that the seaside town would have been the perfect setting for a visit from sea monsters. This was, however, a big story to tell on a live-to-tape TV budget, so allowances must be made. Very much as in "Dunwich," the Leviathans' plan involves their own offspring: Jeb Hawkes, played once again by Pennock, who grows quickly to adulthood. His counterpart in the novella, Wilbur Whateley, is born of a human mother and an otherworldly entity – in Lovecraft's oeuvre, any type of mixed parentage guarantees physically repulsive offspring – while Hawkes had been birthed of two Leviathans and given over to human (if possessed) parents, and is thus rather more conventionally attractive. He also has a brother.

Ultimately, the Leviathans begin manipulating victims in their dreams, a power clearly inspired by Lovecraft's retroactively named "Dream Cycle," a series of works (including the novella *The Dream-Quest of Unknown Kadath*) in which characters visit, or are visited by, the sometimes terrifying beings who reside within the "Dreamlands." Ultimately, "Dunwich" is a horror story about a family secret, whereas *Dark Shadows*' Leviathan storyline ends with the culmination of an ages-long war between those creatures and werewolves, thus drawing in local lycanthropes Chris Jennings and Quentin Collins. Still, Lovecraft was and remains a bit more of a deep dive, even for horror fans. Dracula, Frankenstein, and Wolf Man references are near-universally recognized, while pulling from Lovecraft for daytime soap audiences was a bit bolder.

Of course, the show was never entirely limited to the TV screen. Before Barnabas was even a gleam in an ambitious producer's eye, publisher Paperback Library began a series of tie-in novels written by Dan Ross. There's no need to quibble about continuity either with the show, or between it and the various books, movies, audios, reboots, comic books, and newspaper strips – they can all be made to fit into a kind of *Dark Shadows* metaverse with just a little imagination. It's all just Parallel Time.

The first book, *Victoria Winters*, was released barely six months after the show's first broadcast and re-told, with some significant variations, the series' earliest storylines centered around the decidedly un-supernatural arrival of Victoria Winters. Given *Dark Shadows*' love of time travel and parallel dimensions, it's not hard to wrap one's mind around the idea that Vicki could have developed an infatuation with Collins cousin Ernest, a violinist with a mysterious past whom no one could be bothered to mention on television.

Just as the show did, the books came around to incorporating the explicitly supernatural in their own sweet time. The fifth book, 1968's *The Curse of Collinwood*, introduced zombies (the faux-Haitian kind rather than the Romero variety), while the sixth saw Barnabas Collins well and truly take over as the lead. (The show eventually dealt in reanimated corpse-style zombies, with several main characters brought back from the dead as mindless berserkers. Before the series' end, an army of zombies would destroy Collinwood itself).

In the novel *Barnabas, Quentin and the Mummy's Curse*, by Dan Ross, yet another in the endless stream of Collins cousins/squatters arrives and takes up residence on the property surrounding Collinwood, this time in the gate house. This is the heretofore unmentioned Professor Anthony Collins, retired from the Boston Historical Museum. Of course, if you're inclined toward imposing on the moody, catty, but nonetheless thoroughly accommodating Collinwood Collinses, you might as well bring some friends along. The good professor brings four, each of whom will become a murder suspect, and one of whom is cousin Quentin Collins in disguise... for some reason.

As one does, the professor also brings several archaeological artifacts to study while he's living at Collinwood, including the titular mummy. Specifically, it's Pharaoh Rehotip, who we later learn had himself suspended in a death-like state in order to impress his subjects and bring glory to Osiris with his resurrection. His brother Seotris was meant to provide the potion that would restore Rehotip to life but, as in all the best cursed mummy narratives, there was a double-cross: Seotris never bothered to wake his brother up. Luckily, Anthony has the potion, the mummy, and an utter lack of any sort of scientific scruples. He's unexpectedly successful, however, though he hadn't reckoned on several thousand years' worth of physical and mental degradation. Rehotip flees and hides, there are some murders which turn out to involve a poisonous lizard, and the creature is ultimately destroyed.

It's haphazardly plotted, but the signifiers of the cursed mummy genre are all present: there's a curse on Rehotip's sarcophagus that's ignored, as well as a backstory involving Egyptian gods and a wronged Pharaoh. There's no real thematic connection between Rehotip having been wronged by his brother and the mummy's vengeance – which mostly involves him shambling around at night while a lizard haphazardly kills people – but it's at least the outline of the type of mummy story that we might well have gotten had *Dark Shadows* continued on television. It's hard not to imagine that the show would have done it with a bit more panache, even given the novel's lack of budgetary constraints.

There was another weirder and more intriguing spin on pseudo-Egyptian themes around the same time, even if it didn't involve a mummy per se. A 1971 run of the relatively short-lived *Dark Shadows* newspaper strip threw a major twist into the Collinwood mythology, even if it was never mentioned again. Dr. Samar, an expert in rare diseases, has come to town on a hunt for her long-lost husband. Very long-lost, in fact – she's actually the goddess Isis in human form and her husband is the god Osiris. It's not long before she realizes that the amnesiac Osiris's human form is none other than that of Barnabas Collins.

The Mummy (1932) took post-Howard Carter Egyptian exoticism and constructed the mummy narratives almost whole cloth – the plot revolves around Boris Karloff's high priest Imhotep (named for the real-life ancient architect), who is revived in the modern era and begins a decade-long quest to find his lost love, Ankh-es-en-Amon. He discovers her soul (he thinks, at least) in the body of a modern Egyptian (played by the Austrian-American Zita Johann) and decides that the best thing to do is murder her and make her a mummy. In that story, she successfully appeals to Isis for aid. The *Dark Shadows* newspaper strip put a clever twist on this story, not only placing Barnabas in the role of the lost love, but giving him an origin that long predates his encounter with Angelique Bouchard.

Yet another mummy appeared in issue #6 of Gold Key's *Dark Shadows* comic ("Awake to Evil," published in 1970), in which mummified Egyptian sorcerer Amen-Ra causes havoc in Collinsport. The Gold Key line, though divergent from the TV show in several respects, utilized a variety of classic monsters – and introduced a ton of theretofore unmentioned Collins ancestors to the mix.

The *Dark Shadows* newspaper strips (top) gave Barnabas Collins an unexpected new origin as Egyptian god Osiris – with amnesia. Egyptian mummy lore was also featured in *Barnabas, Quentin and the Mummy's Curse* (bottom), one of several spinoff novels by Dan "Marilyn" Ross.

Dark Shadows was a collaborative effort, created and produced by Dan Curtis, developed by Art Wallace, and brought to life by numerous writers, directors, and actors. Curtis had a literary streak, and it showed in spades. In addition to the above examples, the soap mined the Pygmalion story from Greek mythology for the creation of Amanda Harris, while Reverend Trask's fate of being sealed up alive behind a brick wall was inspired by Edgar Allan Poe's "The Cask of Amontillado," and Count Petofi's severed hand riffed on W.W. Jacobs' "The Monkey's Paw."

Numerous other literary works were incorporated into *Dark Shadows'* plotlines as well, including Charles Dickens' *Nicholas Nickleby*, Emily Brontë's *Wuthering Heights*, Henry James' *The Sense of the Past*, Poe's "The Tell-Tale Heart," Shirley Jackson's "The Lottery," Patrick Hamilton's *Gas Light*, and more. Curtis went on to produce seminal, award-winning classics like *The Winds of War* and *War and Remembrance*, while regular show directors like Lela Swift kept dozens of moving parts in line, most of the time, on an inconceivably tight schedule and with no margin for error. The players were essentially producing a new, live play five days a week, and they certainly didn't expect that we'd still be watching decades later.

Even the evocative, if necessarily repetitive, music of Robert Cobert lent to the unmistakable atmosphere which was the key to the show's success. Suggestive mood and a stylized setting were the foundations for everything. The fake fangs and dangling bats were invitations to shudder or to laugh – to willingly suspend disbelief or to go along for fun, even as the actors played the material with deadly earnestness. It wouldn't work without either. The prestige film projects that made monsters into pop-culture phenomena relied on atmosphere in the same way, and filmmakers quickly learned to inject some humor into them, but they weren't generally low-budget affairs. Rarely in the history of monsters has so much been made with so little – a triumph of people and imagination over expensive effects.[12]

---

[12] Sadly, *Dark Shadows* was canceled before the creators were able to present all of the stories they'd hoped to tell and all of the classic monsters they'd hoped to reimagine. Series writer Sam Hall, in a 9 October 1971 *TV Guide* article titled "Here's What Really Happened to Barnabas & Co.", outlined how he'd envisioned each main character's fate, neatly wrapping up many of the show's unresolved plotlines. It's a fascinating read, though much of the future history detailed in that essay has since been negated by the licensed novels and audios.

I Like the Dark: An Exploration of the Monstrous Feminine in Val Lewton's *Cat People* Duology

by Corinna Bechko

Imagine a monster. Maybe it has fur and claws. Big teeth are a popular option. Tentacles and slime rarely go out of style. But no matter the form, this hypothetical creature almost certainly has something else that makes it scary. The secret ingredient looks a lot like strength, but that's not quite it either. Even a penchant for violence doesn't get to the core of this beast. Instead, its true test is our lack of control. After all, as many stories for children preach, a tame monster is really just a helpful member of the community that looks a little different.

Strength, like a horse harnessed to a buggy, is comforting and useful. But if that horse spooks and runs amok, trampling bystanders and pulling that buggy over a cliff, fear is the result. The only difference is that in the first scenario, the horse is controlled by the driver. In the second, the horse — or perhaps the horse's fear — is in charge. Few people would call a horse a monster, but give it the agency to pull the buggy over the cliff on purpose and it becomes one. The dread the second scenario engenders is made acute by the very familiarity that allows the occupants of the vehicle to climb aboard, confident they will make it to their destination. Knowing that doesn't always happen is terrifying. Of course, there's a corollary, too: Encountering a monster is frightening. But *being* a monster is freeing. No wonder there are so few classic film monsters presented as unabashedly feminine.

But wait, what about the Bride of Frankenstein[1] or Dracula's harem of beauties or...? Well, there just aren't that many others. And those cited above have something rather tiresome in common: they are defined, if not outright directed, by their male counterparts. They may be iconic and interesting in their own right, but they are hardly free to create chaos as they see fit, or to menace victims on their own behalf. In short, they lack agency, quite literally in the case of Dracula's brides. They might be tragic, but they are ultimately afterthoughts, and it's pretty rare that they get to have any fun. Even Universal's 1960 film *The Leech Woman* posited a woman who killed only once because she was wronged. After that, her desire was to be beautiful enough to win over the man of her dreams.

Dig a little deeper, though, and it becomes clear that not all classic monsters are so rigidly constrained. Universal's stable of Halloween mask-inspiring characters might define the classic horror genre for the general public, but they were far from the only scary films being made at the time. One of them, Val Lewton's *Cat People*, even caused quite a stir upon its release despite, or perhaps because of, the protagonist being both a monster and a woman.

Cat People in Context

The year was 1942. The world had already gone through one unimaginably horrible global conflict and was now in the midst of a second. In the United States, the sale of new cars had been suspended as every scrap of steel was needed for the war effort. The Voice of America began broadcasting overseas. And perhaps significantly, the law creating the Women's Auxiliary Army Corps (WAAC) was signed by President Franklin D. Roosevelt. The social order was changing fast, although few would realize the implications until well after Victory in Europe Day, still three years in the future. Even so, the absence of young men was already being felt as more women moved into the workforce to

---

[1] We'll take it as a given here that everyone knows she's the monster's bride, not the scientist's.

take up the slack. Not everyone was happy about it, but most thought it was a temporary evil.

For many women, though, this was heady stuff. It's rare that money doesn't translate into a certain amount of independence. And although there had always been working women, most of them had been relatively invisible, laboring on farms or in sweatshops, or taking in washing. Some few rose to prominence in other fields, but it was a hard climb. Yet now there were whole cities' worth of women being recruited to work in military support positions, in airplane factories, and even on the enormous secret project that would eventually yield the atomic bomb. Flush with extra cash, is it any wonder that some of them went to the movies?

Meanwhile, things were changing in Hollywood, too. During the height of the Depression, escapist fantasies were the name of the game. But now Americans seemed to want more realism in their entertainment. Films set in urban environments were common. So was propaganda, as befitted a country newly at war. But horror films still largely dealt with villages tucked into vaguely European countrysides. Over at Universal, 1941 saw the release of *The Wolf Man*, the first entry of what would become a storied franchise. But by 1942, the studio was already putting out its fourth Frankenstein film, *The Ghost of Frankenstein*. Clearly, there was room for something fresh and new.

Into this milieu came Val Lewton,[2] himself an immigrant from Yalta, in what was then the Russian Empire and is now part of Ukraine. He and his sister Olga had been brought to the United States when he was five by their mother, Anna Leventon, a writer who entered the film industry well before Val ever imagined doing so. He grew up in the household of his famous aunt, Alla Nazimova, an actress of some renown whom poet and critic Dorothy Parker once described as the finest Hedda Gabler[3] she had ever seen. It was an upbringing both eccentric and uniquely American, supported completely by the creative output of two strong sisters, one of whom (Alla) semi-openly dated women. It was an unusual arrangement for the time but not unheard of, proving that American society has never been monolithically nuclear despite protestations to the contrary.

Val, for his part, took a winding path into producing motion pictures. He was a journalist (fired for concocting a story), a writer (mostly of serialized

---

[2] Born Vladimir Ivanovich Leventon (Hofschneider).
[3] The title character of playwright Henrik Ibsen's *Hedda Gabler*.

novelizations of other people's films, a strange Möbius strip of a job for such an original mind), and a publicist for David O. Selznick (during which time he supposedly did some uncredited writing on *Gone With the Wind*, including the famous reveal of endless wounded soldiers – despite the fact that he expected the film to be a huge flop). But it's the films he produced at RKO for which he's most remembered. His first assignment there set the tone for much of what was to come, and yet was never quite surpassed. His job was to be responsible for everything about the film as long as it didn't go above its $150,000 budget or run longer than 75 minutes. There was one final caveat: the film he produced had to at least sort of fit the title provided to him: *Cat People*.

Val Lewton's aunt was actress Alla Nazimova, famous for her 1907 performance in Henrik Ibsen's play *Hedda Gabler* (poster art by Sigismund Ivanowski). Pictured are Lewton playfully battling Nazimova (left) and his mother Nina (right).

The result is a stunningly beautiful 73-minute film which cost RKO a reported $134,000 but banked, by some estimates, $4 million at home and double that amount worldwide. Directed by Jacque Torneur and utilizing some of the sets left over from Orson Welles' *The Magnificent Ambersons, Cat People* had a deceptively simple plot: mysterious girl meets super-normal boy. Chaos results.

Simone Simon gets top billing on this *Cat People* poster.

But wait, that's not quite right. There are no boys or girls to be found here. Both of these characters are fully adults, endowed with the agency to chart their own courses, a fact that plays out over the course of the film. So, let's revise that plot. Man falls for woman, but woman has a secret. She believes she will become a vicious giant cat if she allows passion to overcome her, so she won't consummate their marriage. Man is patient, but meanwhile his open book of a coworker is looking more and more appealing. Desperate, woman goes to see a psychiatrist, but his boorishly paternalizing – not to mention creepy – advances ensure that there is no help to be found in that quarter. Too late, she realizes that jealousy and rage are also types of passion. The psychiatrist is seemingly killed, and she is mortally wounded. The man and the other woman end up together, but not by vanquishing the evil beast. Instead, their worldview is shattered and we know that neither of them will ever feel that life is normal and comforting again. The mysterious woman may be dead, but her shadow lingers.

Centering the Working (Cat) Woman

Given Val Lewton's upbringing, it makes sense that he would create more nuanced portrayals of women than the average 1940s fare. DeWitt Bodeen is credited with the screenplay, but Lewton was a driving force behind the structure of the story. It takes nothing away from Bodeen to notice that this same respect for the feminine runs through every film produced by Lewton. What's interesting here, however, is that all of the women in Cat People not only work for a living but value their careers.

From the very first scene, we're told that Irena (Simone Simon, who gives a heart-wrenching performance throughout), the most sympathetic character in the film as well as the monster, is not only a wage-earner but someone who makes art for a living as a fashion designer. This is not a job that's a stopgap between a father's house and marriage. It's a career that takes talent and perseverance to pursue, especially for a recent immigrant to New York City. Can it be a coincidence that Midge Wood has practically the same job in Alfred Hitchcock's 1958 masterpiece Vertigo? Given that both auteurs say a lot about their characters through detail, probably not. Irena's job says that she is disciplined but has a streak of the unpredictable before we know much else about her.

Speaking of working, Irena's foil, Alice Moore (played with confidence and grace by Jane Randolph), is someone who is passionate about her career, too. She knows Oliver (a suitably square Kent Smith), Irena's husband, because they both work at the same office, designing watercraft. Alice is not a secretary, though; she's Oliver's equal, and like Irena, she in no way needs Oliver for security, money, or social status. Even Theresa Harris, the only woman of color featured in the film, is shown as someone who runs the café at which she works, not as a "mere" server. These days, it's common to see women in definable jobs on film, but it's also still common for ladies to be "punished" on screen for showing too much independence. That's what makes seeing so many women in *Cat People* acting independently – entering and leaving relationships of their own volition, walking the streets of New York on their own, and making their own decisions – feel so revolutionary to this day.

Simone Simon as Irena, *Cat People*'s feline femme fatale.

It's also why Irena's affliction, weather real or imagined, feels so tragic. She is not a clockwork woman set in motion by her creators to illustrate a morality tale about what befalls bad girls who don't do as they're told. Instead, she's an individual with a unique personality and background. She's as vulnerable as she is dangerous, madly in love with Oliver but scared of what she might do to him, as she confesses soon after they wed. We see her fear and his tenderness, but we also notice that it is Oliver who moves into Irena's apartment, not the other way around. He does so despite the fact that it's so near the zoo that they can hear the lions roaring, a sound that is "natural and soothing" according to Irena, and the leopard screaming "like a woman."

Throughout it all, both Irena and Alice retain their dignity, cloudy mirrors of each other who nonetheless could have perhaps been friends under different circumstances. Irena is jealous of the brash and forthright Alice, but not without reason. As Alice says, "That's what makes me so dangerous. I'm the new kind of other woman." She never schemes to take Oliver from Irena, but rather tells him straight out that she loves him. Despite that, she does the best she can to help him help Irena, setting up an appointment with Dr. Louis Judd, a psychiatrist with an interest in the occult. It's never explicitly stated in this film that this is Judd's specialty, but in *The 7th Victim*, a Lewton production released the year after *Cat People*, Judd reappears at a party full of Satanists.

Judd is cocky about his abilities, and it is telling that he is also the only character to suffer for his overreach. "And what if *I* were to kiss you?" he says, leaning forward as if he means to try to tempt out the cat. "I only know that I should not like to be kissed by you," Irena replies before leaving. Later, at the climax of the film, she does allow the kiss, but she does so rigidly, showing no emotion. It is left to the audience to realize that she has been pushed to the edge, that this is an act of rebellion, not of obedience. The monstrous creature within her is unbound, embodying her rage and sadness, while Judd is apparently killed despite defending himself with a sword. Irena dies, too, but not before returning to human form. Her last act is to release the leopard in the zoo below her apartment, as if to drive home the point that freedom can be dangerous even though the desire for it never disappears.

Of Cats and Kittens

Cat People was a complete story unto itself, but it was also a huge success. Even in the 1940s, that meant a sequel was inevitable. And so Lewton's team was handed a new title, minus a plot once again. 1944's *The Curse of the Cat People* was no doubt intended by the studio to replicate the formula of the first *Cat* film. Instead, they got a weirdly charming, dark suburban fairytale, a continuation of Irena's story in the most oblique way possible. The main cast remains mostly unchanged, as does the scriptwriter, Bodeen. Robert Wise shares directing credit with Gunther von Fritsch this time, dampening some of the inventive flair found in the original, but Val Lewton's touch is still felt throughout.

The Curse of the Cat People failed to live up to the success of its predecessor.

The setting is at least seven years after the original story. Alice and Oliver have married and had a child, Amy (Ann Carter), who is now six years old. Alice has become a housewife, but their kid is not the all-American, no-nonsense daughter that might be expected from such a couple. Instead she is a dreamer and a loner, taking after someone she has never met: Oliver's first wife, Irena.

Like the first film, almost everyone aside from Oliver is female. Also like that film, he seems completely out of his depth when asked to deal with these mysterious creatures. But unlike in *Cat People*, there is no way to read Irena as a monster here. Although she still occupies the liminal space between the real and imagined when she appears to Amy dressed in a diaphanous dress that sparkles with captured starlight, she is a soothing influence, someone who will believe in and encourage the child when no one else is willing to take her seriously. It is almost as though Irena has bested her inner demon by releasing the leopard and has ascended into a peaceful, perhaps even beatific state in death. It is not lost on the viewer that she often appears outside. Walls can no longer hold her. In the first film, she had told Oliver, "I like the dark. It's friendly." At the time, this seemed a peculiar, menacing thing to say. But when we remember it here, we see that she makes the statement true for Amy, showing her that dreams and fantasies can lead to a richer life, no matter what her father has to say on the subject.

Naturally, Oliver and Alice worry about their strange, imaginative daughter, especially when her invented world interferes with the real one. And they can't help thinking of Irena, fearing that the shadow of her bizarre obsession portends a similar malady in Amy. They are never cast as villains for their protective tendencies, though, even as they discourage her from befriending an aged and befuddled actress (a vibrant Julia Dean). Indeed, their fears are realized when the actress's daughter Barbara (played deliciously by Elizabeth Russell), blinded by jealousy of her mother's affections, attempts to strangle Amy. Her loss of control is far from supernatural, but nonetheless born of impassioned rage. It's apparent that unleashing our inner monsters can happen without resorting to the uncanny.

Interestingly, it is Irena who saves Amy. She does so not by unchaining her own demons, but by tricking Amy into showing Barbara unfettered affection, something she is obviously in need of receiving. Barbara can't help but be charmed, and we are left with the impression that Amy will have a new champion in her corner as Irena fades from view. Even Oliver is changed afterwards for the better, convinced now that he must meet Amy on her own emotional terms in a way that he could never do with Irena. Both families are strengthened, thanks to the intervention of a reformed monster. Or is it thanks to her invention? We are left to draw our own conclusions, even as we acknowledge it might not matter where the truth lies as long as the dream is memorable.

Sympathy for the Devil Cat

Taken together, these films may be 143 of the strangest minutes in classic monster history. Irena's cat/woman dichotomy could have been a sexist retelling of the Wolf Man story, a tale of female hysteria and the dangers of untamed lady folk. Instead, we get a sympathetic portrayal of a working woman with deep insecurities who isn't believed when she tells the truth about herself. Her happiness is denied to her not because of what she does, but because of a past she can't escape. Like many classic monsters, this makes her a tragic and sympathetic character. We are as frightened *for* her as we are *of* her. We want her to find love, but know it is as impossible for her as it is for the Creature from the Black Lagoon, Frankenstein's monster, or the Wolf Man.

The difference, though, is that even when she loses control of the monster cat inside her, she maintains her humanity. The scenes in *Cat People* staged at a pool and on a darkened city street as Irena stalks Alice are among the scariest and most inventive moments of 20th-century film. Jump scares get a bad rap these days, but when the bus pulls up with a loud hiss just as we think the leopard is about to strike, we react as if it's the first time the trick has been pulled – and, at the time, it very nearly was.

In contrast, the 1982 remake (also called *Cat People*), directed by Paul Schrader and written by Alan Ormsby, leans heavily into the idea that humanity might not be something worth retaining. In this erotic retelling, much of the subtext is made text as New York's concrete canyons are traded for the closer-to-nature steamy streets of New Orleans. The idea of love as sacrifice comes full circle as Irena chooses to become a docile beast literally caged by her beloved rather than retain her freedom and principles, as she does in the original. In a way, it gives Irena a twisted version of what Alice ends up with in *Curse of the Cat People*, minus the child. It also remains one of only a handful of films to portray a zookeeper in a positive light – an interesting claim to fame for a story so concerned with captivity both accepted and imposed.

As for the 1942 version, the fact that this *Cat People* is set in New York City in the same year it was released makes if feel worlds away from the Gypsy caravans and haunted castles popular in other classic monster fare. This is our world, *Cat People* tells us, but that doesn't mean we don't have to be afraid of monsters. City lights can't chase away all our fears, and they might even enhance our worst impulses. It's a starkly adult concept, but not one without a corollary. Embrace the darkness, *The Curse of the Cat People* replies, and you may find wonder as well as horror. Monsters hide in the shadows, and that's exactly why some of us like the dark.

Godzilla vs. Continuity: Toho's Shōwa-Era Shared Film Universe

by Rich Handley

From *Alien vs. Predator* and M. Night Shyamalan's *Unbreakable* trilogy to the Marvel Cinematic Universe (MCU) and DC's Arrowverse, shared universes have become all the rage. A shared universe comprises multiple movies created independently by different writers, directors, and/or casts that, though designed to stand on their own merits, are incorporated into a larger storyline combining each film's characters and concepts. With the MCU, that crossing over was by design, but that hasn't always been the case with other franchises, particularly those involving classic monsters.

One of the first, the Universal Monsters, can be maddening when it comes to continuity, with viewers forced to jump through Möbius strip-like mental hoops in a vain effort to make sense of the contradictions.[1] That doesn't make the movies less enjoyable, yet one can't help but roll one's eyes and chuckle when things don't add up. Anyone who has followed Toho's giant monster films knows this is something Toho and Universal have in common.

---

[1] See Joseph Berenato's essay "A New World of Gods and Monsters: Universal Studios and the First Shared Cinematic Universe."

Oh, No – There Goes Tokyo

Japanese film production and distribution company Toho is the studio behind the long-running Godzilla series, which has been going strong since 1954. Toho has produced an impressive variety of movies since its launch in 1935, but it is arguably best known for its *kaiju* (giant monster) and *tokusatsu* (special effects-heavy) offerings, particularly those featuring its most popular creations: Godzilla, Mothra, King Ghidorah, Rodan, and Mechagodzilla.

There have been 36 movies starring Godzilla as of press-time, up to and including the impending release of *Godzilla vs. Kong*, with more in the planning stages. Watching them all, even the weaker entries, can be greatly satisfying, but no one with a rational mind would describe Toho's shared universe as having a cohesive continuity. The films often contradict each other, the timeline has been rebooted multiple times, and movies that supposedly take place within the same reality seem incompatible with one another. Regardless, the series is eminently rewatchable, which makes the Godzilla franchise rather unique, as fans of other universes might not be so forgiving.

Consider how annoyed some MCU fans might be if, say, Iron Man's origin changed from one film to the next; or if the studio decreed that only movies 1, 7, 14, and 23 were canon and the rest never happened; or if each alien incursion were presented as the first, with those from prior films ignored. Ticket sales would plummet and the internet would be awash with melodramatically outraged fans accusing Marvel and Disney of destroying their childhood. But that's not typically the case with Toho's fan base. When things change (and they frequently do), Godzilla fandom tends to simply shrug and accept it, hoping the next movie will be as enjoyable as the last. It usually is, too.

The Godzilla films are often remembered as goofy stories with silly-looking monster costumes, hilarious English dubbing, and throngs of terrified masses running through the streets as Tokyo is toppled for the two-dozenth time. But there's a lot more to the series than that. For one thing, the movies need to be viewed in their original Japanese, with English subtitles. Dubbing can be painfully bad, particularly when American voice actors make racially stereotypical or downright bizarre acting choices. There's not a single Japanese-made Godzilla film that isn't magnitudes better when viewed with subtitles instead of dubbing. It's an entirely different experience, and the franchise's reputation has suffered from the dubbed versions being more widely known.

The first movie, 1954's *Gojira*, offered a poignantly powerful metaphor for the United States' atomic-bomb testing of the 1950s, as well as its bombing of

Hiroshima and Nagasaki a decade prior. The film was inspired by *The Beast from 20,000 Fathoms*, a 1953 Warner Bros. science-fiction production and one of the very first atomic monster movies ever made. That had featured a giant reptilian creature attacking a major city after being awakened by the detonation of an atom bomb, with stop-motion animation by visual effects master Ray Harryhausen.

While it's undeniable that the Godzilla series evolved over time into something more comical and family-friendly, *Gojira* is a genuine masterpiece of filmmaking, providing insight into how World War II and the subsequent bomb testing profoundly affected the Japanese people. For them, the cinematic debut of Godzilla – or Gojira, as the creature is called in the original Japanese – wasn't about an actor in a rubber monster suit stepping on miniature buildings and model trains. Rather, it was a testament to how the nation had suffered during the war and in its aftermath. Japanese audiences recognized what the monster represented, and it resonated strongly.

"The theme of the film, from the beginning, was the terror of the bomb," producer Tomoyuki Tanaka was quoted as saying in a *Virginia Quarterly Review* article.[2] "Mankind had created the bomb, and now nature was going to take revenge on mankind." Director Ishirō Honda, in that same article, expressed a similar sentiment: "After the war, all of Japan, as well as Tokyo, was left in ashes. The atomic bomb had emerged and completely destroyed Hiroshima... If Godzilla had been a dinosaur or some other animal, he would have been killed by just one cannonball. But if he were equal to an atomic bomb, we wouldn't know what to do. So I took the characteristics of an atomic bomb and applied them to Godzilla."

It's a bit odd, then, that Godzilla would become heroic in later movies, actually *protecting* mankind from *kaiju* and aliens alike. It's telling, too, that the version of this America-critical movie that is most known to Americans is a remarkably different story – one starring an American actor. In 1956, a heavily edited English-language adaptation of *Gojira* was released outside Japan as *Godzilla, King of the Monsters!*. This version not only changed the order of events, but also replaced most of the Japanese dialogue that could be viewed as criticizing the United States, while a good deal of new footage was inserted

---

[2] Ryfle, Steve. "Godzilla's Footprint." *Virginia Quarterly Review*. Winter 2005: https://www.vqronline.org/vqr-portfolio/godzilla%E2%80%99s-footprint.

starring Raymond Burr (later of *Perry Mason* and *Ironside* fame). The actor, playing American news correspondent Steve Martin, spends the movie standing on the sidelines passively observing and commenting on events,[3] which really slows it down.

This was done to make the movie more marketable to a U.S. audience, but it shouldn't have been. The end result, combined with cringeworthy dubbing, is an inferior film. What had originated as a tragic metaphor for war, with strong acting and depth of characterization, was reduced to a mere monster flick with flat voice acting and far less substance. The characters of Daisuke Serizawa, Kyohei Yamane, Emiko Yamane, and Hideo Ogata have noticeably more screen time in the Japanese version and thus seem more lifelike, whereas in the American adaptation, they become background players in their own movie so Raymond Burr can have more time to stand around silently frowning. It's no surprise much of the film's impact was lost on audiences in the West.

Up From the Depths, Thirty Stories High

From the standpoint of a shared film universe, the problem the above represents should be apparent: If the Godzilla films form an ongoing continuity, which version do we count as canonical? The original Japanese release with the metaphor intact? The badly dubbed Raymond Burr vehicle that the rest of the world watched? Or both, despite the differences? This dilemma would only be compounded by later films, particularly *Godzilla Raids Again*, *Varan*, and *King Kong vs. Godzilla*, each of which would receive the same butchering treatment from the studio.

The first 15 Godzilla films, released from 1954 to 1975, comprise what is known as the Shōwa era, corresponding to the reign of Japanese Emperor Hirohito (posthumously known as Shōwa), who died in 1989. This was followed by seven more movies produced between 1984 and 1995, during the Heisei era (representing the reign of Emperor Akihito, who abdicated in 2019 and will be called Heisei once he dies); six films that hit theaters from 1999 to 2004, known as the Millennium series; and four released from 2016 to the present (three of them animated), collectively dubbed the Reiwa era even though that period

---

[3] And never once delivering a standup comedy routine while playing a banjo and wearing a fake arrow through his head – which will likely make no sense whatsoever to readers under age thirty.

didn't actually start until 2019, when Naruhito (who will posthumously be known as Reiwa) became Japan's current monarch.

Each series has its own continuity (or multiple continuities, in the case of Millennium and Reiwa), with the Shōwa films largely ignored by later series other than the first movie. Two American adaptations have brought the atomic monster across the ocean: TriStar Pictures' much-maligned 1998 film starring Matthew Broderick, directed by Roland Emmerich, and Legendary Pictures' far more acclaimed 2014 outing starring Bryan Cranston, from director Gareth Edwards, which has spawned two sequels (and counting) after breaking non-bad at the box office.

In 1978, after the Shōwa era had ended, Godzilla starred in a self-titled Hanna-Barbera cartoon best known for foisting upon the world his cowardly nephew Godzooky and a cringeworthy theme song. The monster has also been featured in Japanese TV shows aimed at children, including *Ike! Godman* (1972–1973), *Ike! Greenman* (1973–1974), *Zone Fighter* (1973), *Godzilland* (1992–1996), and *Godzilla Island* (1997–1998). And in August 2019, the Web series *Gojiban* debuted on Toho's official YouTube channel,[4] performed by puppet theater group Atelier Koganemushi and featuring puppet versions of Godzilla and his offspring, Minilla (Shōwa) and Godzilla Junior (Heisei). These shows complicate the franchise's already convoluted continuity, for Toho considers *Zone Fighter* an official part of the Shōwa series, while the others stand outside the movies' events. Meanwhile, TriStar's film was absorbed into the Millennium line, along with its spinoff TV show, *Godzilla: The Series*.

For our purposes, we'll focus on the Shōwa era. What is it that qualifies this era as a shared film universe, rather than just a string of sequels? Well, in addition to 15 Godzilla films, the Shōwa run incorporated seven non-Godzilla movies into the fold – *Rodan* (1956), *Varan* (1958), *Mothra* (1961), *Atragon* (1963), *Frankenstein vs. Baragon* (1965), *The War of the Gargantuas* (1966), and *King Kong Escapes* (1967) – bringing the total up to 22.[5] The Heisei era also included non-Godzilla films (the *Rebirth of Mothra* trilogy), while the post-

---

[4] https://www.youtube.com/channel/UC5XRZP9kwJ5g0rYqPpBaPrA

[5] Or 23, if you count *The Mysterians*, which I don't for the purpose of this essay (more on that later). I realize some fans do not view these seven (or eight) films as part of Godzilla continuity, much like the 1933 *King Kong* film does not take place alongside *King Kong vs. Godzilla* or *King Kong Escapes*. Your mileage may vary, but I'll let my reasoning speak for itself.

Shōwa movies acknowledged four *kaiju* films of that era: *The Mysterians* (1957), featuring Moguera, which would return in Heisei's *Godzilla vs. SpaceGodzilla*; *Gorath* (1962) and *Dogora* (1964), which would be worked into the backstory of the Millennium series' *Godzilla: Tokyo S.O.S.*; and *Space Amoeba* (1970, a.k.a. *Yog – Monster From Space*), which featured Kamoebas, a *kaiju* whose corpse would show up in *Tokyo S.O.S.*

Confused yet? Just wait, because it gets more complicated still. At least 11 separate timelines exist in the Godzillaverse, and that's without the various novels, comics, cartoons, kids' shows, and video games, which have continuities of their own.[6] It's the Shōwa-era films, though, that are most familiar to Western filmgoers, thanks to their having frequently aired on U.S. television in the 1970s and 1980s.[7] Unfortunately, these were the heavily edited, English-dubbed translations, but the advent of DVDs and Blu-rays has enabled audiences outside Japan to experience these wonderful movies the way they were always intended to be experienced: in Japanese, with their cut footage restored, and without any peculiar American additions.

What makes the Shōwa Godzilla films worth watching again and again is that the series, though formulaic, presented a plethora of story types, with the 22 films approaching the subject matter from some truly unexpected directions. Along the way, they also introduced some regrettable story gaps large enough to walk a giant fire-breathing dinosaur through, as the writers played fast and loose with internal logic and inter-film continuity. And it all started with...

Gojira (1954, a.k.a. *Godzilla, King of the Monsters!*)

A radioactive dinosaur threatens Tokyo until a reclusive, philosophically troubled scientist uses his latest invention to destroy the creature, sacrificing his own life rather than letting his work become a superweapon.

---

[6] For more information, see
https://wikizilla.org/wiki/List_of_Godzilla_film_continuities and
https://godzilla.fandom.com/wiki/Continuity.
[7] Amusingly, *M*A*S*H*'s Walter "Radar" O'Reilly seems to have watched the films before they were even made. In the episode "Springtime," he invites a nurse to go see *Firstborn of Godzilla* (which is not an actual film title), remarking, "I saw the original, before Godzilla got married" (which never happened in any of the films). The Korean War, during which that show was set, ended in 1953, whereas Godzilla would not make his theatrical debut until a year later. Then again, Radar *was* amazingly skilled at procuring things.

The original *Gojira* is so much more than just a mere monster movie.

In his inaugural outing, Gojira is a terrifying monstrosity and certainly not a friend to humanity. His emersion from the ocean depths causes one shipwreck after another, he's described as feeding on humans to survive, and ancient fishermen are said to have sacrificed women to prevent Gojira from eating everyone in sight. In later films, shipwrecks no longer seem to be an issue, and the monster — hereafter called Godzilla — is never presented as carnivorous (which could indicate the villagers of Odo Island have built a less-than-accurate legend around the beast). A scientist postulates that the monster is a dinosaur from the Cretaceous period: "an [intermediate] creature somewhere between the marine reptiles and the evolving terrestrial animals." Having survived the millennia by ingesting deep-sea organisms, he has returned to the surface to feed, roused by experimental nuclear detonations carried out by the United States that have drastically altered its natural habitat.

As this first film explains, Gojira was an ordinary dinosaur that absorbed an enormous amount of atomic radiation. Later entries would change his origin story as necessary, because who needs consistency? Here, Godzilla grows enraged at having lights shined on him, as he prefers darkness. The sequels, on the other hand, would show him walking around in bright sunlight with no problem and even sunning himself on a beach. He tramples and melts electric lines as though they're not even there, whereas other movies would show him alternately absorbing electrical energy to grow stronger or finding electricity extremely painful.

As noted, the American adaptation features reporter Steve Martin dispassionately observing events, with a Japanese narrator translating from the sidelines. New scenes involving Martin are inserted into the previously shot footage,[8] but these mostly consist of him reporting back to his home office about the events of the Japanese version instead of the filmmakers actually showing what has transpired, violating the cardinal narrative rule of "show, don't tell." The focus is now on the American observer instead of the Japanese cast, resulting in a highly altered story. Martin talks Emiko into urging Doctor Serizawa to use the Oxygen Destroyer to eliminate the monster, drastically reducing the emotional impact of Emiko's betrayal of her fiancé's trust since it wasn't even her idea now. Serizawa is particularly marginalized to make room for Burr's addition, making the scientist's self-sacrifice less monumental since the audience barely knows him or his philosophical conundrum.

New scenes were also added for an Italian re-edit made in 1976 by director Luigi Cozzi, nicknamed *Cozzilla* by fans. Cozzi had faced exhibitor resistance to

---

[8] Kind of like *Back to the Future Part II*, but with no manure... well, other than the dubbing, which reduces Kyohei Yamane to repeatedly mispronouncing "phenomenon" as "phenonemum."

showing a black-and-white film in Italy, so he instead licensed a negative of the American cut and used it to create a new movie utilizing a rather psychedelic color palette, adding in graphic stock footage of destruction and death, along with a new soundtrack and World War II newsreel footage – and, admittedly, it's surprisingly effective.[9] Toho now owns the Italian version and retains the negatives, which means there are three official yet vastly different versions of *Gojira*.

So to which version's continuity should the sequels be beholden? Which is part of the shared universe? The obvious answer would be the Japanese original, but the situation isn't so clear-cut, for when the Heisei series launched in 1984 with *The Return of Godzilla*, an American adaptation was created as a sequel to *Godzilla, King of the Monsters!* rather than *Gojira* – and, yes, Raymond Burr even returned to reprise the role of the wild and crazy guy he'd played 30 years prior. Then...

Godzilla Raids Again (1955, a.k.a. *Gigantis, the Fire Monster*)

Another member of Godzilla's species fights a fellow monster, Anguirus, then goes on to attack Osaka until the Japanese military buries this new Godzilla in an avalanche of ice.

During the climax of *Gojira*, the atomic dinosaur is shown dissolving entirely thanks to Serizawa's Oxygen Destroyer. So how did Toho turn the movie into a long-running series? Simple: by introducing a second Godzilla to take his place thereafter. The first sequel, *Godzilla Raids Again*, was released the following year, and in a rare case of human characters returning in later movies, Doctor Yamane made another appearance. This made sense, for in *Gojira*'s final scenes it was the scientist who'd noted, "I can't believe that Godzilla was the only surviving member of its species... but if we keep on conducting nuclear tests, it's possible that another Godzilla might appear somewhere in the world again." As it happens, he was right.

Alas, American edits created cringeworthy continuity snafus, since the movie was released overseas as *Gigantis, the Fire Monster*, with the creature called Gigantis rather than Godzilla, even though it's very clear the actor is wearing a Godzilla suit. In the Japanese original, he's simply a second member of Godzilla's species. *Gigantis* opens with a newly added dramatic narration

---

[9] *Cozzilla* can be viewed here: https://www.youtube.com/watch?v=l1qRxEY0USQ.

about a hydrogen bomb's mushroom cloud, along with a montage of missile warnings around the world and, bizarrely, a vague cautioning about space exploration:

> As the missiles and rockets scream through the upper atmosphere, man hopes ultimately to reach other planets, seeking to find the answers to worlds outside his own. But as he attempts to unlock the mystery of the universe in which he dwells, are there not darker and more sinister secrets on this planet Earth, still unanswered, still baffling and defying man? With each step forward, does he not take several steps back? This, then, is the story of the price of progress to a little nation of people.

It really isn't, though. In fact, the narration has precious little to do with the rest of the movie, which contains no space-travel elements. Following the opening credits, main character Shoichi Tsukioka begins narrating the film (which he doesn't do in the Japanese version), with a focus on Osaka City's tuna fishing industry, accompanied by stock footage of rural workers. This creates a different cinematic experience since the movie is now told from Tsukioka's point-of-view, so viewers learn more about the character's inner workings – and, well, about tuna fishing.

Unfortunately, the Americanized script often makes little sense, and *Godzilla Raids Again* is a far better film than *Gigantis, the Fire Monster*. Gigantis and Anguirus are both described as "fire monsters," even though Anguirus displays no fire-breathing ability, and even though Godzilla himself expels atomic breath, not flame. The dialogue in the Yamane scene is particularly nonsensical, as it claims Gigantis is a member of the Anguirus family, despite their clearly being from different species. The film that Yamane shows in *Raids* (containing footage of Anguirus, as well as from *Gojira*) is replaced in *Gigantis* with an irrelevant documentary about Earth's formation, climate change, and silly-looking fire-based creatures that he claims once ruled the planet, which in no way furthers the plot. Plus, where the heck would he have found recorded footage from prehistoric times?

Godzilla remains light-sensitive in this movie, which is attributed to his retaining memories of the hydrogen bomb tests. As such, the military can lure him away from land with citywide blackouts and decoy flares – a tactic that might have been helpful in the sequels but is never used again. He's also drawn to a city on fire following the explosions of several buildings. Imagine how different the other sequels might have been had Godzilla's hostility toward bright light continued to manifest.

The movie introduced the series' second *kaiju*, Anguirus (or Angilas — the spelling changes from one film to the next in the English subtitles). After several battles, Godzilla fatally bites a chunk out of Anguirus's neck, then sets him on fire, causing his body to burn away along with half of Osaka City. This, of course, doesn't stop Anguirus from showing up in other movies, alive and entirely unburnt — or from becoming Godzilla's pal, because that's how this franchise rolls. A fleet of planes drops numerous bombs to bury Godzilla in an avalanche of ice, which he could probably melt away with his atomic breath and glowing atomic spine, but oddly does not. And there he remains until his next appearance. But first...

Rodan (1956, a.k.a. *Giant Monster of the Sky, Radon; Rodan! The Flying Monster!*)

Giant insects called Meganulons, as well as a pair of flying pterosaurs each known as Rodan, terrorize a small mining village located near a volcano.

A year after *Godzilla Raids Again* hit theaters, Toho introduced its latest *kaiju*: a pair of giant *Pteranodon*, each called Radon in Japan but Rodan internationally.[10] The two Rodans can level cities with the force of their flapping wings. They can also emit a burst of gas from their mouths as a weapon — an ability the species never displays in other films, even when that would have proved extremely useful. The U.S. translation opens with an English-narrated sequence about American military forces carrying out hydrogen bomb testing, unaware their efforts will awaken "a horror still undreamed of." The film is then (as with *Gigantis*) narrated from the perspective of its protagonist, Shigeru Kawamura, resulting in a different viewing experience. You may notice a pattern emerging regarding how overseas releases changed the early movies.

Rodan remains one of Toho's finest monster films. The scenes of the two *Pteranodons* wreaking destruction are exciting, considering when these movies were made and the low budget involved. The Japanese cast members turn in

---

[10] The name "Radon," a contraction of *Pte**RA**no**DON***, also recalls Ladon, a serpent-like dragon from Greek mythology. For English-speaking audiences, the producers changed it to "Rodan" out of concern that viewers might mistake the monster as being related to radon, a radioactive chemical element, because American audiences are often assumed to be stupid. See also the James Bond film *License to Kill*, which had been titled *License Revoked* until that was changed during post-production after a polled audience associated the term with driving. (OK, point taken... American audiences *are* stupid.)

strong performances and are given interesting characters to play, and the English dubbing isn't nearly as distracting as in other movies. One common complaint about Toho's films is that the acting is terrible, but that claim is inaccurate. The *voice acting in the U.S. releases* frequently leaves much to be desired, but in the original Japanese, the actors typically come off as far more natural. *Rodan*'s voice actors were well-chosen, though, including *Star Trek*'s George Takei, *Kung Fu*'s Keye Luke, and *The Rocky and Bullwinkle Show*'s Paul Frees.

Rodan lost his toothed beak and chestnut color after his 1956 debut.

At the time of its release, *Rodan* was not yet part of Godzilla's continuity. It was merely a separate *kaiju* film that stood brilliantly on its own. So when Toho later incorporated Rodan into the Godzilla films, this retroactively created a noticeable gaffe in *Rodan*. The discovery of the Meganulons (which would return decades later in the Millennium series' *Godzilla vs. Megaguiras*) leaves the masses in stunned shock, as though they've never seen a giant monster before. Then, when the first Rodan shows up, scientists suddenly realize prehistoric creatures long thought extinct now roam the Earth. There's no mention of Godzilla's first two movies, not even when the theory is put forth that the creatures may have been awakened by bomb testing – which, keep in mind, is exactly what roused the first Gojira (and presumably the second).[11]

A physicist in the film even comments, "We are in the age of advanced science. It is not a dream to travel to space now. It's hard to believe in the existence of such a thing in nature." Hard to believe, sure... if it weren't for the three dinosaurs (two Godzillas and Anguirus) who'd just run rampant through Japan, leveling cities and generally causing widespread mayhem. Yet when Rodan joins the Godzilla lineup, characters know who he is, confirming that this film is indeed within the same continuity. What's more problematic is that both original Rodans are incinerated when a missile bombardment levels the volcanic mountain containing their nest. So who, then, is the Rodan in the Godzilla movies? A *third* Rodan, perhaps? Meanwhile...

Varan (1958, a.k.a. *Varan the Unbelievable*)

An expedition to study a new species of butterflies culminates in a scientific team encountering a deadly creature called Varan, worshipped by local villagers.

Two years later, Toho unveiled another *kaiju* in the form of a triphibian reptile called Varan whom superstitious villagers worship as their mountain god, Baradagi. No mention is made of Godzilla or other previously introduced monsters, which makes sense since *Varan* was released as a standalone film. Varan/Baradagi would later return in *Destroy All Monsters*, though, making this movie part of the Godzilla franchise in hindsight.

As with *Rodan*, this created a retroactive continuity problem, since no one in *Varan* takes the idea of a living prehistoric monster seriously, indicating they've never heard of Anguirus, the Rodans, or the Godzillas. A character even scoffs, "This is the twentieth century. How can you be so foolish?" and says he finds it "unbelievable that Varan could still be alive after millions of years." If this is the same continuity as the previous movies, which it is, then everyone in

---

[11] On the other hand, as proofreader John Hazlett astutely notes: "After the appearance of the Meganulons, but before Rodan first appears, doctors are attempting to jog Shigeru's amnesiac memory by showing him pictures of prehistoric life. The final picture they show him is of the Meganulon he killed, which makes sense; but in a world where these bugs are the only prehistoric monsters that have ever appeared, why would they expect pictures of a *Triceratops* or *Pteranodon* to trigger Shigeru's memory? It's almost like they half-expected a giant Mesozoic reptilian to also have been awakened, too – an expectation that only makes any sense if it's happened before..."

Japan should find prehistoric monsters commonplace by now. His reaction should be, "Oh, man, not *another* one!"

The movie's English-language release is virtually unrecognizable. Just as *Gojira* had become a Raymond Burr film for U.S. viewers, *Varan* was re-edited as *Varan the Unbelievable* for overseas release, with a team of American heroes undertaking an unrelated mission, played by a new cast of actors. While the monster scenes from *Varan* were reused, it's otherwise an entirely different movie. The original is about researchers visiting an island in search of a rare species of butterflies, whereas the U.S. adaptation concerns a heroic U.S. Navy commander, his submissive Japanese wife, and his loyal Japanese soldier sidekick evacuating a village so the Americans can test a chemical designed to desalinate water. Both Asian actors no doubt cringed their way through every subservient line; the movie might as well have been renamed *Varan the Whitewashed*.

One *could* view both versions as separate stories since they've been released separately on DVD. However, that would mean the monster would have to die twice and the villagers would need to undergo the same physical actions in two sets of circumstances. Conversely, the stories could be happening simultaneously at different parts of the island, but that doesn't work either since they don't jibe well – in fact, they don't even appear to take place on the same island. The Japanese version is set in the mountains of Tōhoku, in Iwaya Village, on the main island of Honshū, with Varan dying at Tokyo's Haneda Airport. Meanwhile, the American adaptation occurs on Kunashira Shima, in the Kuril Islands,[12] with the final battle being fought in a fictional city called Onita. Plus, Varan is called Obaki in the U.S. release,[13] despite the movie not being titled *Obaki the Unbelievable*.

Ultimately, Varan is destroyed by being tricked into swallowing two bombs. As such, his return in *Destroy All Monsters* throws continuity to the wind (though, hey, if Anguirus and Rodan can come back from the dead, Varan might as well, too). This is one instance in which the American iteration comes in handy, for it ends with a narration noting that the monster could have survived in the ocean depths. Thankfully, this was followed by...

---

[12] Which, incidentally, has been Soviet territory, not Japanese, since the end of World War II.

[13] Or Obake – the spelling has been inconsistent throughout the years.

Mosura (1961, a.k.a. *Mothra*)

An uncontacted culture is discovered on Infant Island, home to a giant creature called Mothra. When a capitalist steals her egg, the peaceful deity goes on the offensive to retrieve her offspring.

The benevolent Mothra is among Toho's most popular monsters – and she arguably isn't even a monster at all.

It's no wonder *Mothra* is so beloved by *kaiju* fans. It's a beautifully made movie helmed by Ishirō Honda, who not only directed some of Toho's best films (including *Gojira*, *Rodan*, and others discussed below)[14] but also collaborated with master filmmaker Akira Kurosawa. The movie features some of Toho's most lifelike human characters, a healthy dose of humor mixed in with the drama and destruction, and a wonderful twist on the *kaiju* formula: the monster isn't the benevolent Mothra, but rather human greed and corruption.

The movie stands out among Toho's monster films for its cinematic scope and creative costuming. It makes great use of music thanks to the introduction of tiny twin faeries – or "Shobijin" ("small beauties"), as they're dubbed by Senichiro Fukuda, delightfully portrayed by Frankie Sakai – who serve as liaisons between Mothra and her human worshippers. And as silly as that may sound, the premise works well, with Japanese twin-sister vocal group The Peanuts lending their haunting voices and endearing personalities to the faerie roles. The fact that the Shobijin have continued to appear in the movies is a testament to how well viewers connected with the adorable little singers.

---

[14] For a charming (albeit fictional) account of how he came to do so, watch *Legends of Tomorrow* episode "Tagumo Attacks!!!", in which Honda, portrayed actor Eijiro Ozaki, is inspired by DC Comics' time-traveling heroes to create Godzilla (https://arrow.fandom.com/wiki/Ishir%C5%8D_Honda).

Yet again, no one mentions Godzilla's first two movies or other Toho *kaiju*, so the later incorporation of Mothra into the Godzilla franchise could have compounded existing continuity issues. This time, thankfully, no characters claim to have never seen a monster before, and when the threat of Mothra coming to rescue the faeries first looms, the idea of a giant creature meets little scoffing. As such, it's far easier to smoothly slip *Mothra* into the shared universe than it is for either *Rodan* or *Varan*. On the other hand...

King Kong vs. Godzilla (1962)

A drug company looking to boost the ratings of its sponsored TV shows kidnaps King Kong from his home on Farou Island, but the ape gets loose and ends up fighting Godzilla.

Toho's King Kong (left) reimagined the famous giant ape from RKO Pictures (right).

Continuity took an unexpected turn in the third Godzilla film, released seven years after *Godzilla Raids Again*. Godzilla faced off against another giant creature in the movie, but it wasn't an original Toho creation this time: it was Toho's reimagining of King Kong, the giant ape from the same-named RKO Pictures film, created by Edgar Wallace and Merian C. Cooper, and its sequel, *Son of Kong*, both released in 1933. Toho's Kong is not the same ape as in those films, nor is this movie part of their continuity. This Kong hails from Farou Island (instead of from the U.S. films' Skull Island) where the natives view him as a god.[15] He's larger, he can generate electricity from his hands, and he is addicted to berry juice.

---

[15] Monsters are worshipped by a great many superstitious cultures in Toho's movies; Kong isn't the first (see *Varan* and *Mothra*), nor would he be the last (see *Atragon* and *Godzilla vs. Mechagodzilla*).

When Japan discovers Farou Island, several characters laugh at the idea of a giant ape, with one remarking, "A large monster? He must be joking!" Now, they can be excused for not knowing about Rodan, the Meganulons, Varan, or Mothra, since those creatures' films had yet to be shoehorned into Godzilla lore, but how could they possibly find the existence of large monsters laughable, when *King Kong vs. Godzilla* was a direct sequel to the first two Godzilla films? Godzilla is even found on the same icy island in which he was buried in *Godzilla Raids Again*, so there's no doubt about that.

In 1963, as expected, an American production team heavily altered the movie for English-language release.[16] The producers inserted new footage to reframe *King Kong vs. Godzilla* as a newscast, incorporating stock footage from *The Mysterians*.[17] The newscast idea wasn't a bad one, but the execution was weak, with actors Michael Keith and Harry Holcombe playing a reporter and a museum expert who sit around commenting on the action instead of letting the plot unfold. Adding insult to injury, the soundtrack by Akira Ifukube was largely replaced with music from non-Toho sources, including Universal's *Creature from the Black Lagoon* and *Frankenstein Meets the Wolf Man.* This was an egregious error, as Ifukube was a brilliant composer; his soundtrack to *Gojira* is a large part of why that movie and the entire franchise are so revered.

The added news scenes compound the continuity issues created by the existence of two versions of the movie. In the American cut, the world is shocked to find that prehistoric creatures exist, despite this being the third Godzilla movie, and one character even theorizes that Godzilla could have been trapped in the iceberg for a hundred million years, ignoring the first two films entirely! In both versions, there's also the issue of Godzilla's reaction to electricity; previously, Godzilla had trampled electric lines as though unaware they existed, but in this movie, a million-volt shock leaves him visibly injured. It could be that the higher voltage affects him more, but later movies would seem to rule out that explanation.

Whether one watches the Japanese or American iteration, *King Kong vs. Godzilla* marks the point at which the films began transforming from a dark

---

[16] Note to future filmmakers: please don't do this. It's unnecessary and more than a little racist.

[17] Remember how I said I don't count *The Mysterians* as part of the Godzilla series? This is one reason why: because its footage was incorporated into *King Kong vs. Godzilla* in a different context.

metaphor to lighthearted romps in which Godzilla ends up in humorous fight scenes more symbolic of the World Wrestling Federation than of the evils of atomic power. Godzilla's battle with Kong is at times exceedingly silly, with the dinosaur clapping excitedly as he hurts the gorilla. The human characters, meanwhile, are mere caricatures, not at all cut from the same cloth as the realistically depicted human casts of *Gojira*, *Rodan*, *Mothra*, and...

Atragon (1963)

Captain Hachiro Jinguji, a renegade World War II-era military officer who'd rejected Japan's surrender, builds a super-powered submarine, the Gotengo, to help his nation defeat the West, but his plans change when the legendary lost continent of Mu tries to conquer the world.

When the Mu Empire – which had colonized the world 12,000 years prior, including Easter Island, then sank into the ocean overnight – attempts to take over the planet, Captain Jinguji reluctantly agrees to use the *Gotengo* to defeat the invaders, abandoning his plan to rebuild the Japanese Empire. At first glance, the Honda-directed *Atragon* might seem an unusual title to include in this discussion. It's highly enjoyable, but its connection to Godzilla is not readily apparent.

What ties *Atragon* to the franchise is that this advanced underwater civilization threatens to sic its serpent god, Manda, on mankind if they resist subjugation. As with Varan, Manda would return in *Destroy All Monsters*, retroactively pulling *Atragon* into continuity. Manda and the *Gotengo* would also come back during the Millennium series' *Godzilla: Final Wars*.

Interestingly, none of *Atragon*'s characters seem to find the idea of Manda absurd, nor do they deny the existence of giant monsters. As such, there's little about this movie that outright contradicts Shōwa-era Godzilla continuity, making its incorporation into the series relatively seamless. Unlike the otherwise excellent...

Mothra vs. Godzilla (1964, a.k.a. *Godzilla vs. The Thing* and *Godzilla vs. Mothra*)

Businessmen try to make money by charging tourists to view Mothra's egg. The moth-god is not pleased about this, but still protects mankind when Godzilla suddenly attacks.

Considering the popularity of 1961's *Mothra*, it's little surprise that the gentle giant would make her way into the Godzilla franchise, and her presence in *Mothra vs. Godzilla* makes for one of the better entries in the series. Unfortunately, it's difficult to reconcile the two films as occurring within the same continuity, even though they demonstrably[18] do. When Mothra's faeries show up, for example, no one recognizes them, which is odd since the humans *have* heard of Mothra — and odder still, since the Shobijin had become famous celebrities in *Mothra* after being kidnapped by villainous Clark Nelson and forced to perform for the viewing public.

The Shobijin claim Mothra's egg has been buried underground for many years, even though the film *Mothra* was released only three years prior — and the egg hatched in that movie spawned a larval Mothra. The new Mothra is now an adult, so even if she had grown up within days and hatched her own egg immediately, it still couldn't be more than a few years since the egg's burial. When this one hatches, two larvae emerge, resulting in twin Mothras, a surprising development that will have exactly zero impact on future films. For reasons unclear, mama Mothra has only a short time left to live and seems old and frail, even though she's a toddler's age. Plus, Mothra now can emit clouds of poisonous yellow powder, something she didn't do in the 1961 movie (granted, she may simply have had no reason to release the substance during her debut appearance).

Meanwhile, Godzilla's ever-changing relationship with electricity continues to confuse, as Japan hits him with 20 to 30 million volts, two years after it had trouble generating even a million volts in *King Kong vs. Godzilla*. Though initially stunned by the blast, Godzilla quickly recovers and trashes the electric lines. When the voltage increases, it just makes him angry instead of damaging him and he melts the infrastructure, proving the writers really weren't sure what role electricity should play. That trend would continue as the series progressed.

Oddly, Infant Island seems to vary greatly between *Mothra* and *Mothra vs. Godzilla*. In the 1961 film, the island's interior is a lush jungle, whereas the only greenery visible is now located near the sacred spring, as though the filmmakers had misplaced the gorgeous matte painting in the interim. On the other hand, the red juice mentioned by rescued sailors but not actually shown in *Mothra* makes an appearance here, as the heroes are invited to partake of the beverage upon arrival. Next up...

---

[18] Or would that be... de-monster-ably?

Ghidorah, the Three-Headed Monster (1964)

The spirit of a dead Venusian possesses a human princess to warn mankind that a monster from space, which destroyed her people, will attack Earth as well. Few heed her warning, and when Ghidorah attacks, Godzilla helps humanity repel the alien monster.

King Ghidorah is often cited as Godzilla's most recognizable and most dangerous foe.

A decade after Godzilla first terrorized Tokyo, his most popular foe debuted in *Ghidorah, the Three-Headed Monster*. King Ghidorah – a triple-headed flying serpent from outer space, visually reminiscent of the three-headed dragon in 1939's *Vasilisa the Beautiful*[19] and inspired by Eiji Tsuburaya's dragon design for Toho's 1959 film *The Three Treasures / The Birth of Japan*[20] – along with the Venusian spirit were the first extraterrestrials introduced into the Godzilla

---

[19] The Soviet fantasy-based monster film, directed by Alexander Rou for Soyuzdetfilm (now Gorky Film Studio), is well worth watching: https://www.youtube.com/watch?v=sKR_H5fSuVI.

[20] Tsuburaya, a special effects director on multiple Japanese science-fiction movies and TV shows, helped to create the Godzilla film series and was responsible for the monster's stop-motion animation. He also created the *Ultraman* franchise. Toho's advertising department, in fact, referred to Tsuburaya, Ishirō Honda, and Tomoyuki Tanaka as "The Golden Trio."

universe, with others soon to follow.[21] Despite the rather fake-looking manner in which his necks bobble on their puppet strings, there is something undeniably menacing about the ever-screeching Ghidorah, and it's clear the writers agreed, given how often they brought him back.

Ghidorah and *The Three Treasures* were both based on Yamata no Orochi, an eight-headed, eight-tailed dragon-serpent of Japanese mythology, later featured in Toho's *Orochi, the Eight-Headed Dragon / Yamato Takeru* (1994), as well as in 2019's *Godzilla, King of the Monsters*. In *Godzilla, Mothra and King Ghidorah: Giant Monsters All-Out Attack* (2001), the connection is cemented when Teruaki Takeda notes that in ancient times, Ghidorah had been known as Yamata no Orochi; in the Godzilla films, the creature is apparently not yet fully developed and thus only sports three heads.

Ghidorah, the Three-Headed Monster officially added Rodan to the Godzilla roster, with a newly constructed costume that updated his face, wings, and neck. Rodan is said to have been resurrected by gasses accumulated in the volcano's crust, making it clear that the movie *Rodan* happened within this continuity, even though it doesn't add up since both *Pteranodons* were incinerated in *Rodan* – plus, the gases apparently only resurrected *one* of them, since the other is nowhere to be seen. Still, Toho's shared film universe was now in full swing, and a flimsy retcon was certainly a better solution than not having at least one Rodan be part of it. He was simply too cool a *kaiju* to ignore.

The Shobijin are back to being popular celebrities, and during a television appearance, they reveal that one of the Mothra larvae has passed away. (See? No impact.) The other, still a baby, is keeping the peace on Infant Island. The moth-god gains a new ability, as she communicates telepathically with Godzilla and Rodan to convince them to gang up on Ghidorah and save the planet – the first of many times in which the one-time atomic terror would now serve as Earth's protector. This, though, raises the question of why she didn't try to communicate the last time they met... not to mention how this could even be possible, given that Godzilla's brain, according to the American-made scenes added to *King Kong vs. Godzilla*, is about the size of a Milk Dud.

---

[21] The American dubbing changes all Venus references to Mars, which technically constitutes a continuity error but actually makes more sense since Mars is far more believable as a world that once sustained human-compatible life.

From this point forward, the Shōwa-era films each contain lighthearted scenes to delight the children in the audience, such as one in this movie in which Godzilla and Rodan, instead of fighting each other tooth and claw, smack a boulder back and forth for a while as though playing volleyball. They also each laugh uproariously as Mothra sprays the other with ~~Silly String~~ moth-like silk. During the battle, Rodan drops Godzilla directly onto an electric tower, but he comes away unscathed. Perhaps electricity only hurts him on Tuesdays...?

That being said, *Ghidorah, the Three-Headed Monster* is among Toho's most enjoyable offerings, and the film is notable for featuring some of the most three-dimensional human characters ever to grace a Godzilla movie. In particular, there's the wonderfully portrayed Princess Maas Selina Salno of Selgina (Akiko Wakabayashi), who is thought to have died early in the movie but later is found preaching to the masses as an alien-possessed prophet of doom. Her performance alone makes the film worth watching, but it's certainly not the only reason to do so. Much like...

Frankenstein vs. Baragon (1965, a.k.a. *Frankenstein Conquers the World* and *Frankenstein vs. the Giant Devilfish*)

A feral boy in Hiroshima, who has the irradiated heart of Frankenstein's monster, grows to enormous size. Misunderstood and hunted, he ultimately saves Japan from a ravaging monster called Baragon.

If the above description raises an eyebrow, that's certainly understandable, as Frankenstein's monster is not something one would expect to find in the Godzilla franchise.[22] Then again, if faeries and extraterrestrials can show up, why not Mary Shelley's famous mad scientist, his reanimated creature – and some Nazis who show up as well?

As with *Atragon*, *Frankenstein vs. Baragon* is easy to overlook as a chapter in Godzilla continuity. Most of the movie centers around the plight of the feral boy as he grows increasingly larger and unfairly becomes the target of mankind's fear. The Godzilla connection is a subtle one and it comes retroactively, thanks to the introduction of a reptilian *kaiju* called Baragon who, like Varan and Manda, would later return in *Destroy All Monsters*, making *Frankenstein vs. Baragon* a Godzilla-related tale after the fact.

---

[22] On the other hand, as Greg Mitchell's essay "The Enduring Legacy of Classic Monsters in *The Monster Squad*" notes, the Toho and Universal Monsters franchises nearly crossed over at one point.

No mention is made of any prior monster attacks, though the sight of Frankenstein (as the feral boy is nicknamed) getting larger doesn't seem to shock the other characters, indicating they could have seen other giant creatures before. Still, when faced with the proposition that some dinosaurs may have survived extinction by hiding underground while the Earth cooled, a scientist comments, "I won't say it is impossible to happen, but I can't agree with you either, since such a thing is highly improbable." Those supporting such an idea are treated with extreme skepticism, despite mankind having witnessed several dinosaurs roaming the Earth in the other movies.

The re-editing of *Frankenstein vs. Baragon* would result in yet another continuity issue, for the international version, titled *Frankenstein vs. the Giant Devilfish*, would later restore footage shot for but ultimately removed from the American cut. Because of this, a *third* version of the movie exists, which Tokyo Shock released on DVD in 2007. In the original Japanese, Frankenstein and Baragon battle until the ground beneath them collapses, swallowing both. But in the international version, Frankenstein tosses Baragon from a cliff, after which a giant octopus suddenly appears for no discernable reason and continues the scuffle. It's random and jarring and it comes out of nowhere, with Frankenstein fighting the cephalopod until both fall into the sea and fail to resurface, leaving incredulous viewers to wonder what the hell just happened.

This goes to show that Tōhō and tight continuity go together about as well as peanut butter and motor oil. But it doesn't matter, as the movie is nonetheless one of the studio's greatest, most beloved achievements, and anyone who hasn't watched it should check out the subtitled Japanese version, which avoids the arbitrary octopus battle tacked on like a neon sticky note. Don't be put off by the movie's title; the feral Frankenstein, as played by Koji Furuhata, is a relatable and human character, and one would be hard-pressed to watch the movie without cheering for him to survive. Nick Adams and Kumi Mizuno also turn in strong performances as Doctors James Bowen and Sueko Togami, respectively. Considering their onscreen chemistry, it's no wonder both would soon return (albeit as different characters) in another movie, titled...

Invasion of Astro-Monster (1965, a.k.a. *Monster Zero* and *Godzilla vs. Monster Zero*)

King Ghidorah returns to Earth as the extraterrestrial Xiliens attempt to conquer the planet. With help from Godzilla and Rodan, mankind overthrows the alien invaders.

Ghidorah's return makes *Invasion of Astro-Monster* a direct sequel to *Ghidorah, the Three-Headed Monster*, providing solid inter-film continuity. The story ambiguously takes place in the year "196X," but no matter what year of the 1960s it might be, the level of technology seems more advanced than what existed in that decade. (Perhaps it was built by *Atragon*'s Captain Jinguji...?) The World Space Authority suddenly has spaceships able to journey around the solar system within a matter of days, implying interplanetary travel to be commonplace. After all, it's not like they would have been able to come up with the capability of traveling to another world on the spot – it must be something that was already feasible, since that kind of technological leap would take years to implement.[23]

So why isn't mankind zipping around the cosmos in later films, thwarting the multiple alien incursions that threaten the Earth? Moreover, the Japanese military uses a device to incapacitate all three monsters, which reduces them to lying on the ground, helplessly convulsing. In other words, Japan has come up with the perfect weapon to deploy against all *kaiju*, so why isn't anyone using this technology in future sequels to keep them at bay?

Godzilla's evolution from terrifying monstrosity to beloved friend continues – he even does a joyous victory dance – and that sentiment now extends as well to Rodan, who takes on heretofore unmentioned amphibian qualities at the film's end. When the Xiliens, posing as allies, "borrow" the two *kaiju* to battle Ghidorah, a human astronaut assisting in these efforts wistfully remarks, "They cause trouble sometimes, but I can't help feeling sorry for them." Killing thousands of people and destroying entire cities is merely a case of "causing trouble"? Mankind sure has developed selective amnesia, and has forgotten the unprecedented amount of damage each monster has done. Meanwhile...

The War of the Gargantuas (1966, a.k.a. Frankenstein's Monsters: Sanda Against Gaira)

Two Frankenstein-like behemoths, Gaira and Sanda, one savage and the other timid, are hunted by mankind until Sanda destroys his violent brother.

It's frustrating when a wonderful movie spawns an inferior sequel, and *The War of the Gargantuas* seems to go out of its way to prove this true. Although

---

[23] Come to think of it, perhaps *The Mysterians* occurs within Godzilla continuity after all, and the WSA has reverse-engineered the aliens' space-travel tech from that movie. Hmmm...

it's popular among fans, the movie pales compared to *Frankenstein vs. Baragon* in terms of emotional impact and acting quality, and so much of the earlier plot is altered or discarded that it's difficult to view *Gargantuas* as an actual sequel, since the two films are largely incompatible. It's such a loose sequel that it's basically a remake.

Frankenstein, previously portrayed as a feral child who'd lived his life alone in the irradiated ruins of Hiroshima, here is reimagined to have been raised in a laboratory by a caring and attentive human woman – the polar opposite of the creature's former origin story. The scientist who'd previously helped him, Doctor James Bowen (played by Nick Adams), is now Doctor Paul Stewart, with *West Side Story*'s Russ Tamblyn replacing Adams, which is regrettable since Tamblyn phones in his performance, whereas Adams had made Bowen a nuanced character. Actress Kumi Mizuno (Sueko Togami in *Frankenstein vs. Baragon*) now portrays Akemi Togawa, a character so similar, even in her surname, that the producers might as well have just had her reprise her former role.

Ambiguous references are made to *Frankenstein vs. Baragon*, but the only direct link between the two films is the term "Frankenstein," which appears in the Japanese title and is used to refer to the Gargantuas, known as "Frankensteins" in the Japanese dialogue. For the American version, Tamblyn had to re-dub his dialogue to remove all such references.

In one scene, Doctor Stewart muses "Imagine what will happen should Frankenstein appear in this peaceful place" (Tokyo). The implication is clear: Stewart has no knowledge of giant monsters ever having trampled the city. So either Stewart is an imbecile, or else *The War of the Gargantuas* is not part of the shared universe despite its status as a loose sequel to a film that *is* part of it. It would be easy to ignore the movie's existence in Shōwa continuity if it weren't for one thing: the film contains the first appearance of the Maser Cannon, a weapon that would appear in both *Godzilla vs. Gigan* and *Godzilla vs. Megalon*, as well as in several Heisei and Millennium entries.[24] In short, *The War of the Gargantuas* is a continuity mess. As opposed to...

---

[24] So it's settled then. Stewart is, in fact, an imbecile.

Ebirah, Horror of the Deep (1966, a.k.a. *Godzilla vs. the Sea Monster*)

A man steals a boat to find his lost brother and ends up shipwrecked on Devil's Island, where terrorists are producing heavy water and a chemical to keep a giant lobster, Ebirah, at bay. Unbeknownst to anyone, Godzilla also resides there.

Continuity-wise, *Ebirah, Horror of the Deep* jibes relatively well with the rest of the franchise. That doesn't mean it's necessarily a great film, because it's one of the more over-the-top entries in the series, with a villain's lair that seems like something Ernst Stavros Blofeld might construct if he had a shoestring budget. Despite some genuinely enjoyable human characters, particularly Akira Takarada's would-be-criminal-turned-lovable-hero Yoshimura, the movie also features one of the dumbest monster battles ever to appear in a Godzilla film, with Godzilla and the titular crustacean tossing rocks back and forth as though having a friendly game of catch and not a fight to the death.

This is compounded by absurd dialogue during the film's final scenes. As Mothra helps the human characters escape from Devil's Island, they pity Godzilla being stranded there alone and even try to warn him to leave before the island explodes. One hilariously remarks, "He never did us any harm," displaying an appalling lack of knowledge of recent history, or possibly evidence of head trauma. They then cheer happily as Godzilla swims safely out to sea – even though, for all they know, he could very well be making a beeline to Tokyo so he can stomp the rebuilt city.

Meanwhile, Godzilla now suddenly draws strength from electricity. Previously, it had either hurt him or had little effect at all, depending on the whim of the screenwriters. This time, it rejuvenates the beast. Why? Because the movie was originally written for Toho's version of King Kong, not Godzilla, and Kong had generated electricity in *King Kong vs. Godzilla*. Despite this, a jolt of 100,000 volts enrages the atomic dinosaur later in the same film – which is shocking,[25] as he could sustain *millions* of volts in other movies. Continuity, thy name is not Godzilla. And then there's...

---

[25] See what I did there?

Son of Godzilla (1967)

A reporter infiltrates a scientific team on Solgell Island, where weather experiments have mutated giant mantises known as Kamacuras, which try to consume Godzilla's infant offspring, Minilla.

What can one say about a film in which Godzilla has a son so cloyingly cute and annoying he would be more at home in *Mac and Me*? *Son of Godzilla* is part of the official canon, but it's one of the worst movies of Godzilla's Shōwa era... or *any* era of Godzilla... or, really, any era of any movies, period... thanks to the mantis puppets' visible strings, an irritating soundtrack, and every single scene involving the child-friendly Minilla and his smoke rings, Play-Doh-like body, and incessant whining.[26]

It's a shame, too, as the science team, and especially nosy reporter Goro Maki,[27] are entertaining characters whose dialogue sets up a development in later movies. One character describes the island they're on as "a real *monster island*," while another observes, "When the snow melts, Godzilla and the baby will probably live on that island." Sure enough, Godzilla and Minilla inhabit a place called Monster Island in the sequels, evidence that Solgell Island and the soon-to-be-established Monster Island were likely meant to be the same location.

Godzilla and Minilla kill a giant spider called Kumonga by lighting him up in atomic fire. Kumonga returns in *Destroy All Monsters*, however, making the arachnid the latest Toho monster to come back from the dead without explanation. You'd think humanity would be tripping over each other to harvest *kaiju* organs, as they apparently hold the key to immortality.[28] Speaking of returning monsters...

---

[26] Minilla's existence raises the question of who fertilized Godzilla's egg, not to mention whether the dinosaur is male or female. (*M*A*S*H*'s *Firstborn of Godzilla* doesn't seem so out there now, though.) "A Space Godzilla" (https://godzilla.fandom.com/wiki/A_Space_Godzilla), a short story that adapted a planned but never-filmed 16th Shōwa-era Godzilla movie, was published in *Starlog* magazine in 1979. According to this tale, Godzilla is a female alien named Rozan and has a husband called Kurin. It's not a bad story, per se, but Godzilla being an alien in no way fits the movies. Plus, practically every single film calls the monster "he."

[27] Other Goro Makis appear post-Shōwa in *The Return of Godzilla* (1984) and *Shin Godzilla* (2016).

[28] As it happens, this is a central idea in the 2013 non-Godzilla *kaiju* film *Pacific Rim*.

King Kong Escapes (1967, a.k.a. King Kong's Counterattack)

Dr. Who (no relation to the BBC's time-traveler) builds a robot of King Kong, known as Mecha-Kong, to help mine a radioactive element. The evil genius captures the real Kong and forces the ape to do his dirty work, with nary a TARDIS in sight.

Following the release of *King Kong vs. Godzilla*, Toho had hoped to build a new franchise around its version of King Kong, but rights-holder RKO denied it permission to do so. Instead, the studio helped Rankin/Bass Productions co-produce the film *King Kong Escapes*, loosely based on the animated series *The King Kong Show*. The cartoon, from Videocraft International and Toei Animation, was the first Japanese *anime* created specifically for the U.S. market.

Due to RKO's mandate, *King Kong Escapes* was not presented as a direct sequel to *King Kong vs. Godzilla*. This explains the physical differences between the two gorillas, the fact that Kong now lives on Mondo Island instead of Farou Island, and why this Kong can understand Dr. Who's spoken commands issued in Japanese (not Gallifreyan) via a speaker implanted in the gorilla's head.

A continuity issue would later arise involving Gorosaurus, a *kaiju* created for *King Kong Escapes*, when *All Monsters Attack* repurposed footage of the dinosaur for scenes on Monster Island. Gorosaurus's presence in both films means that while *King Kong Escapes* is not a sequel to *King Kong vs. Godzilla*, they're still set in the same universe. So, then, is this the same Kong? If not, there must be two of them – which, granted, is not unprecedented since there are multiple Godzillas, Rodans, and Mothras. But Gorosaurus seemingly dies in *King Kong Escapes*, so there must be two of him as well, unless he's like Toho's other *kaiju* and can come back to life following a fatal smackdown.[29]

The bigger issue, from a shared film universe perspective, is that characters yet again seem unaware of the existence of giant monsters. Several express skepticism at the idea that Kong is a real creature, with one even calling him "fictional." This sheds some doubt on the idea that the events of *King Kong vs. Godzilla* occurred within the same continuity. What's more, during a briefing about the Mondo Island escapade, reporters are astonished to learn there's a

---

[29] I initially typed "fatal ass-kicking," but since there's no evidence Toho's monsters actually *have* asses, I changed my wording. They also have no visible genitalia, making Minilla's existence a head-scratcher. Then again, reptilian cloacae can be difficult to spot. Or, um, so I've heard.

place on Earth where prehistoric reptiles have not gone extinct – which is kind of astounding since they live in Japan, where prehistoric reptiles have been ripping up the place since 1954 on a fairly regular basis. And now...

Destroy All Monsters (1968)

After Earth's monsters are relocated to an island called Monsterland, alien invaders, the Kilaaks, take control of the creatures and force them to attack major cities worldwide.

Destroy All Monsters is often cited as one of Toho's best, and for good reason: for those who enjoy *tokusatsu* and *kaiju* tales (*Destroy All Monsters* qualifies as both), the film is a smorgasbord of colossal creatures causing *kaiju* chaos. In addition to Godzilla, the movie assembles Rodan, Anguirus, Mothra, Gorosaurus, Manda, Kumonga, Baragon, Varan, King Ghidorah and, to keep the kiddies happy, Minilla. In essence, *Destroy All Monsters* is the reason this essay exists, for it's the vehicle that brought non-Godzilla films *Varan, Frankenstein vs. Baragon, Atragon,* and *King Kong Escapes* into the fold, thereby cementing Toho's many *kaiju* films as a shared universe and not just a string of sequels.

Destroy All Monsters takes place at the close of the 20th century, seemingly after all other Shōwa-era films. In the English-dubbed version, the opening narration specifies "The year is 1999," because Americans demand details, dammit.[30] The world's *kaiju* are said to have been relocated to Monsterland (not Monster Island – more on that later), where they live separated from mankind thanks to protections put in place to prevent them from leaving. How this was accomplished is not explained, but noticeably absent are King Kong, Ebirah, the Kamacuras, the Meganulons, the Frankensteins, the giant octopus, and a few others too forgettable to mention.

One can't help but wonder why, if humanity has developed the technology required to move these incredibly destructive and massive beasts to a single

---

[30] From proofreader John Hazlett: "Interestingly, if we take the American date at face value, it creates one of those nifty coincidence-prognostications that sometimes happens with media set in the future (like *Star Trek* correctly predicting the first Moon shot would be launched on a Wednesday). One of the characters in *Destroy All Monsters* says [in the English-dubbed version], 'All I can say now is what I said 20 years ago. Remember that typhoon? We must be on our guard.' In the real world, on October 19, 1979, Typhoon Tip, the largest and most intense typhoon ever recorded, made landfall in Japan after its storm track carried it near the Ogasawara Islands."

place, they wouldn't then find a way to kill them *en masse*. Ah, but then, monsters are our kid-friendly buddies now. In any case, Mothra being among those rounded up makes no sense at all, since she's not even a monster – she's a benevolent entity and mankind's ally. She is also vital to Infant Island, so wouldn't the Shobijin and the native humans have a problem with her abduction and imprisonment? Moreover, Mothra is a larva once more, even though no one mentions her having died yet again since *Ebirah, Horror of the Deep.*

Destroy All Monsters brought several non-Godzilla films into Toho's shared *kaiju* universe – and thus spawned this shelf in my DVD and Blu-ray collection, which features every non-animated Godzilla film from 1954 to present.

Baragon's appearance in *Destroy All Monsters* presents yet another continuity issue, as he looks noticeably different than he did in *Frankenstein vs. Baragon*. In the interim between movies, the costume had been considerably altered so it could be repurposed as different beasts in Tsuburaya Productions' *Ultraman* series. Since suit repairs continued even while *Destroy* was being filmed, an intended Baragon attack on Paris was instead given to Gorosaurus, who thus gained Baragon's ability to burrow underground. This is why a news reporter's account of the Paris attack identifies Baragon as the perpetrator, even though on screen it's clearly Gorosaurus ruffling the croissants.

King Ghidorah seemingly perishes as the Kilaak base collapses. Since no Shōwa-era Godzilla films take place after *Destroy All Monsters* — the rest occur in the 1970s, prior to this movie's events — Ghidorah may be truly dead in this timeline. Or he could just as easily come back to life. Monsters do that, you know. And back to the '70s we go...

All Monsters Attack (1969, a.k.a. *Godzilla's Revenge*)

A lonely latchkey child imagines that Minilla is his friend, which gives him the strength to stand up to a bully, and to escape from harm when murderous robbers kidnap him.

The tenth Godzilla film is an oddball entry. First and foremost, a sizable portion of *All Monsters Attack* takes place solely in the imagination of young Ichiro Miki. Little Ichiro, left alone for much of his day due to his parents both having to work long hours, spends his free time daydreaming (and actually dreaming) about visiting Godzilla's son Minilla — or Minya, as he's called in the American dubbing — on Monster Island. Since Minilla is smaller and weaker than other monsters, Ichiro can relate to him and likes to think of Minilla as his friend.

All Monsters Attack tends to fare poorly with reviewers, as it makes extensive reuse of footage from prior Godzilla films. Plus, its events have no bearing on the larger franchise since they take place inside the mind of a child, and the English dubbing is some of the worst of the series, with Minilla sounding like a cross between Barney the Dinosaur and Disney's Goofy (he sounds entirely different in the original Japanese). Still, the movie has a lot of heart and deserves more credit than it receives.

Ichiro is a victim of a society that forces parents to work excessive hours to raise their children, paradoxically preventing them from being home to do any raising. This leaves him vulnerable to bullies — a plight with which many can empathize. (Unfortunately, the movie blows it entirely in the final scenes, with Ichiro becoming a bully himself. What the heck, Toho?) The film has an out-of-the-box plot that, despite the reused footage, manages to avoid the formulaic motifs on which many Godzilla tales rely. It's juvenile, certainly, but it's also kind of innovative.

One might assume this movie takes place in the real world, since Ichiro loves Toho's monsters and has action figures of them. However, at no point are the *kaiju* described as fictional; there may simply be action figures of the actual Godzilla in this reality because he's well-known and marketable – kind of like how there are trading cards and comic books in our world depicting serial killers, dictators, politicians, and other real-world monsters. On the other hand, Ichiro's imagination includes footage from prior films, and the only way he'd be able to imagine such scenes would be if he'd watched them; this is the strongest evidence that *All Monsters Attack* exists in a reality in which other Godzilla films are fictional entertainment. In fact, the *kaiju* Gabara might not even exist since he only shows up in Ichiro's dreams – plus, the kid's human bully is named Sanko Gabara.

Chronologically, this film takes place years before *Destroy All Monsters*. The creatures' collective home is here called Monster Island, implying the Japanese government moved the captured *kaiju* to Monster Island after *Son of Godzilla* (possibly to the same island in that film, given how many of the Monster Island scenes come from *Son of Godzilla*), then relocated them to *Destroy*'s Monsterland in the future. Why would they do this? You might as well ask why Japan hasn't permanently evacuated Tokyo. Or why anyone in their right mind would live in a place where monster attacks are as common as sunrises. Or what LSD-laced fever dream inspired this next film...

Godzilla vs. Hedorah (1971, a.k.a. *Godzilla vs. the Smog Monster*)

Hedorah, an alien life form from the Dark Gas Nebula, visits Earth to feed on pollution, and Godzilla protects mankind from his own misguided mistreatment of the planet.

How can you go wrong with a monster that farts, vomits, and otherwise spews toxic waste, that inhales factory smokestacks as though from a bong, and that has eyes intentionally designed by filmmakers to resemble giant human vaginas? I dare say you cannot. *Godzilla vs. Hedorah* even features an animated cartoon sequence, making it the most surreal movie of the bunch. Whatever the gas in the Dark Gas Nebula is, it must be hallucinogenic.

By this point, Godzilla is firmly established as a hero and protector, which is simply inexplicable after all the destruction he has wrought. Now he's apparently an eco-warrior, too. A child named Ken Yano delivers a school report in which he says, "The atomic bomb, the hydrogen bomb cast their fallout into the sea. Poison gases, sludge – everyone throws them into the sea. Even sewage. Godzilla would really get angry if he saw this." Meanwhile, the camera shows Godzilla rise from the ocean, gaze in dismay at foamy pollution floating on the water's surface,[31] and then light it all on fire.

Kaiju dolls, such as Ichiro's in *All Monsters Attack*, are apparently quite popular, as Ken has a sizable collection. It's interesting that the much-maligned *Jedi Prince* novels, by Paul and Hollace Davids, feature a young boy named Ken who collects action figures based on the heroes of the classic *Star Wars* film trilogy. Much like Ken Yano's mysterious psychic connection to Godzilla (the boy can sense the monster's impending arrival), *Star Wars*'s Ken has latent mental powers and a mysterious connection to Emperor Palpatine (who is secretly the boy's grandfather). It's not a big stretch to wonder if the husband-wife author team might be *kaiju* fans.

Godzilla's love-hate relationship with electricity comes into play once more, as he takes several three-million-volt charges from a power-line trap set up to kill the Smog Monster, emerging entirely unscathed each time. He can also fly now, by using his atomic breath to propel himself across vast distances – an ability that would have come in handy in, oh, every other Godzilla movie ever made, including...

Godzilla vs. Gigan (1972, a.k.a. Godzilla on Monster Island)

Space cockroaches from the M Space Hunter Nebula inhabit the bodies of the recently deceased in an attempt to colonize Earth, posing as the benevolent builders of a children's theme park containing a giant structure called Godzilla Tower.

Yes, space cockroaches, the walking dead, and an evil amusement park. Is that really any more ridiculous than fire-breathing dinosaurs, moth-gods,

---

[31] The same year that *Godzilla vs. Hedorah* hit theaters, Italian-American actor Espera de Corti (a.k.a. Iron Eyes Cody) famously dressed as a Native American and shed a tear on television upon viewing pollution ruining the environment. Could Godzilla's reaction to the sludge have been an intentional homage to this public-service advertisement for the Keep America Beautiful organization?

electricity-wielding gorillas, tiny faeries, giant Frankenstein's monsters, or Godzilla playing catch with a lobster? No, of course it's not. What is absurd, though, is the villains' plot, which consists of erecting a theme park for kids as a way to teach them about peace. That's remarkably civilized for conquerors. Their bigger plot is to destroy Monster Island since real monsters aren't very peaceful at all... which makes one wonder why they didn't just skip the theme park endeavor and attack the island from the get-go.

Godzilla vs. Gigan offers a warning about the societal danger of relying too heavily on technology and mechanization, and about how difficult true peace can be to attain. Or something. I don't know. Truthfully, the messages fall flat since the movie is largely devoid of a plot or focus, with excessive time spent on *kaijus* doing battle – which, to Toho's credit, are very fun scenes since Gigan looks like a cross between a punk-rock cyborg and a *Hellraiser* Cenobite. The Americanized version adds spoken dialogue between Godzilla and Anguirus that is hysterically incongruous with the rest of the series and makes the duo sound like 1920s Chicago gangsters with emphysema. The Japanese version just features bizarre sounds representing telepathic communication, which is far less zany.

On the other hand, the human protagonists are highly entertaining, particularly Gengo Kotaka, a *manga* artist; Tomoko Tomoe, a karate black belt who several times rescues her male colleagues from danger, single-handedly redeeming the franchise's appalling track record of making women seem weak and helpless; and Shosaku Takasugi, a bandana-wearing hippie who amusingly tries to intimidate Kotaka with a foil-wrapped corn cob. The movie is among the weakest of the Shōwa era, with some of the most ineffective villains, yet this trio makes it surprisingly watchable. Now let's take a little side-step...

Ike! Godman and *Ike! Greenman* (1972-1974)

Giant monsters attack Japan, but an extraterrestrial named Godman defeats each one. Later, God sends Greenman, a robot envoy, to protect children from a devil called Maoh, the source of all evil.

Toho reused several Shōwa Godzilla-related *kaiju* costumes in the television shows *Ike! Godman* and *Ike! Greenman*, with the suits either altered or rebuilt since the aging originals were in such bad shape. These included Gaira and Sanda, Gabara, Gorosaurus, Toho's King Kong, and an evil version of Minilla (which is just as great as it sounds). Kong was simply called "Gorilla," however, to avoid any potential copyright hassles. (*Gorilla vs. Godzilla* – just imagine the possibilities!)

These TV versions of the characters fall outside Toho's film continuity – which is a relief, because having to fit a supreme being and an actual devil into the franchise might have finally taken things too far. Perhaps it's best to think of *Ike! Godman* and *Ike! Greenman* as occupying a Shōwa pocket-universe.[32] And now for something completely different...

Godzilla vs. Megalon (1973)

An underground civilization, Seatopia, angered by the surface world's nuclear testing, unleashes a monster protector, Megalon, to destroy mankind and save their own existence.

It can be difficult at times to remember one Godzilla movie from another, but *Godzilla vs. Megalon* is easy to recall: it's the one with Jet Jaguar, a giant flying robot that looks like a grinning, metal Power Ranger, talks to monsters via sign language, and can grow to enormous proportions. It's not an image that one quickly forgets. In addition, Gigan returns, making this a direct sequel to the prior film. The movie also features flashy race-car-driving action-hero Hiroshi Jinkawa, who knows martial arts and can pull off fast car chases like James Bond. (Cut them some slack. It was 1973.)

The movie, which takes place in "197X" in Japanese but 1971 in English, contains an intriguing and almost certainly unintentional connection to *Atragon*. The Seatopians, survivors of the lost continent of Lemuria, are said to have built the statues of Easter Island. This means they must have been colonized by the Mu Empire, from *Atragon*, since Easter Island was among the lands the Mu had conquered, according to that prior film.

Godzilla vs. Megalon has a certain cheese factor that makes it enjoyable – if for no other reason than as a source of amusement at how out of synch it is with the other films. Godzilla understands sign language now and can thus respond to Jet Jaguar's call for assistance in defeating Megalon (instead of, say, perceiving the robot's frantic arm-waving as a threat and burning it to a crisp). In fact, Godzilla and Jet Jaguar become not only friends but a professional wrestling tag-team act, with the mechanical fighter holding back Megalon while

---

[32] Also, two Godzilla suits had previously been repurposed for the 1960s show *Ultraman* to create the monsters Jiras, Gomess, and Arstron. That show is separate from Toho's *kaiju* mythos as well.

the dinosaur signals his next move to his partner. Godzilla then gets a running start and actually *slides on his tail* to kick their adversary in the stomach, showing that as monsters go, 1970s Godzilla was far more Hulk Hogan than Incredible Hulk.

Let that image sink in for a moment. Next, consider how the series began: as a terrifying metaphor for the United States' irresponsible use of atomic weapons, reminding Japan of the horrors it had experienced during and after the Second World War. Now picture that same metaphorical monster performing wrestling moves while palling around with a brightly colored robot superhero who gives children piggy-back rides. The monster has traded in WWII for the WWF – he's become the kind of *kaiju* who sits vigilantly on Monster Island, ever on call and waiting for humans to summon his help, which he gladly provides.

What's more, Godzilla can come and go as he pleases, despite the defense measures in place to prevent that very thing. Then again, the film *does* open with nuclear testing near the Aleutians sending shockwaves across the globe, which are felt even on Monster Island, so there's no telling how badly this could have damaged the security system. In fact, this could very well account for the need to relocate the creatures to Monsterland by the time of *Destroy All Monsters*. Elsewhere...'

Zone Fighter (1973)

Extraterrestrial superheroes, with help from Godzilla, thwart plans by evil aliens to take over the Earth with an army of giant monsters.

If Jet Jaguar made you roll your eyes, then just wait, because Godzilla wasn't yet done making friends with superheroes. In 1973, Toho produced a TV show called *Zone Fighter*, featuring the Sakimoris, an extraterrestrial (yet still Japanese) family whose world had been destroyed by the nefarious Garogas. To stop Earth from facing the same fate, the Sakimoris transformed into the heroic Zone Fighter, Zone Angel, and Zone Junior. Unlike *Ike! Godman* and *Ike! Greenman*, Toho considers *Zone Fighter* an official part of the Shōwa-era Godzilla film series, set between *Godzilla vs. Megalon* and *Godzilla vs. Mechagodzilla*. Frustratingly, it's unavailable in English, making it impossible for non-Japanese-speaking audiences to experience the entire continuity. (Come on, Toho – release this already!)[33]

The show lasted for 26 episodes, with Godzilla appearing in five installments (4, 11, 15, 21, and 25). The atomic dinosaur served as an ally, helping the family to battle the Garogas' Terro-Beast *kaiju*, with Godzilla and Zone Fighter becoming pals and sparring partners – which sounds ridiculous, yes, but actually matches how Godzilla was being portrayed on the big screen at the time. The Sakimoris even built Godzilla a cave in which to live until he was summoned to face a new threat, because that's what best friends do.

Among the Terro-Beasts were King Ghidorah in episodes five and six, as well as Gigan (who'd been captured by the Garogas after fleeing from Godzilla and Jet Jaguar) in episode 11. Zone Fighter fires explosive missiles at Gigan, killing one of the franchise's most unique *kaiju* – at least until his return in *Godzilla: Final Wars* during the Millennium series. Ghidorah, meanwhile, manages to escape, making him unique since all other Terro-Beasts were fatally defeated. This proves the wisdom of the old adage that three heads are better than one. Then, the following year...

Godzilla vs. Mechagodzilla (1974, a.k.a. Godzilla vs. the Bionic Monster and Godzilla vs. the Cosmic Monster)

Simian aliens create a mechanical monster called Mechagodzilla, which leaves a path of destruction in its wake until lion-god King Caesar awakens to fight the beast alongside Godzilla.

The gorilla-headed Simians were the fifth extraterrestrial invaders to take on Earth in Shōwa continuity, following the Xiliens (*Invasion of Astro-Monster*), the Kilaaks (*Destroy All Monsters*), the M Space Hunter Nebula roach-people (*Godzilla vs. Gigan*), and the Garogas (*Zone Fighter*) – unless one counts King Ghidorah, Hedorah, and Gigan, in which case the Simians were the eighth.[34] The only friendly extraterrestrials seem to be the dead Venusians/Martians, from *Ghidorah, the Three-Headed Monster*. It's easy to forget that alien visitors played a large part in the Shōwa-era Godzilla line, what with all the city-toppling

---

[33] I'm not saying I have a fan-made English-subtitled bootleg DVD of the entire TV show that I acquired on eBay, because that would be illegal. Ahem.

[34] Or the ninth if one counts *The Mysterians*... which, again, this essay doesn't.

and the roaring and the monster fisticuffs and whatnot. It wasn't just horror-based; it was well rooted in science fiction, too.

The penultimate Shōwa film is a bit out there but enjoyable, due to the uniquely Japanese concept of a giant robot that looks like Godzilla but in shiny chrome. Among the visually impressive aspects is the new *kaiju*, King Caesar (or Seesar – the spelling has changed over time), a legendary monster resembling a *shisa*, a traditional Ryukyuan cultural artifact combining aspects of a dog and a lion. Caesar is the fourth *kaiju* "king" to appear in the movies, following King Kong, King Ghidorah, and Godzilla (king of the monsters), and he would later return in *Godzilla: Final Wars*. Unfortunately, the movie is also rather redundant, as it features a woman with psychic visions of a monster destroying Okinawa, making it reminiscent of *Ghidorah, the Three-Headed Monster*, while Mechagodzilla comes right on the heels of fellow mechanical *kaiju* Gigan.

The bigger issue is that all shreds of cohesive continuity are tossed out the window. When Godzilla arises, seemingly fulfilling the prophecy of a monster destroying the world, one character remarks incredulously, "Who would have guessed that the monster would be Godzilla?!" Keep in mind that this is the 14th Godzilla film, which means the world has witnessed Godzilla's destructive power on more than a dozen occasions, regardless of whether he was acting as friend or foe at the time. Who *wouldn't* have guessed that the monster would be Godzilla? The writers were clearly determined to portray the creature as a hero, no matter what, and it thus became inconceivable to mankind that Godzilla would ever want to destroy *anything*. All of the monsters, in fact – Godzilla, Anguirus, and Caesar – are firmly in the "good guys" camp.

Monster Island's defense restrictions are mere suggestions now, as Anguirus and Godzilla simply leave without incident once Mechagodzilla rears its metal head, implying they're *voluntarily* living there instead of trapped. Moreover, Godzilla is struck by lightning during a rainstorm and is incapacitated by the electricity – his entire body glows and he screams in agony. Never try to figure out Godzilla's relationship with electricity. It will give you a migraine. [35] And finally...

---

[35] Proofreader John Hazlett adds: "Even more so, if I recall correctly, similar VFX to when Godzilla is getting hit by lightning is used when he 'calls upon heretofore unknown powers' (as the recap in *Terror of Mechagodzilla* describes it) to first heal himself, and then magnetically pull a flying Mechagodzilla down to earth, implying

Terror of Mechagodzilla (1975, a.k.a. The Terror of Godzilla)

A reclusive scientist controls a peaceful aquatic dinosaur, Titanosaurus, forcing it to attack mankind. Yet more alien invaders, who have revived the scientist's deceased daughter, in turn control him – and together, they unleash a newly rebuilt Mechagodzilla.

If *Terror of Mechagodzilla* had a tagline, it would be "More of the same!" More aliens try to conquer Earth by remotely controlling *kaiju*. Another dinosaur is introduced. And yet again, Mechagodzilla joins the fight, this time controlled by the brain of a dead woman (OK, that part's new). As the final Shōwa-era Godzilla film, it's actually not bad, all things considered, and it's arguably superior to the first Mechagodzilla movie, largely due to the macabre "dead girl in a robot body" reveal. But it features little else we haven't seen before, with one exception: breasts.

Actually, that's not even true, as nudity had appeared before, going all the way back to Godzilla's debut, though you'd be forgiven for not recalling it; these are not American-made movies, after all, so the cameras had not gratuitously focused on it before now. Three topless elderly women from Odo Island can be briefly glimpsed in *Gojira*, then nude pinup magazine photos appear in *Godzilla vs. Megalon*, which is funny since it's an extremely kid-friendly movie. (And, of course, the monsters are naked in *every* film.) Technically, *Terror of Mechagodzilla* doesn't even show nudity at all, since the filmmakers bizarrely used a mannequin's plastic chest instead of the actress's actual skin.

The U.S. translation contains a prologue created to bring audiences up to date on the prior films, but it alters Godzilla's history substantially by claiming the Xiliens created Mechagodzilla, which is not true. It also has Kumonga and Ebirah being sent to Earth by aliens, even though neither was from space, and implies Godzilla's early rampages were caused by bullying humans attacking the poor, innocent beast while he was peacefully minding his own business – and that he'd defeated Mechagodzilla solo, without King Caesar's help. It's all a rather spotty account of things. From a shared film universe perspective, this movie has apparently forgotten how to share.

There's also the issue of characters *still* not knowing that giant monsters exist, no matter how many times giant monsters do their giant monstery thing,

---

(at least to me) that the lightning strikes are *what gave him those powers*. Pass the Excedrin."

as giant monsters are wont to do. In this case, after Titanosaurus attacks a submarine, a marine biologist finds it utterly absurd that a living dinosaur could have survived to modern times. Mind you, he lives in a world containing Godzilla, Anguirus, Varan, Manda, Baragon, and Gorosaurus, all of whom are dinosaurs, not to mention three Rodan pterosaurs. Meanwhile, once-revered mad scientist Shinzô Mafune has been discredited for believing in said dinosaur, despite his also living in that same dinosaur-filled world. It's kind of like a person in New York City being discredited for believing in the existence of subway trains and large pretzels. In the battle between Godzilla and logical storytelling, Godzilla wins every time.

Would You, Kaiju, Have a Fight?
Beat Them, Beat Them – What a Sight!

Godzilla started off as a destructive monster who inspired terror in the masses, but during the course of his 15 Shōwa-era appearances,[36] he quickly evolved into something lovable and revered who provided levity with his silly antics, more associated with Doctor Seuss than with Doctor Serizawa. In terms of continuity, it's inexplicable. Imagine if Universal's monster films had begun by terrifying audiences with Count Dracula, Frankenstein's monster, and the Wolf Man, only to eventually go for giggles by bringing in Bud Abbott and Lou Costello to – oh, wait... bad example. Never mind.[37]

Now, if all of this seems to imply the author of this essay is not a Godzilla fan, let's put that theory to rest right now. The author is a rabid fan who re-watches the entire series, from *Gojira* to present, every couple of years, savoring every single movie, including those no one in their right mind enjoys. But there's no getting around the fact that as a shared film universe, Toho's franchise has more holes than a golf course covered in bagels, pasta colanders, sex dolls, and old socks. The series may have earned the studio a lot of cheddar, but during the Shōwa era, its continuity was like Swiss cheese.

The thing is, though... it doesn't matter. The existence of continuity problems does not make these movies less enjoyable. This isn't the Marvel

---

[36] Plus numerous others that were planned but never made. You can read about them here: https://godzilla.fandom.com/wiki/List_of_unmade_monster_films and https://www.cbr.com/20-unmade-godzilla-movies-better-than-what-we-got/.
[37] https://travsd.wordpress.com/2015/10/02/abbott-and-costello-the-horror-comedies/

Cinematic Universe we're talking about, nor is it *Alien vs. Predator*, *Star Wars*, or *Star Trek*. When things don't quite make sense, fandom doesn't get worked up in a mouth-frothing frenzy and flood the internet with vitriol. Sure, the films are at times so goofy that one expects the next one to be called *Godzilla vs. Mickey Mouse*. Sure, the English dubbing and ill-fitting monster costumes can elicit some laugh-out-loud moments and are really doing the films no favors. And sure, the scripts disrespect female characters far too often in the early years, to the extent that it can be uncomfortable for modern audiences. But these are all reflections of when the movies were produced – historical allowances must be made.

Plus, the series has more to say than people tend to realize. Weighty themes were subtly slipped in among the monster fights, giving viewers something of substance on which to chew. Journalists are portrayed as protectors of the truth, which the media once represented. Corporations are exposed as predatory and evil. The military is shown to be too inefficient and single-minded to get the job done (why *do* they keep attacking Godzilla with planes and tanks if that never stops him?). And Japan, as a nation, shows admirable fortitude in continually rebuilding post-war Tokyo and its other cities, no matter how many catastrophes it suffers... even if it does stretch credibility that anyone would ever want to live there again after, say, the third monster attack.

The bottom line is this: whenever you see Godzilla on camera (as opposed to Godzilla on Gamera,[38] which fans have longed to see but which, alas, has not come to pass), you know you're in for a fun ride – provided Matthew Broderick and Hank Azaria aren't sharing the screen. If Rodan and Ghidorah are involved, you'll double your enjoyment, and any film with Mothra tends to be better than one without, because the accompanying music is so soothing and melodic whenever the faeries come around, you'll want to listen to it again. There's a

---

[38] A turtle-based *kaiju* from Daiei Film who debuted in 1965's *Gamera, the Giant Monster*. His first nemesis was Barugon, whose name and design were remarkably similar to those of Toho's Baragon. The series capitalized on the popularity of Toho's *kaiju* films, but Toho became the movies' distributor starting in the 1990s, following Daiei's bankruptcy. In 1992, Kadokawa Corp. (which absorbed Daiei) approached Toho about coproducing a crossover project, *Godzilla vs. Gamera*, but Toho declined.

reason there have been 21 more Godzilla films and counting since the Shōwa era's 15: they're more fun than a barrel of monsters.

Gamera, Daiei's kid-friendly terrapin *kaiju*, almost shared a crossover film with Toho's Godzilla.

Toho's Shōwa-era films might not always work together or be as cohesive as the movies from some other shared universes, but they don't need to be. Fans don't watch *kaiju* and *tokusatsu* films because they seek Orson Welles-level storytelling and depth of character. Underlying messages and inter-film connections are welcome, of course, but more than anything, fans yearn to see massive monsters pummeling the snot out of each other, while trampling helpless cities in the process. They thrill at watching the military falter, then human ingenuity prevail. They enjoy seeing reporters save the day who aren't played by Raymond Burr.

Most of all, *kaiju* enthusiasts want to be cinematically entertained and musically stimulated. If a giant dinosaur (*not* a giant iguana, Roland Emmerich) breathes atomic fire and destroys skyscrapers, accompanied by an energetic orchestral soundtrack, fans get pretty excited. The franchise may not display Marvel's tightly woven continuity, but it's continuously fun to watch, building-sized warts and all. In the end, isn't that what matters?

The author wishes to thank proofreaders John Hazlett and Patrick Izzo for their invaluable feedback.

Hippie Freaks in Monstrous Clothing: *The Addams Family* vs. *The Munsters*

by Robert Jeschonek

By the mid-1960s, they seemed to be everywhere, and they weren't like *us.* Their strange hair and attire set them apart from common men and women. They ingested substances that were foreign to those who considered themselves normal. They acted in strange ways, sharing customs, slang, and attitudes that were so alien to God-fearing Americans, they were downright *frightening*.

And yet, they were *familiar* to us as well. We recognized the human qualities within these freaks and came to accept their eccentricities because of them. They made us laugh and helped us accept the *other* nonconformists who were increasingly becoming a presence in our world at the time, or at least not fear them as much. They became like friends and neighbors, because we saw them every week... *on television*.

In the sitcoms *The Addams Family* and *The Munsters.*

Freakish Beginnings

By September 1964, when both *The Addams Family* and *The Munsters* premiered on network television (ABC and NBC, respectively), the hippie counterculture had spread throughout the United States in opposition to conformist lifestyles and the Vietnam War. Known for wearing long hair and colorful clothes, hippies had a reputation for engaging in free love, smoking marijuana, taking psychedelic drugs, and eschewing capitalism and the nine-to-five workday world. They often shared utopian belief systems grounded in Eastern philosophy and dreamed of casting off the shackles of industrialization, commercialization, and spiritual paralysis in return for a freer, more grounded, communally oriented existence that emphasized a "back to nature" approach. Even as the "straight" old guard remained dominant, the hippies challenged traditional social mores, culture, and values, intentionally setting themselves apart as "freaks" who didn't fit in with the establishment.

As the hippie movement gained steam, the cultural moment was just right for TV shows about other freaks among us. Two new shows debuted during the same season, competing for attention with a similar theme – the humor found in the eccentric habits of people considered by society at large to be monstrous. It was a rich comic vein that hadn't been fully tapped on weekly TV before, and viewers seemed primed and ready to embrace it. The novelty, however, wasn't the only appeal to the 1964 TV audience. *The Addams Family* and *The Munsters* shared the same subtext, intentional or otherwise: that the strange creatures we sometimes find among us are not always as threatening as they seem, and we might have more in common with them than we think.

"Here are these ghoulish, monstrous, grotesque people moving in, bringing in difference to the neighborhood," said historian Susan J. Douglas in a segment of the PBS series *American Experience*.[1] "It is this kitschy way to work through how to manage whitebread neighborhoods dealing with a very different kind of family moving in."

What better message could be injected into entertainment programming at a time when a swath of America's young people (and some who were not so young) had taken up the freak flag of a new culture, style, and way of thinking that must have seemed almost incomprehensible to the masses who toed the establishment line? The impact was enormous, as Douglas explained on *American Experience*: "People think this is just entertainment, but people in

---

[1] 1964: "Television Reflects Social Change," *American Experience*. Referenced 6/28/19 at https://wpsu.pbslearningmedia.org/resource/amex26-soc-64tv/1964-television-reflects-social-change/.

television are members of our culture, and they imbibe the zeitgeist of the times. Change is everywhere, rebellion is everywhere."[2]

As for the actual hippies, they found an added subtext in those shows, apart from the message that "the other" could be assimilated or at least accepted by the old guard: that it was perfectly all right to be a freak among straights – and probably a hell of a lot more fun than being straight like everyone else.

About the Addamses

The Addams Family show was based on a series of macabre cartoons that appeared in *The New Yorker* beginning in 1938. Created by cartoonist Charles Addams, the characters put a dark spin on everyday life, demonstrating a Goth sensibility before such a thing existed in the common parlance and popular culture.

The Addams Family was based on Charles Addams' comic strip in *The New Yorker.*

The family consisted of a father figure, Gomez, whose idea of fun was crashing toy trains together; his wife Morticia, who dressed all in black and raised flesh-eating plants; their children, Pugsley and Wednesday, who shared their parents' warped outlook and had a torture chamber for a playroom; Uncle Fester, a crazed goofball who could power a lightbulb by plugging it into his mouth; Grandmama, a knife-throwing witch; Lurch, a towering, stone-faced

---

[2] Ibid.

butler who played the harpsichord when he wasn't busy answering the foghorn doorbell and intimidating unwary guests; Thing T. Thing,[3] a disembodied yet reanimated hand in a box; and Cousin Itt, a short fellow with hair so long it covered his body from head to toe. A 1977 TV reunion film would add two more children, Wednesday Jr. and Pugsley Jr.

They're creepy and they're kooky, the Addams family. Front (left to right): Gomez, Wednesday, Morticia, and Pugsley; back (left to right): Uncle Fester, Lurch, and Grandmama.

Inhabiting a creepy mansion filled with ghoulish props and creatures, the Addamses considered themselves as perfectly normal as the straight-laced citizens with whom they came in contact. Nevertheless, their off-the-wall behavior and predilections often drove people to take drastic steps to get away from them and ensure they never encountered them again.

Munsters 101

While the Addamses had their origins in magazine cartoons, the Munsters were based on Universal Studios' classic monster movies of the 1920s through

---

[3] According to the episode "Thing Is Missing," the middle T also stood for "Thing," making his full name Thing Thing Thing.

the 1950s, played for laughs. Since Universal developed *The Munsters*, the characters on that show could wear costumes and makeup similar to those worn by actors in its monster movies, making the connection between the two very clear.

Since *The Munsters* was developed by Universal Studios, the show's producers were allowed to use any likenesses that the studio owned.

The main characters in the cast of *The Munsters* included Herman Munster, a Frankenstein's monster lookalike and the family's patriarch; his wife, Lily, a vampire as well as a homemaker; their werewolf son Eddie;[4] Grandpa,[5] a vampire and mad scientist always cooking up surprises in his lab; and the couple's adopted niece Marilyn, the only family member who didn't look and act like a monster (though the others saw her as a black sheep because of it).

Though the Munsters looked more exotically monstrous than the Addamses, they were often perceived by "normal" people as being just as normal as they were. Herman had a job, Lily tended the home, and Marilyn and Eddie went to school. In spite of their bizarre appearances and behavior, the Munsters were very much mainstreamed into society. In the episode "Family

---

[4] Someone explain *that* one to me.

[5] Grandpa was identified as Count Dracula in several episodes, with the sequel TV series, a continuation of the original called *The Munsters Today*, giving him the full name Vladimir Dracula, Count of Transylvania.

Portrait," they were even selected by a magazine as an average American family.

The residents of 1313 Mockingbird Lane, the Munsters (left to right): Marilyn, Grandpa, Lily, Herman, and young Eddie.

Dueling Weirdos

The Addams Family and *The Munsters* had a lot in common. For one thing, both shows featured distinctive, instantly recognizable theme songs – a horn-and-guitar-driven rock tune for *The Munsters* and a bouncy piece featuring harpsichord and double finger-snap percussion for *The Addams Family*. As different as the two themes were, they both stood out as utterly unique in the TV soundscape of the time.

Perhaps the strongest similarity between the two shows can be seen in the way they both featured titular families of creepy, misunderstood characters with alternative lifestyles in an otherwise homogeneous American landscape. They both supported the paradigm of the nuclear family – with a mother, father, and children living under the same roof – and also upended it, as the members of both families were anything but typical.

The families' homes were also atypical, though located on the streets of nondescript mid-1960s communities. The Addamses and the Munsters each lived in a haunted-house mansion filled with bizarre decorations and scary surprises. The Addams house, at 0001 Cemetery Lane, featured a stuffed bear, a moose head with one antler pointing downward, a swordfish with a cousin's leg sticking out of its mouth, and various torture devices, including an iron maiden and a bed of nails. Meanwhile, the Munsters' home, at 1313 Mockingbird Lane, had a dragon's den under the staircase, a mad scientist's lab in the basement, and copious cobwebs hanging everywhere.

Inhabiting these mansions alongside them were the families' private menageries of offbeat pets. The Addamses kept a pair of ravenous piranha named Tristan and Isolde, an octopus called Aristotle, a full-grown lion known as Kitty Cat, and Cleopatra, a meat-eating African Strangler plant. The Munsters had a pet dragon called Spot, a Transylvanian bat named Igor, and a black cat by the name of Kitty that roared like a lion.[6]

In addition to their taste in unusual pets, the two families shared unique preferences when it came to wardrobe. Both the Addamses and the Munsters wore outlandish clothing that suited their oddball natures but stood out in a crowd of "normals." On the Addams side, for example, Uncle Fester wore a floor-length, fur-collared coat; Morticia wore a tight-fitting, all-black dress; and Cousin Itt wore a bowler hat and sunglasses. On the Munster side, Grandpa wore full Count Dracula regalia, complete with cape and gloves; Lily wore a flowing gown and "bat luck charm" worthy of a female vampire; and Herman had bolts in his neck and dressed in a black shirt, jacket, trousers, and huge, clompy shoes like Frankenstein's monster did in the Universal movies.

Another similarity shared by the two families was their appreciation of unconventional vehicles. The Munsters rode around in the 18-foot-long Munster Koach (built by Batmobile creator George Barris from three Ford

---

[6] Note the similarities between the feline members of each household.

Model T bodies), which looked like a souped-up hearse, complete with plush interior, mobile lab, and rumble seat.[7] As for the Addamses, their car of choice was a Packard V-12 convertible limousine with fiery rocket propulsion and a horn that sounded like a duck's quack.[8]

Cracked Mirror Images

As many similarities as the Addamses and the Munsters shared, and as much as they both spotlighted themes related to welcoming and humanizing the other, the two families were not equal in their outright resemblance to hippies. One, in fact, was clearly more counterculture-friendly than the other, more of a mirror image of the hippies – albeit a *cracked* one.

It's true that, like the hippies, both the Munsters and the Addamses had unapologetic, in-your-face, nonconformist attitudes. They weren't ashamed of their alternative lifestyles or outrageousness; if anything, they were *proud* of them. So what if Dad was Frankenstein's monster or Mom clipped the flowers off roses and made bouquets of the thorny stems? If it was shocking to some, then so be it. Neither family was going to change for the sake of humoring "the squares," just as the hippies had no intention of adhering to establishment norms and rules because others saw them as bizarre or dangerous.

It's also true that both families shared other traits with the hippies. As much as each had certain twisted proclivities and monstrous characteristics, they favored seeking peaceful resolutions to their problems. They sometimes terrified the straights but didn't seem to take pleasure in it. Like the hippies, they avoided violence; some of the Addamses and Munsters had confrontational natures, but they usually curbed their impulses (though they could have done no end of damage to the "normal" folks who strayed into their orbits).

Like the hippies, the two families were also tolerant of differences in others. They saw diversity as a good thing and embraced people of every stripe without regard to race, nationality, creed, or peculiarity. Bigotry and discrimination had no place among the Addamses, Munsters, or hippies. But when you got right down to it and looked closely, one family stood out as the most hippie-like. One clan had the strongest counterculture cred... and it wasn't

---

[7] https://munster.fandom.com/wiki/The_Munster_Koach
[8] https://e3sparkplugs.com/blog/which-was-the-best-spooky-family-car-the-munsters-koach-or-the-addams-familys-packard-v-12/

the one with the fun-loving Frankenstein's monster and the boy with too much facial hair and the grandfather cooking up concoctions in his lab like Owsley the LSD wizard. The Munsters may have hosted a wild party of teenyboppers and beatniks once,[9] but they never really gave off a hippie vibe – unlike the Addams Family, who had more similarities to real-life hippies than Thing could shake a finger at.

Altogether Ooky

There's a line in Bob Dylan's song, "Ballad of a Thin Man," that goes like this: "Because something is happening here, but you don't know what it is, do you, Mister Jones?"[10] Could there be a better way to describe how average folks must have felt when they first encountered the hippie subculture – or first entered the home of the Addams Family?

The Addams' house was full of bizarre, often surreal, sights and sounds. The characters who inhabited the place seemed like they were from another, freakier reality where "normal" standards and values were turned inside-out. A grown man blew up toy train sets for fun while his wife fed meat to her garden and their daughter played with her headless doll, Marie Antoinette. It was either the weirdest, most horrific scene or the most hilarious put-on ever.

It probably warmed the hearts of many a hippie. Surrealism, put-ons, absurdism, and all manner of oddities fit right in with the hippie mindset and the psychedelic point of view that took hold among many in the counterculture. The rejection of seriousness and the embracing of the silly and strange were very much part of the hippie ethos, a way of exposing the stagnation and corruption the hippies saw at the root of mainstream Western culture.

The Addamses demonstrated their rejection of that same culture as well, from their exotic apparel, bizarre mannerisms, and Goth mentality to their detachment from the daily working world. None of the core family held a steady job or put in regular shifts at any kind of workplace. Gomez, Morticia, Fester, and Grandmama seemed to be independently wealthy and spent their time on leisure activities for their own edification and amusement. They didn't rant about the essential demoralizing nature of the working world, but it truly meant nothing to them (except as an occasional lark, like when Uncle Fester got

---

[9] "Far Out Munsters," 18 March 1965.
[10] "Ballad of a Thin Man," from *Highway 61 Revisited* by Bob Dylan (Columbia Records, 1965).

a job as an insurance salesman[11]) – just as the hippies refused to buy into the predominant system of work, consumerism, and traditional interpersonal relationships. Life, to the hippies, was about seeking bliss and passion in connections to others and the world around them, not chasing promotions, pay raises, material things, and superiority and power over others.

In other words, they followed the gospel of Gomez Addams, who approached every moment with wild-eyed, childlike exuberance.[12] Gomez didn't work and didn't care about keeping up with the Joneses. He went after each new bright and shiny pursuit with demented glee, whether it was backing a political candidate[13] or planning a vacation to the moon.[14] And his passion for Morticia, often ignited by her seductive incantations in French, was intense and all-consuming, nothing like the chaste and reserved marital love portrayed in the majority of TV comedies at the time. Clearly, Gomez and Morticia were as much sexual beings as the hippies, and their lifestyle was anything but mired in conventional mediocrity.

Liberated libidos weren't the only lifestyle choice the Addamses had in common with hippies, either. Drug use was widespread throughout the counterculture, and marijuana and LSD were practically sacraments. Just as the hippies smoked joints and dropped tabs of acid, Gomez and Morticia Addams occasionally smoked a hookah. The unidentified smoldering substance inside the smoke-filled device could have been pot as easily as tobacco. The visual of the two upstanding citizens (upstanding in their own eyes, at least) partaking of the smoke from an exotic-looking pipe system had to have had at least a subliminal impact on viewers who were familiar with the imagery and implements of casual drug use as practiced by the hippies. Maybe they came to the realization that smoking a little dope might not be so bad, after all. The hippies, for their part, might have come to a different conclusion altogether – that the Addams Family were pretty cool, though their show aired on a TV network that benefitted The Man. They might have been corporate shills, but they were up to some downright revolutionary stuff under the noses of the network bosses who pulled their strings.

---

[11] "Crisis in the Addams Family," 12 March 1965.
[12] John Astin, who played Gomez, later portrayed a hippie in the *Night Gallery* episode "Hells' Bells," which first aired on 17 November 1971.
[13] "Gomez the Politician," 9 October 1964.
[14] "The Addams Family Splurges," 29 January 1965.

Hippies in the Family

When you consider all the fundamental similarities between hippies and the Addams Family, you might wonder why you didn't notice them before. You might also be surprised that there are *more* where they came from. In fact, two members of the Addamses' extended family could have been considered actual full-fledged hippies. Recurring character Cousin Itt was the ultimate longhaired freak, a creature who looked like a shambling mass of floor-length hair. He did his own thing and spoke in gibberish that couldn't be understood by "normal" people (much as hippie-speak might have sounded nonsensical to average folks outside the counterculture). Itt was so bizarre and far-out, he made Fester and Lurch look like straight-laced squares.

Then there was Morticia's sister Ophelia, whom Gomez almost married before he proposed to Morticia.[15] Ophelia, who became a recurring character in the second season of the show, looked like a total flower child, wearing daisies in her hair and carrying a big bouquet of posies wherever she went. Blonde and lighthearted instead of dark and gloomy like Morticia, she acted like a free-spirited hippie girl (though she also had a domineering streak and wasn't afraid to use judo flips on Gomez when he displeased her). Appropriately enough, when Ophelia's betrothal to Gomez didn't work out, she ended up falling for the other resident hippie type in the extended family, Cousin Itt.

The Better Monsters of Our Nature

Looked at decades later, long after the hippie movement had its peak, *The Addams Family* still resonates with the flavor of the counterculture of the mid-'60s. The show's characters had hippie-like qualities and delighted in abnormality so extreme, it was revolutionary for television of the era. And yes, they elevated a message – intentional or otherwise – about acceptance of the other in American society, no matter how different or alarming that other might seem. By defanging the creeps and creatures, they paved the way for eventual rapprochement between hippies and squares, a bridging of the gap between those who at first might have seemed overly uninhibited and those who might have seemed too constrained.

That isn't to say that *The Munsters* didn't also play a role in getting the message out. Herman and his family let their freak flags fly proudly, giving

---

[15] "Morticia's Romance: Part 1," 24 September 1965.

viewers a weekly dose of oddball antics that any self-respecting hippie would have applauded. The Munsters made it okay to be scary and ridiculous at the same time, to be monstrous yet benevolent in the face of daily struggles to fit in with an entrenched conformist society.

Together, the Addamses and the Munsters did the same work as the earlier monsters who had inspired them – they helped humanity to face its fears of a changing world. In the 1930s and '40s, the creatures of Universal's horror films came along when the terrors of the Depression and World War II threatened to consume us. Before that, scary novels like *Frankenstein* and *Dracula* had arrived in the 19th century when the specters of other conflicts and the Industrial Revolution were the stuff of nightmares. In the centuries before fiction was committed to the printed page, scary stories were handed down through the oral tradition, helping us drag our fears into the light as new challenges rose to confront us – in that way, giving us power and understanding that enabled us to survive and go forth instead of cowering from the dangers ahead.

Or maybe they just let us delude ourselves into thinking we had some measure of control over uncontrollable circumstances. Maybe they made us feel like we could cope in our own little corners of the world, because nothing was as bad as it seemed once you held it up to the light. Not even people who come along wearing peace signs and love beads and long hair... people taking drugs and shirking work and having sex with whomever they pleased outside the bonds of wedlock... people who said traditional ways of life were an empty joke, and *they* weren't the ones who were the *monsters*.

When you get right down to it, whatever our differences or disagreements, those people were our family, friends, and neighbors. They were our fellow men and women, no matter what clothes they wore or how they behaved or what they believed. And if a Frankenstein's monster could love a vampire woman and put up with her bloodsucking father... if a train set-smashing nut and his morbid wife could find happiness with a walking heap of hair and a cadaverous giant butler... then it wouldn't hurt *us* to get along with a bunch of hippies, would it?

That was the gospel according to *The Addams Family* and *The Munsters*, brought to the heart of middle America every week in beautiful, flickering black and white. That was the message transmitted for two TV seasons on Thursday and Friday nights from 1964 to 1966. And what do you know? It turns out the message was right. (Insert *Addams Family* theme song "snap snap" here.)

Dracula Gets Hammered

by Glenn Greenberg

There are roughly 200 movies based on or inspired by author Bram Stoker's immortal classic, *Dracula*. Most of them suck outright, hobbled by low budgets, lazy or unimaginative writing, clumsy or misguided direction, or a combination of all of the above. That, of course, makes the relatively few exceptions stand out all the more.

The Dracula series produced by Britain's Hammer Films from the late 1950s to the early 1970s encapsulates that assessment to a tee. In terms of quality, the series is all over the place, with the movies ranging from excellent to mediocre to "Geez, they weren't even *trying*." The studio had two not-so-secret weapons that never failed to bring class and dignity to the projects they worked on: Christopher Lee as Count Dracula and Peter Cushing as Van Helsing. But even those two gentlemen could not create jewels out of junk.

And yet... quality, or the lack thereof, is in the eye of the beholder. Movies that I consider treasures, other folks – including the people who actually *worked* on them – may consider trash. But *I'm* writing this piece, not them, so for now, you're stuck with my opinions. This brings me to the heart of this matter: an overview of the entire Hammer series, with observations, background information, and a final verdict on each installment.

Let's open the coffin...

Horror of Dracula (1958, U.K. Title: *Dracula*)

Until this movie, the actor most associated with Dracula was, of course, Bela Lugosi, who had brought the character to life (undeath?) on the big screen in the original 1931 Universal classic, and then reprised the role in 1948's *Abbott and Costello Meet Frankenstein*. While other actors played the Count in the intervening years, most notably Lon Chaney, Jr. and John Carradine, only Lugosi left an indelible mark – one that is still highly visible today. But once Lee arrived on the scene, Bela was no longer the only Dracula cemented in the hearts and minds of moviegoers and horror fans around the world. And rightfully so – from his first moment on screen in *Horror of Dracula*, Lee owned the role, delivering a performance that ranged from coldly polite to darkly menacing to frighteningly feral.

Christopher Lee masterfully dons the cape inherited from Bela Lugosi for the first time in *Horror of Dracula*.

Peter Cushing's Van Helsing is a major departure from Stoker's novel, being much younger and far more physically vital, and actively working against Dracula even before the story begins. Nevertheless, he is terrific in the role – distant, methodical, and authoritative most of the time, and yet wonderfully charming, compassionate, and warm when the situation calls for it, specifically when comforting a little girl who nearly falls victim to Dracula's new bride, Lucy Holmwood.

The rest of the cast, which includes Michael Gough as Arthur Holmwood (an amalgamation of three characters from Stoker's novel), Melissa Stribling as Mina Holmwood (a variation of Mina Murray Harker), Carol Marsh as Lucy (a different take on Lucy Westenra), and John Van Eyssen as Jonathan Harker, are all solid, though Gough's Arthur comes off as far more of a milquetoast than any of the characters on which he's based. For devotees of the novel, perhaps the biggest change is the handling of Jonathan, whose storyline plays out quite differently from the way Stoker presented it.

Set in 1885, this first entry in the series – the first Dracula movie to be shot in color, by the way – is widely considered the best of the Hammer bunch. But its flaws become glaringly obvious upon close inspection. It's understandable that what works in a novel doesn't necessarily translate well to film. Changes have to be made to adapt the material into another medium – one with visuals, sound, and actors interpreting the characters and performing the dialogue. And in the case of *Horror of Dracula,* Bram Stoker's several-hundred-page book had to be streamlined and condensed considerably, as screenwriter Jimmy Sangster and director Terence Fisher had only 90 minutes to tell their version of the story. But that doesn't explain some of the creative choices that veered away from the original work and created plot holes and lapses in logic that weren't there originally.

For example, in the novel, Jonathan Harker is a young attorney summoned by Dracula to his castle in Transylvania to help the Count finalize the purchase of an estate in England. In *Horror of Dracula*, Harker arrives at the castle to begin his new job as an archivist for Dracula's library. Harker is *really* there to destroy Dracula, secretly working with Van Helsing. This raises the question: Why would Dracula hire an archivist for his library? Why would a vampire care whether or not his book collection was in order? Did he just wake up one night with an urge to rearrange everything according to the Dewey Decimal System, but decided he didn't want to do it himself? From a character standpoint, and a logical one, this makes absolutely no sense. It's frustrating to know that flaws like this would not be there if the filmmakers had put just a little more thought into the screenplay.

Still, Lee and Cushing are a delight to watch, the production values are strong, as is Fisher's direction, the movie moves along at a nice pace, and the ending is satisfying enough – even though it perpetuates the notion that vampires crumble to dust in the sunlight. That's an invention of the *movies*, not Stoker.

The Brides of Dracula (1960)

This is certainly one of the stronger entries, despite the misleading title – the movie is not about Dracula *or* his brides. Christopher Lee is a no-show, as is the Count. Lee wasn't ready to put on the cape again, reportedly concerned about being typecast. And who could blame him? The 1931 *Dracula* made Bela Lugosi an international star, but look what happened to his career in the years that followed.

Despite its title, *The Brides of Dracula* isn't a film about Dracula or his brides.

Nevertheless, the film is a direct sequel to *Horror of Dracula*, featuring the return of Peter Cushing as Dr. Van Helsing. Terence Fisher is once again in the director's chair, working with a screenplay by Jimmy Sangster, Peter Bryan, and Edward Percy (with uncredited contributions by producer Anthony Hinds). Hammer has to be given credit for respecting Lee enough to not simply hire someone else to play Dracula. To stand in for the still-dead Count, they brought in David Peel to portray Baron Meinster, described in the opening narration as one of Dracula's "disciples," and who looks like a cross between a young, blond Robert Wagner and Conrad Veidt as Gwynplaine in the 1928 film *The Man Who Laughs*. Meinster proves to be just as ruthless as his mentor – perhaps even more so, given the fact that he kills his own mother and turns her into a vampire. While seducing a young schoolteacher recently arrived in Transylvania, he rushes headlong into a dramatic showdown with Van Helsing, and comes closer to destroying the vampire hunter than even Dracula did.

It's an entertaining film, certainly well made, but it can't help but come off as little more than an effort to keep the home fires burning until the lord of the manor returns.

Dracula: Prince of Darkness (1966)

It took eight years, but Hammer finally managed to corral Christopher Lee for a proper Dracula sequel. This one is essentially a haunted house story, with the haunted house being Castle Dracula. The Count has been dead for 10 years, but his castle still stands, serving as a stark reminder of evil and terror for the villagers living in its shadow. When two English couples visiting the countryside find themselves stranded nearby, they end up at the castle, where they are greeted by Dracula's servant, a man named Klove, who has maintained the place for all the years since his master died. That night, Klove snatches one of the men and uses him as fodder to resurrect the Count. Once Dracula is back, he resumes his evil activities, targeting his unwitting houseguests. He even reenacts a scene from Stoker's novel, in which he slices open his chest and forces his intended female victim to drink the blood oozing from the wound, as a means to control her mind.

Eight years after *Horror of Dracula*, Christopher Lee returned to the role of the bloodthirsty count in *Dracula: Prince of Darkness.*

The one thing Dracula *doesn't* do in this movie is speak. He has absolutely no dialogue. In the years following the film's release, Lee said in a number of interviews that he was so disappointed in the lines that were written for him that he suggested that Dracula not speak at all – that he function solely as a voiceless, supernatural presence. As recently as 2011, during a personal appearance at University College Dublin, Lee maintained this account, telling the audience, "I had read the script and I refused to say any of the lines."[1]

However, the film's screenwriter, Jimmy Sangster, asserted in his book, *Inside Hammer*, that it was *his* idea to keep the Count silent. "Vampires don't chat," Sangster explained. "So I didn't write him any dialogue. Chris Lee has claimed that he refused to speak the lines he was given... So you can take your pick as to why Christopher Lee didn't have any dialogue in the picture. Or you can take my word for it. I didn't write any."[2]

With returning director Terence Fisher at the helm, *Dracula: Prince of Darkness* is a solid film – not *quite* as good as *Horror of Dracula*, but certainly within range of it. The ending is somewhat hokey, however, dispatching the Count in a manner that diminishes him as a vastly powerful force to be dreaded and feared. Regardless, Lee demonstrates that he doesn't need to utter a word to be a great Dracula.

Dracula Has Risen from the Grave (1968)

This one has been unfairly maligned over the years, with a lot of the criticism coming from Christopher Lee himself. On numerous occasions, Lee publicly voiced his displeasure about a scene in which the young male hero, Paul, plunges a stake into Dracula's heart, but it fails to destroy the Count because Paul is an atheist and therefore cannot bring himself to say the prayer required to make the staking effective. Lee objected to this heretofore unrevealed bit of vampire lore because it didn't come from Stoker. It's a valid point, but the whole bit about vampires not being able to survive in sunlight didn't come from Stoker either, and Lee never expressed any objection to Hammer using it in *Horror of Dracula*.

With stylish and colorful direction by Freddie Francis, who stepped in when Terence Fisher had to bow out unexpectedly, *Dracula Has Risen from the Grave* is actually one of the strongest films in the series. Written by Anthony Hinds under his pseudonym John Elder, the story is of a more personal nature, with a newly resurrected Dracula seeking revenge on the local monsignor who has just performed an exorcism at Castle Dracula – thus rendering the Count unable to enter his own home. After corrupting a priest, who then becomes his reluctant

---

[1] https://www.youtube.com/watch?v=XY-xzYbEocM
[2] Sangster, Jimmy. *Inside Hammer*. Reynolds & Hearn, 2001, pg. 114.

slave, Dracula targets the monsignor's niece, a young woman named Maria, to become his next bride.

The Count is once again up to no good in *Dracula Has Risen from the Grave.*

The film features interesting characters and compelling interpersonal conflicts, with a strong performance by Lee, who is thankfully given dialogue once more. It also benefits from having Veronica Carlson as the lead female protagonist. In addition to being a talented actress, Carlson was one of the most beautiful women to ever grace a Hammer production. As Maria, she turns in an effective performance that makes you truly care about her character. Even the male romantic lead – usually the weakest element in a Hammer horror movie – is interesting and well developed. Portrayed by Barry Andrews, a dead ringer for the young Roger Daltrey, Paul is likable, fallible, and relatable. He's desperate to prove that he's worthy of Maria's love, and to gain the respect of her uncle, who is appalled when he learns of Paul's atheism.

The plot has more substance than any other film in the series, as it's as much about the still-relevant conflict between faith and reason as it is about the struggle between good and evil. And the ending is a doozie, with a particularly gruesome death for the Count.

Taste the Blood of Dracula (1969)

This one is a major step down. It gets off to a good start, picking up where the previous film left off, but quickly starts to stumble. The story follows three wealthy, middle-aged men who seek out dark, forbidden pleasures together, leading them to hook up with a young, creepy practitioner of the occult called Lord Courtley. He manipulates them into providing the means to resurrect Dracula, and involves them in a black-magic ritual in which he orders all three men to drink some of the Count's remains. They refuse, so Courtley drinks the whole thing himself. Horrified, the three men beat Courtley to death and flee, returning to their seemingly respectable lives. But unbeknownst to them, Courtley's dead body transforms into Dracula, who swears vengeance on the ones who destroyed his servant. The Count targets each of the men's children, compelling them to murder their fathers.

The resurrection process in this movie – along with Dracula's motivation – is confounding. Had the three men each ingested Dracula's remains, how would the Count have returned? Would there have been three of him? Would he have been revived in spirit form, possessing each of their souls? For that matter, by drinking all of the remains, Courtley literally becomes Dracula, so he's essentially gone – the Count has displaced him completely. So why does Dracula care that the men killed Courtley, to the extent that he devotes all of his time and energy to taking revenge on them?

To make matters worse, Lee is given virtually nothing to do. He stands on the sidelines most of the time and has the absolute barest minimum of dialogue. *Taste the Blood of Dracula* epitomizes one of Lee's main complaints about Hammer's Dracula series – that the Count is shoehorned into stories that don't really have anything to do with him. Reportedly, early versions of the script did not even feature Dracula. It was only at the insistence of Hammer's

U.S. distributor, Warner Bros., that the Count was added, and a major effort was made to entice Lee to reprise the role. Otherwise, the movie would not have been produced at all.

As Lord Courtley, Ralph Bates – who, at the time, was being groomed to become Hammer's new major horror star – chews the scenery, spits it out, and then chews it all over again. The other characters and the interpersonal conflicts are little more than watered-down, far less effective retreads of what we saw in the previous film. And the conclusion is both incoherent and unsatisfying. It's as if the filmmakers suddenly realized they had to wrap things up, so they improvised the ending on the spot on the last day of shooting.

Screenwriter Anthony Hinds, once again using the name John Elder, and director Peter Sasdy are responsible for this huge disappointment, so blame where blame is due.

Scars of Dracula (1970)

From the time Hammer started to produce its Dracula sequels, the company's approach was to have all of the movies link together. Dracula's death at the end of one film would be addressed directly in the next one, and audiences would see how the Count managed to return. But *Scars of Dracula* broke from the line of continuity that ran through the first five films and told a standalone story. Supposedly, this break was made because Hammer was seriously considering starting the series over with this movie in the event that Christopher Lee could not be lured back again. Once Lee's services were secured, there was either no time or no interest on the part of the producers to revise the script to make it tie in with the established continuity.

Despite that, *Scars of Dracula*, written by Anthony Hinds (as John Elder) and directed by Roy Ward Baker, is one of my favorites. In this film, Dracula is central to the plot, Lee gets a lot of screen time and dialogue, and there are several direct nods to Stoker's novel. They include a moment in which Dracula scales the side of his castle, and some key scenes involving Dracula and one of the male protagonists that strongly echo the Count's interactions with Jonathan Harker. Former *Doctor Who* actor Patrick Troughton gives a fantastic, memorable performance as Dracula's manservant, Klove – not the same one from *Dracula: Prince of Darkness*, as Troughton's Klove is far more brutish and conflicted about his lot in life.

The simple, straightforward story is about a dashing ladies' man named Paul who is forced to flee his home village after getting caught in bed with the daughter of the burgomaster. Ending up at Castle Dracula, Paul is welcomed by its owner, who was recently resurrected after a bat flew into his resting chamber and vomited blood onto his ashes. (Just roll with it.) Much like Jonathan Harker in the novel, Paul soon realizes that he is a prisoner in the castle, and that his host is anything but a good Samaritan. Some time passes, and with Paul having disappeared without a trace, his brother Simon comes looking for him, accompanied by the beautiful Sarah, with whom both Simon and Paul are in love. Their quest leads them right to Dracula's doorstep, and the Count, as one would expect, takes an immediate interest in Sarah.

The only weak elements in this movie are the ridiculously fake-looking vampire bat puppet that can actually *hover* in mid-air, the silly, unsatisfying death the filmmakers concocted for Dracula, and the character of Simon. As played by Dennis Waterman, he is so utterly bland, boring, colorless, and stoic that he's little more than a walking mannequin.

Jenny Hanley, who plays Sarah, is absolutely lovely, but all of her dialogue was dubbed by another actress. As far as I can tell, Miss Hanley gave a perfectly acceptable performance. Could she have really delivered her lines *that* poorly?

Christopher Lee bashed *Scars of Dracula* for years, saying it was the worst of the bunch. However, the audio commentary he recorded for its 2004 DVD release is eye-opening. Recording the commentary while watching a screening of the movie, Lee admitted that he actually didn't remember it at all – and that he didn't think he had ever seen the finished work. As the commentary continued, Lee, to his own surprise, even made some positive remarks about what he was seeing on screen. It's quite funny to hear Lee ruminate about how the Hammer films had gone wrong, how Dracula became less and less integral to the stories, and how there was not enough adherence to Stoker's novel – only for him to then discover those criticisms don't really apply to *Scars of Dracula*!

Lee also criticized the level of sadism displayed by Dracula in the film, but I think he was off the mark. This was the first time in the Hammer series when Dracula was truly *frightening*, truly *disturbing*. It worked for me. Regardless of how he felt, Lee's performance is impeccable.

Dracula A.D. 1972 (1972)

By the early 1970s, Hammer Films was in decline, with most of the key creative people from the glory days having moved on and audience tastes shifting away from the company's output. Hammer's movies, once considered shocking, daring, and groundbreaking – and even offensive to some – now seemed positively quaint. As the company's box-office success dwindled, budgets were reduced, and in many cases it really showed on screen, with production values on display that never would have passed muster just a few years earlier.

Desperate creative decisions were made to try to keep up with the latest cultural trends, which led to the use of nudity and more blood and gore. To reinvigorate the Dracula series, Hammer decided to transport the Count from his 19th-century setting to what was then the here and now, and to have him face off against a descendant of Van Helsing played by Peter Cushing, who would make his return to vampire hunting after a 12-year absence. Unfortunately, the end result was that the series went completely off the rails.

After a great opening scene, *Dracula A.D. 1972* unfortunately takes a stake to the heart.

The basic idea is not bad at all. The movie, written by Don Houghton and directed by Alan Gibson, begins with an *excellent* prologue set in 1872, in which Dracula and the original Dr. Van Helsing, Lawrence (though it was Abraham in Stoker's novel), have their final showdown aboard a runaway coach in London's Hyde Park. This confrontation completely contradicts the continuity established in the first five movies. The coach crashes and Dracula is impaled on the spoke of one of the vehicle's broken wheels. Van Helsing, mortally wounded, uses the wood from the wheel to stake Dracula, and then dies with the Count. Soon after, a disciple of Dracula arrives, collects the vampire's ashes, and plants some of them, along with the stake, in the ground at a cemetery – the same one where Lawrence Van Helsing is buried.

Cut to 100 years later, at which point the disciple's descendant, who calls himself Johnny Alucard (get it?),[3] gathers a group of young hippies that includes Jessica Van Helsing (played by Stephanie Beacham), the great-granddaughter of Lawrence. Alucard takes them to the now-deconsecrated cemetery, where he performs a black-magic ritual in which he resurrects Dracula, introducing the ancient evil to a whole new world – one in which the Count intends to destroy the Van Helsing line forever. If only the rest of the movie was as good as the opening sequence.

I have no problem with moving Dracula into the modern age. My undying love for Marvel's 1970s comic-book series *The Tomb of Dracula* will attest to that. But *Dracula A.D. 1972* doesn't work as a horror film, because it's not scary at all. In fact, it's downright *boring*. It doesn't work as a Dracula film, because Dracula has less screen time than ever. It doesn't even work as a reunion of Lee and Cushing, because they have barely two minutes of screen time together and their relationship in the 20th century is never established or developed. Cushing's character, Lorrimer Van Helsing – Jessica's grandfather – has obviously never met Dracula before, and doesn't come face to face with the Count until the closing minutes of the film.

But for me, the biggest sin of this movie is that after having been gone for an entire century, Dracula experiences no culture shock whatsoever after he's revived. What's his initial reaction to airplanes? Television? Cars? You'll never know, since it's never addressed. Take away the 1972 element and the same exact story, more or less, could be told in a 19th-century setting. In fact, it was – in *Taste the Blood of Dracula*. The creative laziness here is staggering. Lee and Cushing give it their all, but it's not enough to save this sorry excuse for a Dracula movie.

The Satanic Rites of Dracula (1973)

It's hard to imagine that Hammer could do worse than *Dracula A.D. 1972*, but the company managed to top itself – and not in a good way – with this one. Screenwriter Don Houghton and director Alan Gibson were brought back, so there was little chance that the results would be any better.

---

[3] A nice homage to Lon Chaney Jr.'s Count Alucard, from the 1943 Universal film *Son of Dracula*.

Like its immediate predecessor, *The Satanic Rites of Dracula* is set in the early 1970s and is thoroughly boring. The plot is silly, ill-conceived, and muddled, mixing horror with science fiction and even James Bond thrillers. Resurrected yet again, Dracula poses as reclusive tycoon "D.D. Denham" and prepares to unleash a deadly plague upon the world to destroy humanity. (Uhh, Count? If all the people are gone, what are you going to do for sustenance?)

Peter Cushing returns as Lorrimer Van Helsing in the lackluster *The Satanic Rites of Dracula.*

Peter Cushing returns as Lorrimer Van Helsing, but Joanna Lumley replaces Stephanie Beacham as Jessica. (Beacham turned out to be the lucky one.) Considering that this movie marked the last time that Christopher Lee would ever play Dracula for Hammer, and the last time that Cushing would ever play Van Helsing opposite Lee, it's a travesty. As a cure for insomnia, though, it's ideal.

The Legend of the Seven Golden Vampires (1974)

Despite Christopher Lee's departure, Hammer produced one more film involving Dracula – and it was a real oddity. *The Legend of the Seven Golden Vampires*, written by Don Houghton and directed by Roy Ward Baker, is an uneasy mix of horror and kung fu co-produced by Hong Kong's Shaw Brothers Studio. Set primarily in 1904, it features Peter Cushing as Professor Van Helsing (presumably the one from the original continuity), with Dracula making a cameo appearance.

The plot involves Van Helsing and his associates embarking on a mission to free a rural village in China that has long been terrorized by a cult of vampires. The cult's high priest, a Chinese man named Kah, is actually Dracula in disguise. Dracula had encountered the *real* Kah a century earlier and took on the high priest's physical appearance and identity to escape Transylvania. John Forbes-Robertson stepped in to play the Count in his original, non-Asian form, with his voice dubbed by someone else. Suffice it to say that Forbes-Robertson would not make anyone forget the man whose cape he had inherited. The film, unsurprisingly, was not a box-office success, and it is widely considered a footnote in the Hammer Dracula canon.

And with that, it was all over. Christopher Lee had moved on, and within a few years, Hammer closed up shop. As of this writing, Lee made his final appearance as Dracula nearly 50 years ago. Since then, other actors have donned the fangs, including Frank Langella, Gary Oldman, Gerard Butler, and Luke Evans. But none of them have made the kind of impact, or forged an extended association with the character, the way Lee did. It may be many more years before another actor comes along who can ingrain himself so indelibly in the public consciousness as Bram Stoker's vampire lord, to stand alongside Lee and Lugosi.

But Count Dracula is immortal – he's got plenty of time to wait.

Hosts with the Ghosts: Horror Hosts in Comics and Television, 1940-1969

by Matthew Sunrich

Horror stories have been with us throughout human history.

In our modern world, horror is a vast literary genre with millions of hardcore fans who absorb it through print media, websites, movies, comic books, television series, and video games, but the notion of horror as entertainment is a relatively recent development. Traditionally, horror stories were, among other things, designed to keep children out of trouble. If you tell children not to go into the woods at night because a monster will eat them, they will probably keep to the road. The real reason might be to keep kids from getting lost, but that in itself is unlikely to convince them since it doesn't conjure up a concrete image in the mind. While our modern sensibilities may be shaken by this idea, virtually every culture in the world did it.

So, how did we go from stories concocted to scare the fertilizer (thank you, Michael Palin) out of kids to others written purely for thrills? Tracing this in detail would be far beyond the purview of this essay, so let's just look briefly at some of the more important elements in the development of the horror genre. The first is the work of Edgar Allan Poe. While he didn't invent the horror story, Poe brought it to a wider audience during the 1830s and 1840s and gave it a hint of respectability. The second is the publication of Bram Stoker's *Dracula* (1897), which catapulted horror into the literary realm and was also the first horror novel to be adapted into a full-length film (albeit in the guise of German director F. W. Murnau's *Nosferatu*, starring Max Shreck as the terrifying Count Orlok). The third is a magazine called *Weird Tales*, which began in the early 1920s. Many influential horror writers were featured in this publication, Cthulhu-creator H. P. Lovecraft chief among them, and it was key in the development of the genre.

Horror stories found their way onto radio in the 1930s with shows such as *The Witch's Tale* and *Lights Out*. The former was hosted by "Old Nancy, the Witch of Salem," which is a significant development in the genre. Horror stories, up to this point, were told either from the first-person perspective, by someone actually experiencing the events directly or indirectly, or by an omniscient narrator. The notion of a host harkened back to scary stories told around the campfire, imbuing them both with a particular kind of eeriness and the reverence that a storyteller commands. It also provided a level of consistency, as most horror stories are, by their very nature, episodic. To put it another way, listeners would not be able to identify with recurring characters in the tales themselves, as most would wind up dead or would simply never appear in another installment, but they *could* look forward to hearing Nancy's voice every week.

Comic books, the offspring of pulp fiction and newspaper strips, came into existence around this same time, and it's no surprise that horror themes found their way into their pages. At the beginning, of course, adventure stories and early superheroes, such as Superman, Batman, and Captain America, were the order of the day, but that didn't stop publishers from experimenting. Unlike most comics these days, early Golden Age books were anthologies, featuring a number of different characters and genres. In the pages of Quality's *Hit Comics* #1 (1940), we find a six-page story titled "The Tale of the Haunted Inn." It is the first horror tale ever published in a comic and it's introduced by the Old Crone. She changed her name to the Old Witch with the title's second issue and continued spinning horror yarns until issue #14. She wears a hooded green cloak with a shock of white hair framing her wizened, wart-ridden visage. Only known to hardcore comic fans, she is the first of three hosts to use the Old Witch moniker.

In Archie's *Blue Ribbon* #20 (1942), we find the second horror host. She is never explicitly given a name, but her feature is called "Tales from the Witch's

Cauldron." In her first appearance, she looks like the sort of stereotypical witch you'd expect to see trick-or-treating, with a long black dress, a pointed hat, and sharp teeth for devouring wayward children, but in her second she is dressed in a red cloak and has green skin – borrowed, one can assume, from Margaret Hamilton's portrayal of the Wicked Witch of the West in MGM's *The Wizard of Oz*. In her third, she again has green skin but is back in black, as AC/DC would say. In any event, while she doesn't say very much, she offers readers "The Future Bubble," followed by "The Black Stallion of Death" and "The Warren House Curse" in the subsequent two issues, after which the book was put out to pasture.

Horror stories weren't limited to the silver screen, as these issues of *Weird Tales*, *Boris Karloff Tales of Mystery*, and *The Witching Hour* illustrate.

After these early experiments, horror stories, unfortunately, vanished from comic racks for several years. However, with the end of the Second World War, the popularity of superheroes began to wane, leaving a window for the first comic devoted entirely to horror. *Eerie Comics* #1, published by Avon, appeared in late 1946. It was originally conceived as a one-shot but picked up where it left off a few years later and ran for a total of 17 issues. Unlike *Hit Comics* and *Blue Ribbon*, its stories stood on their own and were not presented by a host. Two years later, William Gaines, publisher of EC Comics, introduced the most famous of all comic horror hosts in *Crime Patrol* #15. Illustrated by Al Feldstein, "Return from the Grave" is presented to readers by the Crypt-Keeper. The host appears again in the next issue with "The Spectre in the Castle." Response to these stories was positive, so the decision was made to make the book entirely horror. As was common practice at the time, the title of the comic was simply changed, first to *The Crypt of Terror* with its 17th issue and then to the familiar *Tales from the Crypt* with its twentieth.

Unlike the rotting corpse known to fans of the HBO television adaptation, the Crypt-Keeper looks more or less like a normal human male in the comics, albeit with long white hair and an overabundance of saliva. "Lower Berth," appearing in *Tales from the Crypt* #33, reveals the Crypt-Keeper's origin and is a rare example of a host actually being featured in a story. Master cartoonist Jack Davis guides readers through a bizarre tale involving a traveling carnival with a sideshow comprising a female mummy from the Valley of the Kings and the corpse of a two-headed man preserved in formaldehyde. One night, both exhibits disappear. Their trail leads to a wedding chapel, where they were apparently married by a blind justice of the peace who found the nuptials odd but simply remarked on the odor ("Five bucks is five bucks"). A year later, the loving couple is discovered in a cave, but they have clearly been busy, as a wailing baby with familiar features crawls from the mouth of the cave as they are carried back to the carnival. This is indeed a weird story that leaves one with far more questions than it answers, but it's exactly the sort of thing one would expect from the brilliant but twisted minds of the EC creators (recall that these were the same "gang of idiots" responsible for *Mad* magazine).

It soon became evident that horror comics were the next big thing, so Gaines rolled out two companion titles in short order: *The Vault of Horror* and *The Haunt of Fear*. The former was hosted by The Vault-Keeper, who had debuted in *War Against Crime* #10, and the latter by the second host to go by the name the Old Witch (Gaines remarked in several interviews that she was directly inspired by Old Nancy from *The Witch's Tale*). If truth be told, EC's Old Witch is virtually identical to Quality's, though EC's is uglier and prefers red cloaks. The Vault-Keeper is kind of a cross between the Crypt-Keeper and the Old Witch, and he wears a green cloak. The triad of EC books is effectively interchangeable, as each one includes stories by each of the hosts, though the hosts' personalities are distinctive.

The Crypt-Keeper has a penchant for puns (the title of the aforementioned story, for instance) and usually sets up and concludes his stories with them. This use of humor was a new idea at the time and would prove immensely influential on horror media. The other two hosts use highly alliterative language and purple prose. Each of the three insists that his or her stories are the best and seizes every opportunity to belittle the others, creating an entertaining rivalry for readers. The stories themselves are certainly horrific, though rarely actually gory, but any discerning reader can recognize the frequent tongue-in-cheek aesthetic. In the final four issues of *The Vault of Horror*, the Vault-Keeper shares hosting duties with a mysterious young woman (possibly a vampire?) named Drusilla. The nature of their relationship is inscrutable. Unlike the others, Drusilla never speaks, but she was a groundbreaking character because she had sex appeal, a quality that would become important in short order.

In 1951, Fawcett, the publisher probably best known for the original Captain Marvel ("Shazam," as he's known today), introduced Dr. Death in the first issue of *This Magazine Is Haunted*. The cover features a graveyard scene with a distressed man crouching down next to a coffin he has apparently exhumed, and its skeletal inhabitant doesn't appear to be as dead as he had thought. In a jagged box above, the ghoulish Dr. Death, resplendent in his top hat and cape, dares us to read his "hair-raising horror stories." The comic ran for 14 issues, concluding in late 1953.

A year after Dr. Death, Fawcett gave readers The Mummy in the premiere issue of the awkwardly titled *Beware! Terror Tales*. On the cover, beneath a tableau in which a terrified man in a tacky, rumpled outfit confronts an array of various monsters, The Mummy remarks, "For 2000 years I have lain in the cold embrace of death — known intimately the blood-chilling secrets of the supernatural I am about to reveal." Compelling stuff, for sure. The series ran for eight issues, wrapping up (heh) in mid-1953. Unfortunately, Dr. Death and The Mummy were the last two noteworthy comic horror hosts to be introduced for more than a decade, as comic-book publishing was about to suffer a major blow.

In 1954, New York psychiatrist Fredric Wertham published a book called *Seduction of the Innocent*, which argued that comic books were harmful to youth and contributed to delinquency. The fact that much of it was exaggerated or just made up whole cloth (what the hell did Wertham have against comics, anyway?) was beside the point; it attracted a lot of attention and eventually led to a Congressional inquiry which culminated in the formation of the Comics Code Authority, a self-regulating body with the responsibility of policing comic-book content (the CCA label on a comic's cover let parents know that the book was "safe" for their child). It should come as little surprise that the lion's share of comics were canceled as a result, including every single horror title. While publishers were not obligated to adhere to the Code, this was during the period when distributors wielded a lot of power, and many of them wouldn't carry books that didn't, so very few companies were willing to see their profits decline.

Curiously enough, while horror hosts were in the midst of disappearing from the pages of comic books, they were coming to life on television. The first of these – and the most famous – was Vampira. In 1953, lovely Finnish-American actress Maila Nurmi, who had posed for artists such as Alberto Vargas and Man Ray, attended a masquerade ball dressed in a costume inspired by Charles Addams' Morticia cartoon character from *The New Yorker* (note that this was a decade before *The Addams Family* sitcom would debut on television). This drew the eye of TV producer Hunt Stromberg Jr., who hired her to host horror movies on his Los Angeles-based station, KABC-TV. Nurmi's husband came up with the name Vampira, and Nurmi herself developed the character. Clad in a form-fitting dress that accented her décolletage, Vampira sat on an antique sofa in her misty, cobwebby attic and addressed viewers in a sultry yet disarming voice while puffing on a cigarette.

Vampira (Maila Nurmi) was television's first and arguably most famous classic-era horror host.

The Vampira Show premiered on 1 May 1954. It only ran for a year, but it proved hugely influential and has a large cult following to this day.[1] It's hard to say whether or not the writers were inspired by the Crypt-Keeper's jokey

---

[1] Horror-punk progenitors The Misfits even included a song about her on their 1982 debut album *Walk Among Us*.

nature, but her monologues were riddled with gruesome humor. While sipping a "vampire cocktail," for example, she remarks that a cherry or an olive would only disintegrate in the drink, so she suggests dropping in an eyeball instead, "if you happen to have an extra one around the house" (and who doesn't?). When asked why her attic doesn't have any electricity, she replies that "electricity is for chairs." She would also gently mock the movie she was hosting. A year after the show's cancellation, Nurmi, desperate for money, agreed to appear as Vampira, to which she had retained the rights, in Ed Wood's *Plan 9 from Outer Space*, which is deservedly considered a contender for the worst film ever made.[2]

In 1957, Screen Gems began offering the Universal Classic Monsters films, including both well-known ones such as *Frankenstein*, *Dracula*, and *The Mummy*, and obscure titles such as *Pillow of Death*, *The Frozen Ghost*, and *Weird Woman*, to television stations, which showed them during weekend nights under the title *Shock Theater*. Stations were encouraged to employ hosts for the features, which gave rise to the horror-host phenomenon. *The Vampira Show* never aired outside of Los Angeles, and this was the norm for television horror hosts. They were a localized experience, which makes them particularly interesting for a number of reasons. For one, it provided something special for people living in a particular area: a host they could call their own – a "secret" to cherish, if you will. For another, it fomented horror fandom nationwide in an unprecedented way, giving fans different experiences to share with others who had never seen their hosts. In short, fans were seeing the same movies, but framed in different ways, weaving a rich tapestry of monster fandom.

Next to Vampira, the best-known horror host is probably John Zacherle. He assumed the role of horror host for *Shock Theater* in Philadelphia in October 1957. Dwelling in a crypt, he dressed in an undertaker's coat and went by the name "Roland" (pronounced Ro-LAND). He was joined by his lab assistant Igor and his unseen wife, who lies in a coffin and is referred to by Roland simply as "My Dear." His persona alternated between irascible and severe, and good-

---

[2] Actress Lisa Marie portrayed Vampira in Tim Burton's 1994 film *Ed Wood*, which explored the genesis of *Plan 9 from Outer Space* (and Wood's other movies), including how the director convinced Nurmi to join the cast. In 1989, Nurmi famously sued actress Cassandra Peterson (TV horror hostess Elvira) for $10 million, alleging she had pirated the Vampira character. Peterson, however, prevailed in the lawsuit.

humored and gregarious. Roland carried out various experiments for the audience, mixing potions and whatnot, and talked in an eccentric way that drew viewers in one moment and repelled them the next, creating a sense of unease. The show had clearly taken a cue from Vampira's, though it ramped the humor up considerably and dispensed with the sexiness altogether.

John Zacherley and a bony friend.

Whereas Vampira had merely ribbed (heh) the films she hosted, Roland flat-out lampooned them, often cutting away from the film for a gag. This technique would later be employed by myriad similar programs, most notably *Mystery Science Theater 3000*. The show was neither afraid to use gory props for shock value nor to be outlandish. Dick Clark, host of *American Bandstand*, nicknamed Zacherle "The Cool Ghoul." In 1958, he recorded "Dinner with Drac," a novelty song with the lyrics, "A dinner was served for three / At Dracula's house by the sea / The *hors d'oeuvre* were fine / But I choked on my wine / When I learned that the main course was me!" It preceded Bobby Pickett's similar but better-known "Monster Mash" by four years. That same year, Zacherle took his show to New York, leaving behind the name "Roland" and becoming "Zacherley" instead. The show was retitled *Zacherley at Large* in 1959. The following year, he edited two collections of horror short stories by such authors as L. Ron Hubbard, A. E. van Vogt, and Theodore Sturgeon. Though he went on to many other projects, he is most fondly remembered as a horror host.

Other notable hosts of the late 1950s and 1960s include Morgus the Magnificent, a mad scientist portrayed by Sid Noel for the New Orleans and later Detroit markets; and Ghoulardi, a hugely popular hippie character played by Cleveland DJ Ernie Anderson, who made no secret of the fact that most of the movies he hosted were stinkers. Anderson was also an outspoken critic of Lawrence Welk and other local television personalities, and he organized softball, football, and basketball games for charity.

I mentioned earlier that comic publishers were not required to have their books approved by the Code, though the majority chose to submit. One of the few that decided to ignore it was Gold Key. In 1962, it published *Boris Karloff Thriller* #1, which changed its title to *Boris Karloff Tales of Mystery* with its third issue. While its content was relatively tame compared to what was found in pre-Code horror books, it is certain that the CCA would have taken issue with most of its stories for the simple fact that they contained things like zombies and mummies, which were strictly forbidden. As the title suggests, the stories are hosted by an illustrated depiction of Boris Karloff.

English actor William Henry Pratt took the stage name Boris Karloff both because it sounded better and because he wished to disassociate his career from his family, who considered acting to be a low profession. After starring in numerous films throughout the 1920s, he landed the role of the Monster in James Whale's *Frankenstein* (1931). The following year, he played Imhotep/Ardath Bey in *The Mummy*. Karloff appeared in films spanning many genres throughout his career but is remembered most for his horror work and has, indeed, become an icon. He has the distinction of being the only real person to appear as a horror host in a comic.

Not unlike the Crypt-Keeper and the other EC hosts, Karloff bookends many of the stories, setting them up and offering concluding remarks. There is nothing humorous or flowery in his language, however – which, depending on whom you ask, can be interpreted as either dull or sophisticated. When you read one of his stories, such as "The Menace of the Missing Mummy" in issue #4, it feels as though you're sitting in the dimly lit study of an English manor house on a crisp autumn evening, fire roaring on the hearth, as he thumbs the spines of the dusty volumes in the bookcase while telling you the story.

In 1964, James Warren, publisher of the popular magazine *Famous Monsters of Filmland*, decided to try his hand at a horror comic in the vein of EC's efforts. Recognizing a loophole that would skirt the Code, he published it as a black-and-white magazine. That magazine, *Creepy*, introduced the first of three new Warren horror hosts, Uncle Creepy. The cover of the first issue was illustrated by EC alumnus Jack Davis and has a playful and cartoonish, rather than frightening, aesthetic. Despite his name, Uncle Creepy – a gaunt ghoul with thinning hair and gnarled, clawed hands, clad in a threadbare suit – is far from avuncular. He seems harmless enough, but he's not the kind of person you'd want to encounter in a dark alley, as it were. It's clear that he enjoys telling his scary stories and is often surprised that readers keep coming back for more. He himself appears in a few stories, most notably "Monster Rally" in issue #4, which serves as an origin story, though he denies it.

Creepy, Tales from the Crypt, and *Vampirella* were not typical comic books.

A couple of years later, Warren launched a second title, *Eerie* (not to be confused with Avon's earlier comic), and introduced a new host, Cousin Eerie. Clad in a Colonial-era getup, Eerie was short and plump, with two prominent bottom teeth protruding from a face not even a mother could love. He only appeared briefly in the first issue, due to its being an "ashcan" composed mostly of reprint material slapped together to secure the rights to the title (Warren and another publisher were each vying for it, and Warren got his to the printer mere hours before his competitor). Not unlike the EC hosts, there was a rivalry between Cousin Eerie and Uncle Creepy, and while name-calling ensued, it was not malicious in any way. Both hosts generously used humor and often made light of the fates of their stories' victims.

It's fair to say that Warren was responsible for reigniting the horror-host craze in comics, because several more would debut during the next few years. Charlton, a long-running comic publisher probably best known for the superheroes that inspired the characters in *Watchmen*, introduced a new horror host in *Ghostly Tales* #55 (1966), known as Mr. L. Dedd. A white-skinned humanoid with horns, dressed in a suit and purple cape, Dedd describes himself as "the only living creature" in the Haunted House, and he presents the tales

"Great Caesar's Ghost," "Army of the Dead," and "A Powerful Tale." Dedd appears here and there throughout the stories to appraise the actions of the characters in a very matter-of-fact way, hanging around until the series ends with issue #64. And in *Ghost Manor* #1 (1968), we meet the third host to go by the name "Old Witch." There's a good chance that she could, in fact, be a *pirate* witch, because she has a patch over her right eye and seems to have a penchant for maritime subjects.

It is interesting to note that Charlton, which operated under the authority of the Code, could get away with publishing horror books. At around the same time, DC eased its way back into the horror game as well, with hosts Cain and Abel in *The House of Mystery* and *The House of Secrets* (their dynamic is similar to that of Uncle Creepy and Cousin Eerie), respectively; Judge Gallows in *The Unexpected*; and Mordred, Mildred, and Cynthia, a triad of witch sisters, in *The Witching Hour*.[3] It seems that the Code had loosened its standards somewhat in the ensuing years, though it wouldn't actually lift its ban on vampires, werewolves, and zombies until the early 1970s. This is coupled with the fact that the comics didn't feature any actual monsters or anything particularly grisly. While ghosts often appear in Charlton's comics, as the titles suggest, the stories can more accurately be described as "suspense" rather than horror, and, like Boris Karloff's tales, they're pretty tame.

Marvel's only horror-host offering, Digger, debuted in *Tower of Shadows* #1 (1969). Digger is a ghastly gravedigger with a passing resemblance to Frankenstein's monster, who carries a shovel and a huge set of keys. The only truly significant thing about Digger is that he introduces Jim Steranko's tale "At the Stroke of Midnight," a masterpiece of sequential-art storytelling and one of the few stories from the title that has proven memorable.

Rounding out the decade is the debut of Warren's third host and arguably the most popular of the bunch: Vampirella. Created by *Famous Monsters* editor Forest J. Ackerman and underground cartoonist Trina Robbins, and brought to life by master illustrator Frank Frazetta, whose gorgeous painting graces the cover of the premiere issue, Vampirella rescued the publisher from the dire financial difficulties it had been facing in previous years. In the tradition of

---

[3] Cain, Abel, Gallows, and the witches would later feature prominently in Neil Gaiman's *The Sandman* and its spinoffs, particularly *The Dreaming*, in which they would be greatly fleshed out (heh) as far more than mere horror hosts.

Vampira, her sex appeal was unquestionably a factor, in that Vampirella's outfit was far skimpier (it was the era of the sexual revolution, after all). An alien from the planet Drakulon, she was originally meant to be nothing more than a host, but she appears in stories in the first couple of issues and becomes a regular feature with issue #8. Clearly, Vampirella was too great of a character and deserved to be a headliner in her own magazine.

It's not hard to see that hosts were hugely important elements in the development of the horror genre. They were quirky and unique and kept things interesting when the features they hosted left something to be desired. Thanks to the loosening of the strictures of the CCA in the early 1970s, horror enjoyed a renaissance in the pages of mainstream comics, but as the decade wore on, the hosts, while not disappearing completely, became less prominent. Warren closed the lid on its coffin in 1983, and DC's horror titles were put to rest around the same time.

On television, however, viewers were introduced to Elvira, Mistress of the Dark, and her show *Movie Macabre*, which enjoyed unprecedented success, quickly going national after its debut on a Los Angeles-based station. In 1986, the bosomy Valley girl entered the world of comics when DC began publishing *Elvira's House of Mystery*, which ran for 11 issues. Elvira, standing on the shoulders of the giants who preceded her, has become the most famous horror host, appearing in myriad commercials, television shows, stage productions, and even her own movie.

On the comic book front, in 2014 Warrant Publishing introduced *The Creeps*, a pastiche of the Warren magazines of the early 1970s with a modern twist. The stories are hosted by The Old Creep, a character similar to Uncle Creepy or the Crypt-Keeper. Warrant debuted a second title in 2020 hosted by Carmilla, a comic-book version of the vampire in Joseph Sheridan Le Fanu's eponymous 1872 novel. Warrant's Carmilla is clearly based on Vampirella, and though the latter is enjoying new adventures at Dynamite Entertainment, she is no longer serving as a host, so it's high time for someone else to fill her boots.

Horror anthologies are wonderful creations that breathe life into a genre in which death is always dominant. They're made just a little better, though, when they're bracketed with commentary by a terrorizing tour guide or a ghoulish grand master of ceremonies. It's that subtle distinction between simply watching or reading a story and having one *told* to you that can make all the difference.

The Plague of the Plague of the Zombies

by Robert Smith?

Why are zombies so scary?

The answer is far more subtle than it might first appear. The immediate answer would seem to be "Because they're zombies. Duh." And it's true that zombies are pretty horrific: they're the walking dead, inexorably coming after you. They don't need to sleep, don't need to eat — except for your braaaiiinnnsss! — and no matter how many you kill, there are always thousands more of them.

However, I'd argue that it goes deeper than that. What makes zombies really work is that they draw on some very fundamental fears that all of us have. One of those fears — very usefully pre-programmed into all of us, thanks to our ancestors — is of being eaten by a predator.

This isn't quite what zombies do, however. Although they want to eat our brains (or our charred corpses in a pinch), they don't seem to need to do so for sustenance. If they did, we'd be seeing a lot more examples of zombies (permanently) dying without food or becoming increasingly more desperate the hungrier they got. Instead, they just seem to want to eat our brains, just because.

Or do they? It's telling that, while the zombies have a number of obvious advantages over us, we have some advantages of our own. We might be frail humans who need to eat, sleep, and not be turned into pale, undead imitations of our former selves, but we can also do things the zombies can't. We can electrify fences, build moats, design shopping malls... in short, the best way to defeat zombies turns out to be our braaaiii–

Wait a minute.

So it turns out that the one thing the zombies want to eat just happens to be our best defense against them. Huh.

Nevertheless, being eaten alive is a pretty fundamental fear. It's the kind of thing that could freeze you into inaction. Even the thought of it is pretty visceral; enough to make you unable to think straight and hence make fundamental errors because of misfiring neurons in your braaaiii–

Wait a minute.

The other thing that most people fear is being felled by a disease. It's at this point I should probably lay my cards on the table: I'm best known for being the academic who published the first-ever mathematical model of a zombie virus.[1] I'm a disease modeler by day and proud science-fiction nerd by night, but I'd always kept my two worlds separate. When my students and I touched the two together, the whole world went mad.

Back in 2009, the fact that a bunch of mathematicians had published an academic article considering a zombie invasion was considered so newsworthy that it briefly became the number-one story in the world. (I freely admit that it was a slow news week!) We even won a Guinness World Record for the first-ever mathematical model of a zombie invasion.

The reason this was so popular was that we had a background in modeling regular diseases. In my day job, I use mathematics to study infections such as HIV, malaria, human papillomavirus, and various tropical diseases – including, subsequently, Ebola, which can be transmitted by the dead. Okay, they don't get up and come after you, but the dead are still an important class when determining control and intervention methods. My experience with zombie models showed me how this could be modeled when the large Ebola outbreak hit in 2014.

Our zombie model first described the infectious process. Humans can be infected by zombies, whereupon they will transition to the zombie class. But humans could also die, and the dead reanimate as zombies. Zombies themselves could be killed, either permanently or temporarily. We then

---

[1] https://mysite.science.uottawa.ca/rsmith43/Zombies.pdf

parameterized the model with data that we carefully studied from classic movies and video games (my students were given the best homework ever!) and found that a single zombie would result in the annihilation of a city of a million people in just four days.

We then refined this model to include a latent class: that period of several hours after one of your friends gets bitten and starts shaking and sweating and shivering, all apparently without anyone in the zombie apocalypse thinking that this might be odd behavior, because they are absolutely guaranteed not to notice until it's too late. We could call this the Charles Beaumont effect, after the transformation seen in *White Zombie* (1932), the first full-length zombie feature film.

Bela Lugosi's *White Zombie* was the first full-length zombie film.

We applied several control options: quarantine (removing zombies from the infectious pool), treatment (which would return zombies to the human state, although without immunity), and more sophisticated, coordinated attacks. You'd think that quarantine would do the trick, but it only slows the apocalypse down by a few days. I realize that a cure seems pretty unbelievable and kind of made up, but stay with me here. Turns out that you end up stuck in an equilibrium: for every zombie you cure, the zombie horde convert one of your shopping-mall buddies from friend to fiend.

Instead, it's the last option that has the best chance of success. Individuals fighting zombies one-on-one aren't very effective, but there's another option: we could pool our resources and attack in force at specific times, then reunite to examine what lessons were learned, before fighting back again more efficiently. This is a subtle, nuanced balance between educational techniques, joint co-operation... and mindless violence.

So what do we learn? We learn that we can only defeat zombies if we can outthink them. That if we get better at fighting them, thanks to pooling our knowledge, then we can eventually eradicate them. It all comes down to our sweet, succulent braaaiii–

Wait a minute.

Zombies aren't a disease exactly; one of my proudest moments was being invited to the Hollywood Director's Guild to talk about zombies and getting into an argument with George Romero about what zombies were. "You think they're a disease?" he said, unbelievingly. "I just thought Hell was full, so they sent them back." He was right, they're not a disease – but they do have the hallmarks of one.

In particular, they have the ability to *transmit*, which is a fundamental property of any disease. Like viruses in your body, they swarm and are not particularly concerned with the loss of any specific individuals. Another thing they have in common with viruses is that they're not quite alive and not quite dead.

Interestingly, not all classic zombie movies correlate zombies and the dead. *The Incredibly Strange Creatures Who Stopped Living and Became Mixed-Up Zombies* (1964) has lead character Jerry being hypnotized to become a zombie, but he doesn't die (until later, when he's shot by the police). The zombies here are disfigured, but only because they've had acid thrown in their faces. So they're a sort of halfway house between the living and the dead, just like this movie is a kind of halfway house between the worst movie you've ever seen and the most fun you can have on a Saturday night at the drive-in.

Viruses have some of the properties of life – they can carry genetic material and replicate, for instance – but they don't have cell structure and thus don't fully qualify for the definition of being alive. There are other similarities, too: in order to infect, the virus has to make actual physical contact with a cell, tearing it open. Sound familiar?

One of the knock-on effects that we see from most of the classic zombie movies is the apocalypse. Romero's *Night of the Living Dead* (1968) conveys it the way that most of us would experience it: on TV. The subsequent genre it spawned did so more directly, although there's much to be said for the power of hearing about the collapse of society second-hand. The apocalypse is an indirect consequence of the zombies, but I'd argue that it's way more in line with the disease side of things.

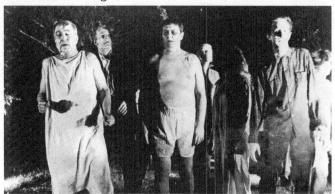

George A. Romero's *Night of the Living Dead* was a watershed moment in cult horror film history.

It's hard to imagine any predators being so efficient that they'd wipe out a whole city. That's just not how predators work. They're more of a "strike quick, kill the weak, then retreat" variety – which is absolutely terrifying if you're one of the weak ones, but it's a rare lion that takes down more than a couple of antelope at once.

A disease, on the other hand, can very quickly lead us to an apocalypse. During the 1918 Spanish flu epidemic, in order to go shopping, you'd have to write a list of what you wanted and slip it under the door with some money, and then retreat. The shopkeeper would assemble a package and leave it outside his door. Once he was firmly inside, you'd approach and pick up your goods. (If only they'd had a shopping mall!)

This kind of thing happens all the time during various epidemics. In a moderate outbreak, you might not go to the football game, but you'd still go to work and your kids to school. With a large outbreak, schools would close, but you'd still have to work.[2] In a severe outbreak, you would hide in your house with your family and a shotgun and take your neighbors off your Christmas list.

---

[2] Editor's Note: By eerie coincidence, Robert's essay was turned in mere months before the COVID-19 pandemic suddenly thrust the world into the very scenario he describes. It's not a zombie apocalypse (yet), but it sure felt like one for a while.

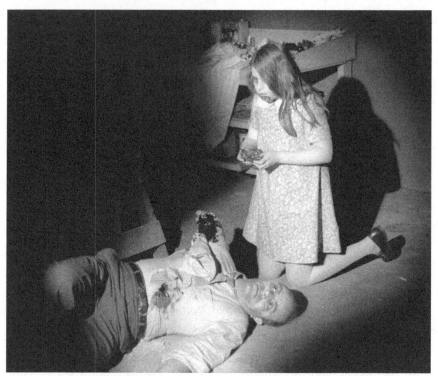

The slow-moving zombies of George A. Romero's *Night of the Living Dead* craved human braaaaaiiinnnsss... and the rest of the flesh, too.

During this kind of apocalypse, be it from a plague or zombies, the structure of society starts to fall apart, as *Night of the Living Dead* so aptly illustrates. People don't (or can't) show up for work, services become interrupted, electricity stops running, gas runs out...

...and aliens arrive and implement Plan 9 in order to raise an army of the undead to save *the entire universe* from humans. You know how it goes. You see? You see? Your stupid minds. Stupid! Stupid!

One of the appeals of the zombie apocalypse, I think, is the return to a simpler time. We can all imagine just what it would be like to have to survive against the odds and against nature, while picking off our enemies one by one. (Being a mathematician by trade, I have precisely calculated my own odds of survival in this regard. They are zero.)

It's an appealing fantasy. "Man against nature"[3] is one of the four conflict

---

[3] We don't generally use "Man" anymore in this context, but I'm leaving the sexist version intact, as I'm primarily talking historically.

narratives in literature. It calls to mind a rugged individualism, with particular echoes of the American frontier or colonial narratives. These sorts of stories are ones we've been telling for a very long time indeed – largely because when we started out, "man against nature" was pretty much our collective day job.

Of course, fighting nature and fighting zombies at the same time is an uphill battle. If the mindless undead don't get you, then an abscess of the tooth or an outbreak of dysentery probably will. Most of us don't have the ability to dig up ore and refine it, so we're going to run out of gas very quickly. Even if you do, then those skills probably don't extend to smelting lead to create more bullets. On the off chance that these are both talents you happen to possess, you may lack the scientific rigor required to develop a vaccine against the virus.

This is because we live in an interdependent society. You have your skills, I have mine, and someone else has totally different skills again. With capitalism, I can use my own talents to make money, so I can pay someone else for the privilege of not having to learn everything. Take away civilization and it's pretty unlikely that any single one of us would survive for long.

That's assuming we survive in the first place. Everyone always likes to imagine that they'll survive the zombie apocalypse, with people zombie-proofing their homes and so forth. Here's the awful truth: on the balance of probability, you're going to die. Since everyone thinks they'll survive an onslaught of zombies, yet the majority of people don't, it's patently clear that most people's survival plans must be flawed. What makes yours so exceptional that you'll be in the 0.001% of survivors?

The answer, like almost everything, is that it's an illusion of control. This, incidentally, is how we cope with diseases. We invest a lot of time convincing ourselves that we'll be safe from infection. A lot of our morality and rituals are based on ancient responses to disease. We bury people six feet under because that was the depth required to stop the plague transmitting from dead bodies. Many religions forbid the eating of certain foods, largely because those foods once carried disease. Monogamy was essentially developed as a way to stop sexually transmitted diseases.

The tragedy is that these illusions can be so strong that they can blind us to tackling new infections (or having a lot more orgies, I guess). When the AIDS epidemic arrived in the Western world, it mostly affected gay men. Straight people believed that this meant they weren't at risk, thus sweeping the issue under the carpet. Doctors even believed that the "rugged vagina" could take a lot more than the "sensitive anus" and hence advised women not to use protection in the early days of the AIDS epidemic. This killed a lot of people.

An analogy for zombies might be homeless people. If the zombie epidemic starts in poor areas, then shambling, grunting "people" might easily be overlooked. My other theory is that the perfect place to start a zombie epidemic would be at a large convention like San Diego ComicCon. Everyone would be taking photos of the cosplay and admiring the commitment to large-scale LARPing. You'd have 100,000 zombies without anyone even raising the alarm... at least until the zombies started trampling on *Star Wars* figurines. Then you'd have a panic on your hands.

So zombies are scary because they represent two primal fears that every human has: being eaten by a predator and being felled by a disease, of which the latter can lead to an apocalypse. But that's broadly true of many other creatures in this fine book. There's a third aspect to zombies that makes them really work, however, and that's the moral dilemma: can you shoot Grandma in the face?

Of course, it's not quite so straightforward as that. No one's asking you to randomly murder Grandma. Not even at Thanksgiving. But if Grandma dies and comes back as a zombie, can you shoot your beloved grandmother?

Better be quick, because if you love Grandma and paused to think about it, then you're a zombie snack already. Indeed, I'd wager most of us would have second thoughts about killing our loved ones. But that means all us favorite grandchildren are now dead, our braaaiiinnnsss eaten by zombie granny.

So who's left? Only the sociopaths. Or people who hate grandmothers. You see the problem here: even if we win against the zombies, we lose.

I Walked with a Zombie (1943) shows this in a number of ways. Paul Holland goes to enormous effort to save his zombified wife, Jessica, while Paul's brother Wesley (who's also in love with her) becomes obsessed with releasing her. Only the Sabreur takes definitive action, using voodoo to force Wesley to stab Jessica to death, whereupon Wesley drowns himself. The victory thus goes to the killer, with the sympathetic characters either dead or traumatized.

There's one thing that distinguishes (most) zombies from the other monsters: the dead come back to life. But why is this so bad? (Aside from the fact that they're trying to eat our grey matter, that is — which admittedly undercuts my argument somewhat.) The dead are so obviously horrific that they're a convenient shorthand for something terrifying. But this isn't true everywhere. In many places throughout the world, the most important day of your life is the day you die. Dead bodies are revered and touched by everyone, cleaned and bathed. In the Western world, we mostly hide them away and don't like to think about it.

Frances Dee, Christine Gordon, and Darby Jones in *I Walked with a Zombie*.

Even here, I'd argue that there's a legacy of disease. Europeans who lived through the Black Plague of the Middle Ages learned the hard way that the dead must be feared and avoided. Clutch the recently deceased body of your loved one in anguish, and you'll soon be taking their place. So we, as a culture, learned to shun the dead.

It's the moment in *The Plague of Zombies* (1966) when Sir James and Dr. Thompson open the coffin, only to find it empty, when we truly realize the horror of what's happened. That this is tied into witchcraft and voodoo – from otherworldly, mysterious foreign lands, where death has a different meaning – just reinforces the way that death rituals are embedded deeply into our culture. Ever since *White Zombie*, death and voodoo and zombies were intimately linked. Bela Lugosi's Murder Legendre controls the dead, raises the dead, and creates the dead (when he convinces Beaumont to kill Madeleine). *I Walked with a Zombie* was still linking voodoo and zombies in 1943, although by this point the zombie genre had branched out; *Bowery at Midnight* (1942), for example, finds Lugosi's Professor Brenner consumed by the living dead with nary a witchdoctor in sight.

Many people in developed countries can go their entire lives without seeing a dead body; however, the 2014 Ebola outbreak was exasperated by burial practices in Sierra Leone, Guinea, and Liberia, because people had a lot of close contact with the bodies of their loved ones.

Returning to pop culture: which is scarier, the fast zombie or the slow zombie? It depends on where you're standing. More recent films have picked up on the idea of the fast-moving zombie, in part because it suits the modern filmic sensibilities for rapidly paced scenes, computer-generated crowds of creatures, and visceral "They're coming right at you!" scares that can be worked into 3D.

Using the disease metaphor we've been developing, let's make a comparison. What's scarier: Ebola or HIV? Neither is particularly pleasant, but Ebola consumes you in a fever, causing you to bleed from every orifice, while HIV is mostly a slow, silent disease, with no symptoms for a decade until you succumb to opportunistic infections.

If you're in an Ebola-infected country and the disease is sweeping across the continent, this is pretty terrifying. (Full disclosure: this has happened to me. Being a disease researcher ain't for the faint of heart.) But if you take a larger view, then Ebola is actually not that scary at all. It largely burns itself up before it can do massive amounts of damage, whereas HIV is a slow and stealthy disease, shambling from one physical encounter to another, slowly taking over the world. HIV is the ninth-worst disease of all time, in terms of the number of deaths (36 million to date), whereas Ebola deaths are a tiny fraction of that number.

So there you have it, straight from science. Fast zombies might seem scary, but only if one is coming right at you. In the long run, it's the slow, classic zombie that can do the most damage, taking down civilization because of its powers of stealth. In other words, the classic zombie is the tortoise and the fast zombie is the hare.

Oh, but there's one last thing to address. How do we stop them? It's not with guns or bullets or violence or individualism. Instead, we rebuild the very thing the zombie apocalypse tries to take down in the first place: civilization. I might not be able to refine ore or smelt lead, but somebody in my community probably can. They might not be able to work on developing a cure for the zombie virus, but I can do that bit. In short, it's the interdependent society we started off with in the first place that allows us to succeed, not as rugged individuals but as cogs in the grand wheel of civilization.

Or, in other words, we simply have to use our braaaiii–

Wait a minute.

Rock Until You Drop: The Enduring Legacy of Classic Monsters in *The Monster Squad*

by Greg Mitchell

Allow me to set the stage: A little girl in a flower-patterned dress happily hums to herself as she plays beside a small pond one sunny day, innocent to the undead horror lumbering toward her from the tall grass. She is alone and unguarded as a shadow descends upon her, startling the girl's gentle song. Two giant boots plant themselves on the grassy bank to her left – boots belonging to a patchwork man made of cadavers, an amalgamation of corpses given blasphemous life by a mad doctor who has stolen lightning from Heaven. The girl looks up into the kind eyes of the gangly giant, seeing past his grisly appearance to the soul he possesses that no creator – save God – could give. And she accepts him.

Since you're reading this book, you no doubt saw this tender scene unfold in James Whale's 1931 groundbreaking masterpiece *Frankenstein*, with Boris Karloff portraying the definitive vision of the misunderstood "monster." But *I* first saw it in 1987's *The Monster Squad*, in which the Monster's iconic encounter with little Maria was recreated in loving detail – with an exciting twist. *Now* the little girl – here named "Phoebe" – not only befriends the

Monster, but also teams up with him to battle Dracula, the Wolf Man, the Mummy, and the Gill-man!

Opening on 14 August 1987, *The Monster Squad* was originally conceived by *Night of the Creeps*[1] writer-director Fred Dekker and his co-writer Shane Black[2] as a modern-day monster rally in the tradition of *Abbott and Costello Meet Frankenstein* – or, as Dekker dubbed it, "*The Little Rascals/Our Gang* meet the monsters."[3] Often dismissed (at least by everyone *I* ever talked to) as a rip-off of the more popular and successful *The Goonies*,[4] *The Monster Squad* occupies a special place in my heart, as it does for many horror fans of a certain age. It is a cult classic that has lived long beyond what, I'm sure, its creators ever believed possible.

For the uninitiated, *The Monster Squad* tells the fast-paced, uncomplicated story of a small, ragtag neighborhood club of monster kids who stumble across an amulet with the ability to open a door to Dumbo... er... *limbo*.[5] For the first time in a hundred years, the stars are mystically aligned, and if a virgin reads the right incantation (and, yes, it *must* be a virgin – Steve *does too* count), the gateway will be opened, swallowing all evil inside black oblivion forever. But the monsters, led by Count Dracula himself, want the amulet for themselves to ensure that their reign continues uninterrupted, and they are not above killing meddling children to obtain it.

Immediately, the film was met with a confusion that lingers even to this day. Is it a kids' movie? Is it too scary for young viewers? Is it a parody? A spoof? A comedy? Adults didn't want to watch it because it had a bunch of kids as its heroic leads. Parents didn't want their *kids* to watch it because it had a bunch of violence and swearing children. Therefore, sadly, virtually no one went to see it

---

[1] Released one year earlier, on 22 August 1986, Fred Dekker's directorial debut *Night of the Creeps* is another homage to science fiction "B-movies" of the 1950s, and is well worth checking out, in this writer's humble opinion.

[2] Earlier that year, Shane Black's "other" writing project – *Lethal Weapon*, directed by Richard Donner – went on to spawn a successful franchise of "buddy cop" movies. More recently, Black wrote and directed *Iron Man 3*.

[3] Burke-Block, Candace. "Directing a 'Monster' Mash." *Ocala Star-Banner*. New York Times Syndicate. 4 September 1987.

[4] Directed by Black's *Lethal Weapon* director Richard Donner in 1985.

[5] These similar sounding words are confused by Squad member Patrick (played by Robby Kiger), who is quickly corrected.

upon its initial theatrical release.[6]

Not even me, I must confess.

As a result, so many would-be fans missed out. What, then, is *The Monster Squad* and why should you care? In short, *The Monster Squad* is a love letter to classic horror – and, on a personal note, it was *my* first introduction to the Universal Monsters.

The cast of *The Monster Squad*: pint-sized monster hunters with 1980s fashion vs. Universal Pictures' creations from the 1930s to the 1950s.

---

[6] According to boxofficemojo.com, *The Monster Squad* opened on 1,280 screens and brought in just under $2 million. During its entire theatrical run, the movie would only earn $3.8 million of its estimated $12 million budget.

I was eight years old the weekend of 14 August 1987, on the verge of turning nine that November. My mom was pregnant and about to give birth to my little brother. I was still at an age when I would take off outside to run loose around the block with my neighborhood gang – and the world was still at an age when parents were comfortable letting their kids do just that. I remember those days so clearly, riding bikes until sundown, spraying each other with the garden hose, racing to one another's houses for sodas, and playing *Legend of Zelda* or *Punch-Out* on a friend's Nintendo video-gaming system.

Now my childhood has become cliché – its own genre, even: "kids on bikes," to which the Squad, as well as the aforementioned Goonies, Elliot and his friends in *E.T. the Extra-Terrestrial*, the Losers Club from Stephen King's *It*, and the Frog Brothers from *The Lost Boys*[7] all belong. You know the type: A group of foul-mouthed latchkey kids, often overlooked by adults, unattended by their parents, and left to raise themselves, who embark on crazy adventures that adults would have a hard time understanding.

More recently, "kids on bikes" have made a huge comeback, in large part due to the success of Netflix's original series *Stranger Things*. But back in the '80s, it wasn't a genre, it was just our *lives*. We were a generation brought up by working parents in oftentimes broken homes. We were all too familiar with empty houses, TV babysitters, fast food, and lots of time to ourselves. We grew up too fast and lost our innocence too quickly. Yet those sacrifices came with trade-offs in the form of self-reliance, teamwork, street smarts, and heightened intuition. As young as in grade school, we were taught that the world was full of strangers offering us delectable treats, but only as bait to lure us to the impenetrable darkness of a non-descript van so that we'd never be seen or heard from again. We were expected not only to run from danger, but to uncover it – to *look* for it, in all its varied guises. The monsters were everywhere, it seemed, waiting for our defenses to be down – just once! – so that they could attack.

That was *my* mindset at eight years old. I was a scared kid, fearful – not of

---

[7] Released a mere two weeks earlier, Joel Shumacher's "hip" vampire update *The Lost Boys* (originally selected to be a directing vehicle for none other than Richard Donner) debuted at #2 its opening weekend, reviving the vampire legend for a new rock-and-roll crowd, making household names of Corey Haim and Corey Feldman, and earning a domestic total of more than $32.2 million against its $8.5 million budget.

the dark, but of the darkness in men's hearts. People were scary, unpredictable tricksters. For many years, I just didn't trust anybody because I didn't trust myself to know the difference between the good people and the bad, between the neighbors and the strangers offering candy. "Better to be safe than sorry," I'd decided. I must confess, as of this writing, that I'm 41 with kids of my own, and yet I'm *still* that scared kid sometimes, distrusting of strangers, fearful of monsters everywhere, posing as people you can trust. The world is a frightening, uncertain place indeed.

It might, therefore, come as a surprise to learn why I always gravitated toward "scary" entertainment. Even before I could articulate the whys, I was drawn to monsters from my first recollections. Before Frankenstein's monster and the Wolf Man, I was obsessed with Bill Bixby's stalwart portrayal of the Incredible Hulk.[8] Long after my memory of those early years of my life faded, my mom would tell me how, whenever someone made the woeful mistake of making mild-mannered David Banner angry, I would hide my eyes as he transformed into the Green Goliath – but I never wanted her to turn off the show. To me, there was *power* in the Hulk. To be afraid, to be threatened, and to have this inner strength bubble to the surface to protect you – even without being aware of it! – was very tantalizing to me.

When Tim Burton's original *Batman* debuted in 1989, I caught Bat-mania along with the rest of the country, and now I understand my fascination was owing to the Dark Knight's horror roots. A small boy victimized by a cruel, uncaring world wraps himself in the very object of his fear to turn the tables on those who terrorized him. In both cases, the monsters were *protectors* of small boys frightened of the world. It was, therefore, cinematic geek destiny that I would discover *The Monster Squad*.

I come from a Christian home, I am a Christian now, and I've carried that faith to my own children. Now, you may or may not know this, but horror is not exactly welcome in most Christian circles. I know... shocker. Neither are Christians welcome in most horror circles. I've spent my entire life feeling

---

[8] *The Incredible Hulk* pilot aired on CBS on 4 November 1977, then a subsequent television series ran from 1978 to 1982, followed by a trio of made-for-TV movies. Bixby starred as tormented Dr. David Banner in search of a cure for his monstrous green alter ego, played by bodybuilder Lou Ferrigno. The series was developed by Universal Television (now NBCUniversal Television), opening up the possibility that the Incredible Hulk could be perceived as one of the Universal Monsters.

caught between two worlds. At any rate, horror was not "approved" in my home, by and large. My mom was always sensitive about that kind of thing, though my dad didn't really care, and I didn't want to upset her sensibilities, so I kept it out of the house. As a youngster, I can't count the times I heard pastors warning of the dangers of "horror movies and rock 'n roll." It was the 1980s! Satanic Panic was still in effect, and we were all one *Friday the 13th* away from total depravity. Unlike most kids of my generation, I didn't even see an "R" rated movie until I was 16 or 17 (it was *Species*, for the record). As a result, most of my horror movie experiences were second-hand.

The twins across the street had an older cousin from the Big City (I actually don't know if he was from "The City" or not, but he always seemed that way to us small town kids), who would sit as a wizened teacher on the front lawn until well into twilight, all us impressionable youngsters gathered at his feet in wide-eyed wonder. Like the great storytellers of campfires past, he would regale us with tales of the R-rated gorefests he'd recently seen. *Phantasm, A Nightmare on Elm Street, Friday the 13th* – all of these I first "saw" in my mind's eye as he narrated the movies' events (no doubt badly, in retrospect). I'll never forget the magic of those evenings, and the images I conjured stayed with me. Oddly, those stories gave me comfort when real-world anxieties plagued me.

Later, as heavily edited slasher fests made their way to late-night syndicated networks, I'd secretly set the VCR timer to catch any Freddy Krueger movie I could nab (he was my favorite, you know) and then quietly wake up extra early on Saturday mornings to watch and re-watch before my parents woke up. Just like when I'd watched the Hulk years earlier, I was petrified by the gruesome-*ish* images (edited for television, remember?), but I couldn't look away. I wouldn't. I would face the horror and would emerge stronger.

All of this was going on while *The Monster Squad* was bombing at the box office. It came and went with very little fanfare. I was only dimly aware of it because I caught a fleeting glimpse of a commercial for it one night. It was only a 30-second spot, but I noticed a Wolf Man and stirred with giddy interest, though I immediately gave up any hope of ever seeing it. It was PG-13. I was eight. My mom was still my mom. It was never going to happen.

Months passed. I continued playing Nintendo with my neighborhood chums, riding our bikes, talking about horror movies I would never see (but that they'd all viewed, naturally, by sneaking into the theater to witness the carnage firsthand). And then... it happened. We were at the neighbor's house and his mom made that most incredible declaration that only a child of the 1980s could ever fully appreciate: "Let's go rent a movie and order a pizza."

How can I describe the horror section of any given mom-and-pop video store in the glory days of VHS? How could my meager mortal words ever capture the otherworldly magic of walking into that section and being met with those fantastic images of macabre art? The movies might have stunk, *but that art*! We kids were given free reign and, lo, the heavens parted and a single pillar of light shone through the clouds of my fearful childhood to rest on a new VHS release that immediately called to me.

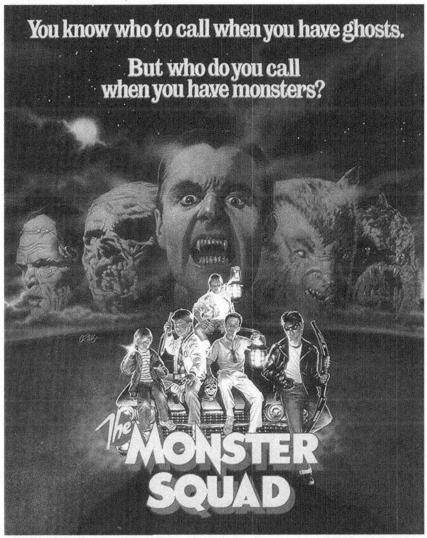

A poster for *The Monster Squad* riffed on the popular tagline of *Ghostbusters*, released in theaters three years prior.

To begin, the original poster was predominantly blue – my favorite color. At the top of the box, like some profane Mt. Rushmore of Horror, were the creatures: Frankenstein's monster, the Mummy, Dracula (with his fangs bared and dripping with saliva), the Wolf Man, and the Creature from the... er... the Gill-man. Directly below them, in a contrast of full-color, was a group of kids, not much older than me, bearing weapons and leaning on the hood of a classic car. They were cocksure, smug, and ready for war with whatever Hell had to throw their way.

The Monster Squad.

The poster wasn't merely a work of art, but an *invitation* to a world of monsters, where young boys were strong and sure and united and, above all, unafraid. We rented it that day and sat on the living room floor, eating our pizza and watching it. After we were done, I asked to borrow it, promising I'd have my parents return it before its due date. I just couldn't part with it. Not yet. My buddy's mom obliged and I watched it again. And again.

And again.

Not long after that, it premiered on HBO (which we couldn't afford), but I convinced my teenaged babysitter to tape it for me. She obliged and I watched it again. And again. Every day for *months*, I watched that tape. Now, decades later, after I've bought the VHS, the DVD, and the 20th Anniversary Edition Blu-ray, I *still* have that old tape from the late '80s that my babysitter made for me.

So that's a lot of reminiscing on my part, but what about *The Monster Squad*? What's the big deal?

The first thing you must understand is that while the movie is billed as a "horror comedy," it is *not* a spoof or a parody or a send-up.[9] It is an earnest, straightforward mission to re-introduce the classic Universal Monsters into the (then) modern world of 1980s slashers. The humor, such as it is, comes as the result of well-meaning but clueless parents struggling to understand the difference between Dracula and Godzilla,[10] or just the stupid stuff that comes

---

[9] Even though the movie's poster riffs on *Ghostbusters*' tagline "Who ya gonna call?" and despite the town square in the final scenes looking suspiciously like *Back to the Future*'s Hill Valley.

[10] Perhaps a set-up, as rumors circulate that at one time Fred Dekker was entertaining a sequel to *The Monster Squad* in which they would indeed have faced off against Godzilla (or some *kaiju* stand-in; see Joey Paur's "14 Fun Facts About Monster Squad" at https://geektyrant.com/news/14-fun-facts-about-monster-

out of adolescent boys' mouths at that age when they've got more balls than brains. For context, 1987 also brought us, arguably, the greatest of the Freddy sequels, *A Nightmare on Elm Street 3: The Dream Warriors*, along with the gore-tastic *Evil Dead II* and Clive Barker's darkly poetic *Hellraiser*. By this point, the kids of the '80s were used to whips and chains and meat hooks and cleavers and amputated limbs and blood by the bucket. Yet *The Monster Squad* turned all that on its ear by resurrecting a more noble breed of monster not seen on the screen in a generation.

The challenge was palpable: After encountering a serial child molester in a striped sweater, with burnt skin and razor claws for fingers,[11] could any youngster be frightened by a middle-aged man with a sharp widow's peak, a high-collard cloak, a frilly shirt, and fangs? That answer is, if the iconic Count is played by Duncan Regehr, *yes*.

The film featured reimagined designs for the Wolf Man, the Gill-man, the Mummy, Count Dracula, and Frankenstein's monster (in the box) that were updated for a then-modern audience yet reverential to the monsters' classic origins.

---

squad). As crazy as that may sound, the idea would not have been without precedent, as giant versions of Frankenstein's monster were featured in Toho's Godzilla universe, in the films *Frankenstein vs. Baragon* and *The War of the Gargantuas*. See Rich Handley's essay "Godzilla vs. Continuity: Toho's Shōwa-Era Shared Film Universe" for more information.

[11] That's Freddy Krueger, as dreamt up by horror master Wes Craven for the *A Nightmare on Elm Street* franchise.

In the 1990s, Francis Ford Coppola would seek to update the Dracula legend in his artistic tour de force *Bram Stoker's Dracula*, with Gary Oldman as the titular (and, this time, tragically romantic) bloodsucker, sparking a trend of modern updates and "new spins" that carry on to this day. *The Monster Squad*'s director, Fred Dekker, however, thankfully did not take that approach. *The Monster Squad* isn't a reboot or an update or a reimagining of the classic monsters – it's a literal transplant of the ghouls of cinema's yesteryear into the 1980s, without irony or self-abasement. This isn't a joke or played for laughs. It's not campy or corny (except where, perhaps, a meager budget demanded such). In my mind, this is the last ride of the original Universal Monsters – a tale of the old gunslingers coming out of retirement one last time to show the new generation how it's done.

While legal reasons demanded that Dekker give his monstrous stars a different *visual* spin, the *spirit* of these characters remains entirely unchanged from their Universal predecessors. Dracula is suave, but not a caricature, as some have portrayed him. He is conniving and brilliant and savage. He is a monster, using sex appeal only as a weapon. Frankenstein's monster, brought to life this time by Tom Noonan,[12] is the epitome of childlike innocence trapped in the quilted flesh of a misunderstood creature. While the Wolf Man's human counterpart has no name in this film, Jonathan Gries' few scenes immediately draw us in as we feel his Lon Chaney-esque despair at his curse, and by the end we see him not as a villain, but as a victim of fate longing for release.

To this day, Michael MacKay remains the only Mummy I've ever seen who is convincing as a walking skeleton. Silent and slow, he is nonetheless unrelenting in his pursuit of these kids – a specter of mortality that is permanent and unmovable. The Gill-man is pure animal lethality, wild and free with seemingly no motive to join Dracula's cause but to perhaps rise up against humans who have, no doubt, hunted his kind to near-extinction. What's more, the "man in the suit" is none other than Tom Woodruff, Jr. – a legend in the special effects industry. Along with and under the supervision of master craftsman Stan Winston,[13] the same man who gave us James Cameron's

---

[12] Horror fans will recognize Tom Noonan from many roles, perhaps most immediately as Francis Dollarhyde in 1986's *Manhunter*, based on the novel *Red Dragon* by Thomas Harris.

[13] Stan Winston (1946–2008) designed the Wolf Man's prosthetics in *The Monster Squad* based on his own face! Not only was he perhaps the most influential special

Terminator, the Predator, and the dinosaurs of *Jurassic Park*, Woodruff, Jr. and partner Alec Gillis[14] achieved the impossible and updated the look of the classic monsters (to avoid those pesky lawyers who'd drive a stake into the heart of anyone's fun), while still making their creations instantly recognizable as their Universal counterparts.[15]

Top row, left to right: Frankenstein's monster (Tom Noonan), Count Dracula (Duncan Regehr), and the Mummy (Michael MacKay); bottom row, left to right: the Gill-man (Tom Woodruff, Jr.), the Wolf Man (Carl Thibault), and Abraham Van Helsing (Jack Gwillim).

Let's not forget the music! In an era of synth-heavy arrangements, Bruce Broughton composed a lush orchestral score to accompany our time-displaced

---

effects artist of his time, but Winston was also a director on the 1988 creature feature *Pumpkinhead*, utilizing the talents of the same team who did the effects on *The Monster Squad*, including Tom Woodruff, Jr. as the title monster.

[14] Alec Gillis and Tom Woodruff, Jr. would go on to open their own special effects company, StudioADI, and supply practical effects for many fantasy projects for decades, including director Andy Muschietti's big-screen adaptation of Stephen King's *It* – which, incidentally, involves kids on bikes fighting monsters.

[15] In 2004, writer-director Stephen Sommers – under the official Universal Studios banner – would seek to essentially capture what *The Monster Squad* did unofficially, with *Van Helsing*. Hugh Jackman stars as hunky monster hunter Gabriel Van Helsing as he tangles with the Universal Monsters – only this time with CGI, rousing adventure music by Alan Silvestri, and very little *actual* horror.

monsters, evoking the grandeur of the Golden Age of Hollywood, but still managed to have fun with some quirky synthesizer shenanigans when the kids were livin' it up in the '80s.

While the movie is relatively gore-less (and ultimately way tamer than my mother would have believed in 1987), its kill count rivals that of any Jason Voorhees summer outing. But the lack of blood and guts leads some to believe we must classify *The Monster Squad* as a "kids' movie," with a derogatory emphasis. It's true: the film was my first real gateway into horror movies, as it was for many of us. But it's only a kids' movie in that it's *about* kids. In actuality, it's a story told through an adult lens. It never talks down to children, but rather challenges them to adulthood, nodding at their struggles with an understanding "I get it."

The then-28-year-old director stated of older filmmakers trying to reach a young audience, "It sometimes comes off as cheesy. It doesn't come from the heart, and physically and age-wise I still touch that."[16] Indeed, these kids must grow up – faster than their peers – if they want to survive this night of horrors. And that is the true appeal of *The Monster Squad*, at least to me. The kids in the movie are *us*.

We know very little about most of their personal lives, but we are given enough glimpses to know that they come from different walks of life. Sean is the stern-eyed leader, seeking solace in his horror obsession in the midst of his parents' inevitable divorce. Patrick is our calm Everyman trying to keep the mood light when the red stuff starts flowing. Everyone's favorite "fat kid," Horace,[17] is just trying to get through the day without suffering more torment from his peers (and he finally *commands* their respect in one of the most cheer-worthy moments in horror film history). Quiet Eugene is obviously younger than the rest, but he's just as valued a member as any. And my personal favorite, Rudy, is the chain-smoking, leather jacket-wearing "cool kid" who supposedly killed his dad – at least, according to Phoebe, but what does she know? She's five.

Along the way, the Squad grants honorary membership to the Scary German Guy down their street, whose experience living as a Jew during the

---

[16] Burke-Block, Candace. "Directing a 'Monster' Mash." Ocala Star-Banner. New York Times Syndicate. 4 September 1987.
[17] Immortalized in our hearts by Brent Chalem, who tragically died in 1997 of pneumonia.

Holocaust taught him more about *real* monsters than any person should ever have to know. They even violate their one and only rule by inducting Sean's little sister, Phoebe, into their hallowed halls once she arrives with her very own Frankenstein's monster wrapped around her pinky. "*Now* can I be in the Monster Club?"

They're disparate heroes, all with their own inner demons, their own home situations. They come for different reasons, with different things to prove to their parents, their peers, and themselves. But they are all united in their love of monsters. In fact, it is this love for monsters that convinces Sean that they alone are qualified to act in order to save the world from the forces of evil. "Nobody can do a thing about it but us," he proclaims. *They* are the experts. All those afternoons "wasting time" watching monster movies, studying the minutiae of mythology and fantasy, being misunderstood by adults, and scoffed at by the other kids – in the end, it proves to be the world's only real hope against Dracula's posse of Old School spooks. If that's not a validation for geekhood, I don't know what is.

The movie is smart, too. Nearly ten years before *Scream*[18] broke the fourth wall and dazzled us with the concept of the "hip" horror movie in which the characters had seen all the same scary movies their audience had, *The Monster Squad* knew its Universal Monster history – and celebrated it, hiding savory Easter eggs throughout. This is a movie written by the Initiated *for* the Initiated – a secret language from one monster kid to another.

Together, the Squad stands strong against fantasy monsters made real, and with very little navel gazing. There's an almost John Wayne-type of swagger to these kids, as they quietly acknowledge that they'll have to become adults to get the job done, and they do it. To some of you who've seen the movie, I'm sure it sounds like I'm overselling it, but I can't express enough how empowering this film has been for me since that day the skies parted to reveal it to my young eyes. I was terrified of growing older, especially of becoming a teenager! Teens were cannon fodder for the likes of Michael Myers and Freddy and Jason. I was sure that some mythical bogeyman waited for me in high

---

[18] Released in December 1996, directed by Wes Craven, and written by Kevin Williamson, *Scream* brought the slasher genre back from the dead – for better or for worse.

school, and there were days when I was petrified I wouldn't survive to adulthood. Remember that feeling?

But the kids in *The Monster Squad* did it, so I could, too. They showed me how – by finding my tribe, by standing by my friends, by "getting the job done" even if it meant having to grow up faster than I wanted. In a fight against Dracula and the Wolf Man, Sean and his Squad never lose their childlike love for monsters, even accepting Frankenstein's monster as one of their own. I still think about that. With the world spinning off its axis and human monsters on all sides, I find comfort now in the "good monsters" of horror. They're faces to our fears, yes, but sometimes they – the Incredible Hulk, Batman, the Monster, even Godzilla – can fight *for us*, too. We can find kinship with the things that initially frighten us and see that they're not so scary after all. They're *more* than that. They inspire us to rise to the challenge, to shake our fists at the dark and say, "I'm not afraid."

Even as I type this, Hollywood continues to struggle with how best to revamp the classics for *our* modern age. I'm sure there will be some successes[19] in a sea of overwhelming failures (I'm looking at you, Tom Cruise[20]). I would hope, however, that more future filmmakers will take a cue from Fred Dekker and Shane Black, and allow the classic monsters to return without "improvement" – to allow them to speak as they did when they first shocked and horrified audiences. I think they still have something to say about us, our culture, and our darker natures that we must combat, nearly a century later. We would do well to listen.

---

[19] 2020 saw the release of *The Invisible Man*, written and directed by *Saw* co-creator Leigh Whannell, to much praise for its re-envisioning of H.G. Wells' original concept. Elisabeth Moss plays a victim of emotional and physical abuse who believes her ex-boyfriend, thought dead by suicide, continues to haunt her as an invisible predator.

[20] Cruise starred in 2017's *The Mummy* – an attempt to jumpstart the ill-conceived "Dark Universe" of interconnected monster movies (which also includes 2014's grandfathered-in *Dracula Untold*) that draw more inspiration from big-screen Marvel Studios superhero slugfests than anything resembling Boris Karloff or Bela Lugosi.

Your Monster and You: An Afterword

by Lou Tambone

Inside each of us, there are monsters.

It's not something we'd like to admit, but they are there, nonetheless. They may take different forms, tangible or otherwise. They can be thoughts, actions, ideas, ambitions, habits, dreams and nightmares, or even diseases. Perhaps this is why many of us love monsters so much. They're an innate part of us.

I'm a firm believer that, much like our lycanthrope friend Larry Talbot, humans "suffer" from a form of duality in their personalities. Sometimes it's simple, like behaving professionally at the office during the week and then partying all weekend long. Other times, it's more severe and can be destructive or even fatal, like a mental illness. This duality lives in all of us and manifests itself in various ways, voluntarily or involuntarily.

Sometimes, I'm keenly aware of the duality in myself. Other times, I catch it later on and it makes me worried. Why did I behave that way? What triggered my reaction? Which of those people is the *real* me? The answer to that last question, of course, is "both." Much like a yin-yang, two parts combine to form one, yet they are still individual. Without darkness, there could be no light. Evil could not exist outside of the context of morality.

I like to think that when we watch a monster film like *The Wolf Man*, we subconsciously tap into that duality in our souls. We find something oddly relatable in the monsters we see on the screen, but we can't quite put our fingers on what it is. That duality, the monster inside, grabs a handful of popcorn and watches the film along with us, gently elbowing us in the ribs and pointing at the screen as if to say, "See that? That's us."

The concept of duality was a common theme in horror films, especially those that dealt with werewolves.

Sigmund Freud, the father of psychoanalysis, is famous for equating dreams with hopes and fears, among other things. If you think about it, monsters may be an extension of Freud's philosophy on dreams. Our natural fear of death is what makes certain monster films scary in the first place. When a monster goes on a killing spree, we are afraid because it reminds us of our own mortality. We sometimes even feel the need to check underneath our beds or in a closet after watching a scary film for fear of a monster lurking, waiting for the right moment to strike.

But whether it's about duality or our hopes and fears, monster films do one thing exceptionally well, besides scare the living daylights out of us: they make us take a good look at ourselves. By shining a light on the big bad monster, we can discern the qualities in ourselves that are similar and (hopefully) make the proper adjustments.

I guess what I'm trying to say is that these works are not only designed to make you jump out of your seat. They are important. But they're not just important for their place in cinematic history; they're life lessons — dark, scary life lessons. Don't play God. Don't give in to your animal instincts. Don't judge too harshly those who look or behave differently. Stop looking for the fountain of youth. Don't destroy the world we live in. *Never* go against nature.

Monster films help us to identify the monsters inside of us, but it's up to us to face and ultimately overcome them.

* * *

When I was asked to serve as coeditor on this book, my immediate response was, "Yes, of course." This was driven by a few facts. First, I have worked with Rich Handley before and we have a wonderful rapport as collaborators. I consider him a good friend. Second, my enjoyment of monster films throughout the years — I, too, was a monster kid — filled me with a guilt-ridden sense of obligation. We all owe a lot to these films. Third, I had learned of the passing away of Jim Beard's wife, Becky, as noted in Rich's introduction.

I regret to say that as of this writing, I have yet to meet Jim in person. That's something I hope to rectify in the future. Rich wanted to make sure we honored Jim's vision as he stepped away from the book to mourn. I was humbled to think that he felt I could rise to the occasion, and I hope that I have. Thanks for reading.

About the Contributors

Sam Agro is a writer, illustrator, and some-time performer. In his day job as a storyboard and background artist, Sam has worked on such animated series as *Teenage Mutant Ninja Turtles, Ewoks, The Ripping Friends,* and *Bunsen Is a Beast.* He has also created storyboards for live-action films like *Fly Away Home* and several entries in the *Saw* horror movie franchise. In addition, Sam writes and draws for the comics industry, including DC's *Looney Tunes,* Mr. Comics's *Revolution on the Planet of the Apes,* and Alterna's *Horror in the West* and *Monstrosity.* His prose fiction story "We Apologize for the Delay" appeared in the volume *Gods, Memes and Monsters,* from Stone Skin Press UK, and Sam has completed several essays for Sequart anthologies. When all this isn't enough to keep him busy, he writes and performs improv and short plays with comedy troupe The Canadian Space Opera Company. Sam lives in Toronto, Canada, with his incredible wife, Beth, and their neurotic cat, Little V.

Leah Battle works and lives in California's Coachella Valley. She's been a professional artist since 1982 but has been an artist nearly all her life. Leah studied under Tony Askew and Cynthia Martin (not the comics illustrator) in Santa Barbara, and was a student of fine arts and art history at Santa Barbara Community College. Her passion for animals turned professional when she started a business illustrating pets. The business was eventually featured in a *KEYT News* segment series called *Businesses That Work.* After 20 years of pet illustration, she was invited to participate in creating sketch cards for licensed properties (*Star Wars* and *Lord of the Rings,* among many others), and she was chosen as an artist for *Star Wars* Celebration in 2010. Since then, Leah has worked on personal commissions, has dipped a toe into the basics of photography, and has more recently looked to different avenues of creativity. Her preferred mediums are colored pencils, markers, and digitally created works. She has illustrated two covers for Sequart and is currently working on several personal projects.

Jim Beard became a published writer when he sold a story to DC Comics in 2002. Since that time, he's written official *Star Wars* and *Ghostbusters* comic stories and contributed articles and essays to several volumes of comic book history. His work includes the novel *Spider-Man: Enemies Closer*; coediting and contributing to *Planet of the Apes: Tales from the Forbidden Zone*; a story for *X-Files: Secret Agendas*; *Gotham City 14 Miles*, a book of essays about the 1966 *Batman* TV series; *Sgt. Janus, Spirit-Breaker*, a collection of pulp ghost stories featuring an Edwardian occult detective; *Monster Earth*, a shared-world giant monster anthology; and *Captain Action: Riddle of the Glowing Men*, the first pulp prose novel based on the classic 1960s action figure. Jim also currently provides regular content for Marvel.com, the official Marvel Comics website.

Corinna Bechko has been writing comics since her horror graphic novel *Heathentown* was published by Image/Shadowline in 2009. She has worked for numerous comics publishers, including Marvel, DC, BOOM! Studios, and Dark Horse, on titles that include co-creating *Invisible Republic* for Image Comics and co-writing *Planet of the Apes*, *Star Wars: Legacy Volume II*, and *Savage Hulk*, as well as writing *Aliens/Vampirella* and *Miss Fury* for Dynamite. She is a zoologist by training and has worked closely with nonverbal orangutans and chimpanzees.

Joseph F. Berenato, a writer with *The Hammonton Gazette*, received an M.A. in writing from Rowan University in 2015. He is the author, editor, and coeditor of several anthologies and essays for Sequart and other publishers, analyzing various aspects of pop culture – and he has been eagerly awaiting the chance to write about monsters since his introduction to the orange Crestwood House books that hooked so many other monster kids. You can find him online at @JFBerenato and jfberenato.weebly.com.

Joe Bongiorno, a New York native, runs a small-press publishing company, The Royal Publisher of Oz (theroyalpublisherofoz.com), and is the creator of The *Star Wars* Expanded Universe Timeline (starwarstimeline.net), The Royal Timeline of Oz (oztimeline.net), and The *X-Files* Chronology (xfilestimeline.net). Joe wrote the *Star Wars* novel *Supernatural Encounters* and two books in the *Black Sabbath: The Illustrated Lyrics* series. He coedited *The Cyberpunk Nexus:*

Exploring the Blade Runner Universe and has contributed short stories to *Oziana* magazine, as well as essays to Sequart's anthologies on *Battlestar Galactica*, *Star Wars*, and *Planet of the Apes*. Joe currently lives in an ever-expanding library, where he caters to the demands of five cats and two dogs.

Greg Cox grew up watching classic horror films on *Nightmare Theater* in Seattle. Nowadays, he is the *New York Times* bestselling author of numerous novels and short stories, including the official movie novelizations of *War for the Planet of the Apes, Godzilla, Man of Steel, The Dark Knight Rises, Ghost Rider, Daredevil, Death Defying Acts*, and the first three *Underworld* movies. In addition, he has written books and stories based on such popular series as *Alias, Buffy the Vampire Slayer, CSI: Crime Scene Investigation, The Green Hornet, Farscape, The 4400, Leverage, The Librarians, Riese: Kingdom Falling, Roswell, Star Trek, Terminator, Warehouse 13, Xena: Warrior Princess, The X-Files, Zorro,* and assorted Marvel and DC superheroes. Greg has received five Scribe Awards from the International Association of Media Tie-in Writers, as well as the Faust Award for Life Achievement. He lives in Lancaster, Pennsylvania. Visit him online at gregcox-author.com.

Kelli Fitzpatrick is an author and educator based in Michigan. She is a winner of the *Star Trek: Strange New Worlds* contest and writes for Modiphius's *Star Trek Adventures* game line. Her essays on *Star Trek, Battlestar Galactica, Blade Runner,* and *Firefly* appear in print from Sequart and ATB Publishing, and online at both StarTrek.com and Women at Warp (womenatwarp.com). Kelli leads writing workshops and is a passionate supporter of gender representation and the arts. She can be found online at KelliFitzpatrick.com and @KelliFitzWrites.

Glenn Greenberg is an award-winning editor and writer. He worked extensively for Marvel Comics and DC Comics on such properties as Spider-Man, the Hulk, Superman, *Star Trek*, Star-Lord, the Silver Surfer, Thor, Iron Man, and Dracula, as well as Web-based tie-in projects for the film *Superman Returns* and the weekly comic-book series *52*. His work has also appeared in such publications as *TIME Magazine For Kids, Scholastic News, Time Out New York, Back Issue,* and *Smoke*. Glenn has also written several works of prose *Star Trek* fiction for Simon and Schuster, and has now made the jump to *The X-Files* for a fiction anthology published by IDW. He avidly covers all aspects of popular culture – including *Star Wars*, of course – on his blog, "Glenn Greenberg's Grumblings" (glenngreenbergsgrumblings.blogspot.com), and welcomes anyone and everyone to check it out.

Rich Handley is the editor of Eaglemoss's *Star Trek Graphic Novel Collection*. He has written books about *Planet of the Apes, Back to the Future,* and *Watchmen*, as well as licensed *Star Wars* and *Planet of the Apes* fiction. Rich has co-edited Titan's Scribe Award-nominated *Planet of the Apes: Tales from the Forbidden Zone*; eight Sequart anthologies discussing *Planet of the Apes, Star Wars, Battlestar Galactica, Hellblazer,* and (now) classic monsters; and three Crazy 8 Press anthologies about the 1966 *Batman* TV show. He has also contributed essays to DC's *Hellblazer: 30th Anniversary Celebration*; IDW's five *Star Trek* and three Eisner Award-nominated *Star Wars* comic-strip reprint books; BOOM! Studios' four-volume *Planet of the Apes Archive* line; Sequart anthologies about *Star Trek* and *Blade Runner*; and ATB Publishing's *Outside In* series focused on *Star Trek, Buffy the Vampire Slayer, Angel,* and *The X-Files*. Rich writes a *Star Trek* column for HeroCollector.com and is the managing editor of RFIDJournal.com.

Robert Jeschonek is an envelope-pushing, *USA Today* bestselling author whose fiction, comics, and non-fiction have been published around the world. His stories have appeared in *Galaxy's Edge, StarShipSofa, Fiction River, Pulphouse,* and many other publications. Robert has written official *Doctor Who* and *Star Trek* fiction and has scripted comics for DC, AHOY, and others. His young adult slipstream novel, *My Favorite Band Does Not Exist*, won the Forward National Literature Award and was named one of *Booklist's* Top Ten First Novels for Youth. He also won an International Book Award, a Scribe Award for Best Original Novel, and the grand prize in Pocket Books' *Strange New Worlds* contest. Visit him online at bobscribe.com. You can also find him on Facebook and follow him on Twitter (@TheFictioneer).

Ross Johnson lives in snowy upstate New York with his husband and two wonderful, but unnecessarily large, dogs. He co-hosts the long-running current affairs radio show *The Sound of Tomorrow* (soundoftomorrow.com), where he discusses trends in politics and pop culture, with a focus on queer and women's issues. Ross writes and performs for several regional comedy television shows, and occasionally shows up onstage. The big, grown-up-looking book he's reading is very often concealing a few comics.

Greg Mitchell is a screenwriter and a novelist, and the author of *The Coming Evil Trilogy* and *Infernal City*. His eclectic career includes eight novels, including the kid- and monster-kid-friendly *Dracula vs. Great White Shark*, as well as several short stories and two Syfy Channel original B-movie creature features – *Snakehead Swamp* and *Zombie Shark* – and he is the cowriter of the non-fiction work *Back in Time: The Unauthorized Back to the Future Chronology*, with Rich Handley. Greg lives with his wife and two daughters in northeast Arkansas.

Robert B. Nejman, a man who is pure of heart and says his prayers by night, may become a wolf when the wolfbane blooms and the autumn moon is bright. Rob was born on a bayou in the Bronx and toiled on a small sea monkey farm in his youth to make ends meet. Once the ends met, he saddled up a greyhound and trekked out to the great West Coast, where he exported more than a million pounds of scrap metal, made a few short films, and acquired a collection of quaint and curious volumes of forgotten lore. Currently, Rob can be found wandering the streets of Los Angeles in search of treasure or a decent slice of pizza.

Charles R. Rutledge is the co-author of three books in the *Griffin & Price* supernatural suspense series, written with James A. Moore. He has written two novellas that bring Bram Stoker's Dracula into the present day, *Dracula's Revenge* and *Dracula's Ghost*. Charles owns entirely too many editions of the novel *Dracula*, keeps actual soil from Transylvania in an envelope on his desk, and is rarely seen in daylight.

Frank Schildiner is a martial arts instructor at Amorosi's Mixed Martial Arts in New Jersey. He is the writer of the novels *The Quest of Frankenstein*, *The Triumph of Frankenstein*, *Napoleon's Vampire Hunters*, *The Devil Plague of Naples*, and *Irma Vep and the Great Brain of Mars*. Frank is a regular contributor to the fictional series *Tales of the Shadowmen* and has also been published in *The Lone Ranger and Tonto: Frontier Justice*, *The Joy of Joe*, *The New Adventures of Thunder Jim Wade*, *Secret Agent X* Volumes 3, 4, 5, and 6, and *The Avenger: The Justice Files*. He resides in New Jersey with his wife Gail, who is his top supporter, and two cats who are indifferent on the subject.

Robert Smith? is the author of *Who Is the Doctor*, *Who's 50: The 50 Doctor Who Stories to Watch Before You Die*, and *The Doctors Are In* (ECW Press), as well as a *Black Archive* volume on *Doctor Who and the Silurians* (Obverse Books), all guides to the wonderful world of *Doctor Who*. Robert is also the editor extraordinaire of the *Outside In* series of pop-culture reviews with a twist (ATB Publishing), covering *Doctor Who*, *Star Trek*, *Buffy the Vampire Slayer*, *The X-Files*, and more. In his day job, Robert is a professor of biomathematics and a world-leading expert on both pandemics and zombies. Really.

Matthew Sunrich fell in love with monsters during the Universal revival of the 1970s, when action figures, books, lunchboxes, costumes, and posters sporting their ghastly visages were everywhere. Frankenstein's monster quickly became his favorite and remains so to this day. Through the ensuing years, he became a major horror fan, with *Creepshow, The Texas Chain Saw Massacre,* and *The Return of the Living Dead* being his favorite films. He also collects horror comics, such as *Creepy, Eerie, Vampirella,* and *Nightmare,* and enjoys horror fiction, particularly the works of H. P. Lovecraft. Matthew has authored two books, *Drawn Swords: An Unauthorized Exploration of Red Sonja and the Artists Who Brought Her to Life* and *Someone Shot the Hip, Young Conductor,* a short-story collection. He has contributed essays to *A Long Time Ago: Exploring the Star Wars Cinematic Universe* and *A Galaxy Far, Far Away: Exploring Star Wars Comics,* both published by Sequart.

Lou Tambone is an independent musician, freelance writer, and UI/UX designer from New Jersey. A lifelong fan of pop culture, he was an early HTML adopter, creating and maintaining some of the first *Star Wars* fan sites under the starwarz.com banner. As well as the occasional magazine and Web piece, he's been published in anthologies from Sequart covering the *Planet of the Apes, Battlestar Galactica,* and *Star Wars* franchises. His editing credits include *The Cyberpunk Nexus: Exploring the Blade Runner Universe, Somewhere Beyond the Heavens: Exploring Battlestar Galactica,* and *From Bayou to Abyss: Examining John Constantine, Hellblazer.* When he's not reading or writing, Lou is usually making music or rehearsing with one of his many bands. During his "spare time," he tries to remember to eat and breathe.

ALSO FROM **SEQUART**

FROM BAYOU TO ABYSS: EXAMINING JOHN CONSTANTINE, HELLBLAZER
SOMEWHERE BEYOND THE HEAVENS: EXPLORING BATTLESTAR GALACTICA
THE CYBERPUNK NEXUS: EXPLORING THE BLADE RUNNER UNIVERSE

A LONG TIME AGO: EXPLORING THE STAR WARS CINEMATIC UNIVERSE
A GALAXY FAR, FAR AWAY: EXPLORING STAR WARS COMICS
A MORE CIVILIZED AGE: EXPLORING THE STAR WARS EXPANDED UNIVERSE

OTHER BOOKS ON SCI-FI FRANCHISES:

BOOKS ON GRANT MORRISON:

BOOKS ON WARREN ELLIS:

ON TV AND MOVIES:

OTHER BOOKS:

DOCUMENTARY FILMS:

For more information and for exclusive content, visit Sequart.org.

Made in the USA
Las Vegas, NV
13 July 2022

51426767R00184